WALTER REED

DOCTOR IN UNIFORM

WALTER REED
DOCTOR IN UNIFORM

BY L. N. WOOD

ILLUSTRATED BY DOUGLAS DUER

Julian Messner Inc.   New York

PUBLISHED BY JULIAN MESSNER, INC.

8 WEST 40TH STREET, NEW YORK

921
R

8718

PRINTED IN THE UNITED STATES OF AMERICA

BY MONTAUK BOOK MANUFACTURING CO., INC.

ILLUSTRATIONS

WALTER REED

DOCTOR IN UNIFORM

CHAPTER ONE

WALTER REED had not been in bed long, but he realized, as he became conscious of the light shining weakly on his face, that he must have dropped asleep almost at once. Startled, he opened his eyes. His father, dressed only in his long white nightshirt, was bending over him, shading with his hand the candle whose feeble beam picked out the heavy scattering of white in the full beard and luxuriant hair that only four years earlier had been a dark brown. In the wavering hollow of light scooped by the little flame out of the dark room, the bedposts, it seemed to the thirteen-year-old boy, loomed close, the rest of the furniture shrank into the protective dark. The shutters, open when he and his brother Chris went to bed, were drawn now. Fully awake, Walter felt the cold certainty even before his father spoke.

"The Yankees are coming, Pa?" he asked in a low voice.

Chris, two years older than Walter, stirred on the other side of the big bed and sat up.

"Yes," Pa answered quickly. "Joey Rogers is just in from the country. Sheridan's men were there today. He and Jeff got away with their team. They're down in our barn now, saddling Bess and Turnip."

Walter and Christopher slipped quickly out of bed and began drawing on their trousers. They knew what to do.

It was the spring of 1865, the fifth spring of the Civil War. Petersburg had been under siege since June, 1864, and the countryside for miles around was at the mercy of the Yankee invaders. At that little Virginia city Robert E. Lee's half-

starved, half-clad army—Lee's Miserables, they called themselves, in allusion to Victor Hugo's somber classic—were still
desperately, stubbornly, checking the advance toward Richmond, the Confederate capital, of Ulysses S. Grant's overwhelming forces.

The once thriving rural town was now the crucial theater
of war. No longer did the high, canvas-covered wagons, drawn
by six great horses decked with bells, rumble over the plank
road into the city with hogsheads of tobacco and sacks of corn
and wheat. The *bateaux*, similarly loaded, were gone from the
canal and the river. The prosperous tobacco factories had
stopped operating: they had long since been converted into
military hospitals.

During the cold weather, military activity at the besieged
city had been desultory. The occasional cannonades drove the
ladies, with their reading and sewing, to the "bomb-proofs,"
holes six feet deep and covered with heavy timbers and packed
earth, where they listened quaking to the martial thunder.
During the uncertain intervals of quiet, the town was gay with
the merriment of soldiers and civilians who could not be sure
of waking to a tomorrow. There were dances, weddings, receptions—and, because of Grant's raids against the surrounding
railroads, almost nothing to eat at any of them.

Even while inaction prevailed at the siege, the surrounding
countryside was ceaselessly, anxiously, on the alert. There was
no telling when Union raiders, clad in their camp-stained blue
uniforms, would trot into the yard and scour house and barn
and grounds. The purpose of their raids was not only to provide
Federal troops with necessities, but to prevent food, clothing
and anything else of value from reaching the Confederates.
It was no wonder that families developed considerable skill in
concealing valuables. Important papers were jammed into
chinks in the wood pile, silver was tossed down the well, and
food stuffed into cooking utensils and hastily buried a couple

Silver was tossed down the well . . .

of feet deep in the flower bed or vegetable patch. Livestock was driven into the thickest available woods, and hobbled. Then, when the raiders came, the report that others had been there before them had all the air of truth.

As the Yankees combed the country in widening circles in the first months of 1865, Lemuel Sutton Reed, the Methodist minister stationed at Lawrenceville, some fifty miles south of the siege, had made what little provision a man of peace and a man of God could make to protect his property against enemy foragers. He had told his two youngest sons, Walter and Christopher, so young that even the desperate Confederate army could not use them, to be ready to hide the horses on short notice in the thickets along the banks of the Meherrin River. Now the time had come.

As the boys dressed rapidly, the father's eyes were on his youngest son. Walter was a lean, wiry boy with blue eyes and straight brown hair. Good temper and quick-witted humor lay behind his serious and attentive expression. The shadow of the war, that had lain for so long over all of them, seemed to his father not to have darkened his youth, but rather to have touched it with a becoming gravity.

The boys were dressed now. Pa hugged them both without a word.

"Don't worry about anything. I'll take good care of Walter, Pa," Chris promised him, pressing his hand. "We'll be all right, and the horses, too."

"I know you will, son. You boys have always looked after each other. I can trust you both to act wisely. Jeff will go with you to see where you hide. Then he'll come back tomorrow and fetch you more food, and let you know when it's safe to come out. Now off with you."

They slipped down the stairs, Pa leading the way with the candle. A quiet, hasty good-by to Ma, and they were out in the damp spring night. The rain had been dripping down, softly, steadily, for a week, but tonight it had stopped and there was a thick mist. They made their way to the stable, where, feeling their way in the unfamiliar dark, Joey Rogers and Jeff, one of his father's hired farm hands, were saddling the horses. A few whispered words, and they were mounted, filing past the dark, wakeful house and down the village street.

The embrace of the sodden dark made Walter shiver. Through the black he could barely distinguish the bulk of the familiar houses on either side. There were no lights showing. They rode past the deserted schoolhouse—it had not opened at all this term—at a trot, and the horses' feet squelched loudly in the hock-deep mud. The damp, fresh smell of the earth suggested spring, but there was nothing but hope to suggest that it would ever clear. The weather had made this road a mud-hole, but those leading into Petersburg, he had heard, were little better than morasses. Even the plank road was submerged in sticky red gumbo, stirred up by days of rain and renewed military operations.

Trotting along at the end of the short procession, with every sense alert to catch any sound that might mean someone was approaching, Walter forgot the wet and cold. As a matter of fact, he thought, we're very lucky to have such murky weather. No one will be abroad on a night like this—except maybe another neighbor stealing off into hiding. In the dark he smiled to think what a fright they would give each other if they met.

A couple of miles out of town they turned off the main road into a lane that shortly dwindled to a wagon track. Low-growing branches smacked wet in their faces as Joey led them off the trail into a narrow path. Jeff began to mutter complaints then to pray, a rapid chattering. Walter listened to him uneasily.

"Hush, Jeff!" Joey told him sharply. "Do you want to wake up the whole county?"

The boy did not answer. He was quiet, but his teeth clicked together with chill and nervousness.

"Are you cold, Jeff?" Walter called softly.

"He's not cold—just scared to death," Joey's irate whisper carried back to him. "He's afraid of the dark."

Walter suppressed a chuckle. "We don't have to be afraid of the dark, Jeff," he reassured him. "It's the best friend we could have right now."

"No Yanks will ever find us on a pitchy night like this," Chris encouraged the frightened boy, "and Yanks are all we've got to be scared of. The dark never hurt anybody. I hope you know where you're taking us, Joey," he added.

"I've hunted all over this country," Joey told him. "Indeed, I know every foot of it, light or dark or blindfold. We'll come out on a steep little bank at a bend in the river. It's deep there, and the thickest trees you've ever seen in your life. No raiders, not even Sheridan's, are going to stumble across us there."

The woods seemed to be getting thicker, the night, if that were possible, blacker. Turnip struck his foot on a root, shook his head and blew indignantly. This was no kind of jaunt for a respectable ministerial mount, even for a circuit rider's horse who was used to almost anything. Some of the boys' tension relaxed in the safe, quiet darkness. Chris began to whistle almost inaudibly, and a tuneless hum from the front of the line indicated that Joey was busy with Dixie. But Jeff, unimpressed by the assurances of his companions, resumed his muttered prayers.

Walter lost track of time and distance. For hours and miles, it seemed to him, he had been warding off the swish of branches and straining his eyes into the absorbent blackness. He was beginning to be conscious of fatigue, but in spite of it felt increasingly alert, as though each nerve were becoming tighter and more sensitive. This night could have no end, had had no beginning; it had been going on for all remembered time. Automatically he held up his arm to fend off the slap of the wet boughs, tightened the reins as Turnip stumbled again. The darkness and his weariness seemed to merge, both of them to fold around him warm and suffocating. Then he remembered: Pa had closed the windows—the miasma was bad for Ma.

He was half out of the saddle before he felt himself slipping. Jerking himself back, he shook his head hard to clear it.

"Joey, where are we?" he called in a whisper.

"Almost there."

In a daze Walter finally dismounted. The ground felt unfamiliar to his chill feet and stiff legs. He could feel, rather than see, the little clearing amid the dense trees, sense the stream flowing swift and full at the foot of the bank. The tired boys unsaddled their horses and tied them at the edge of the thicket. With quick strokes of his hatchet Chris cut pine boughs for them all to lie on. Using their saddles as pillows and wrapping themselves in blankets, they fell asleep without even a whispered good-night.

A bird call, and the rays of the early sun pointing through the branches, woke the sleepers. The sun was shining again! It was a glorious, a perfect, spring day, warm, with an opal sky that would become a brilliant blue as the sun rose higher. The boys sat up, stretching and smiling sleepily, then looked at each other blankly.

Jeff was gone.

In hiding the horses the boys had done all they could to insure their safety. Now they had nothing more to do until they received word that the raiders were gone from the neighborhood. High spirits, long suppressed by wartime anxieties, bubbled up again. The first day they wrestled, told tall tales, built themselves a rough shelter of pine boughs in case of rain, and, between relief and fatigue, slept again. Their anxiety over Jeff's disappearance evaporated gradually.

"After all," Chris reminded Joey, "we knew he wasn't going to stay with us. He's just gone off to get us some more food, the way Pa said he would."

"I don't see why he lit out before anybody was awake," Joey grumbled. "He was supposed to wait till later, so's he wouldn't get back till late evening, not straggle in in broad daylight for the Yankees to nab him."

"I guess he didn't like the notion of being out after dark again," Walter remarked. "I'm afraid you maybe hurt his feelings, Joey, saying he was scared last night."

"Oh, I didn't mean to—I was kind of jumpy myself. I was sure glad you fellows were along."

"Don't worry about it," Walter advised him. "He'll come back tomorrow or next day, with some food, and maybe news. I hope. . . ." His voice trailed away. As far as the war was concerned, even he knew now, there was nothing left to hope for, except its quick conclusion. And he had done nothing to help! When he had told Pa how that made him feel, Pa had consoled him. There was always plenty to do in the world, he had explained, and his turn would come soon, just a few more years.

What shall I do when I'm a grown man? Walter wondered. He had thought about it many times, but had never been able to decide. Now he sat on the edge of the bank above the river, forgetting the horses, forgetting the war, his intent blue eyes staring unseeing at the water.

Joey strolled over and sat beside him.

"What are *you* going to be when you grow up, Joey?" Walter asked.

"Why, a farmer, of course," Joey answered. "What else would I be? I'm one already. Like my pa, and my grandpa, and his pa. Rogers are always farmers."

"I guess it's nice being a farmer," Walter agreed with the unspoken assumption, "planting things, and seeing them come up and helping them grow. And making plenty of food for everybody," he added longingly. It had been four endless years since anyone he knew had had plenty of food.

"Not for me," Chris remarked, joining them. "Farmers never get a chance to read anything. They work so hard that they haven't time to study things. I'm going to be a lawyer, and a city man. Maybe I'll go to New York."

"There?" Joey was shocked. "That Yankee town?"

"Oh, we'll all be friends again by the time Chris is ready to go," Walter explained trustfully. "I'd like to go there myself, and then maybe out west. But I'd like to see such a big city first. Pa says 'most a million people live in it."

"No!" Joey exclaimed incredulously.

"Really," Chris assured him. "Pa told us so."

They were all silent, contemplating the awesome figure. It

was too big for Joey. He dismissed it. Anyway, he didn't believe it.

"What are you going to be, Walter?" Joey finally inquired.

Walter answered slowly, "I don't know. I haven't made up my mind. Maybe a minister, like Pa. Or maybe a schoolmaster. I want to do something," he hesitated a moment seriously, "whatever it is, that will *help* people."

"You better not be a schoolmaster, then," Joey advised drily, recalling his own regrettable educational experiences in which a hickory switch had figured largely. He stood up and stretched, thinking how good it was to feel the spring sun again on the top of his head. "Let's take the horses down for a drink," he suggested. "They're acting awfully restless."

By sunset they had to admit that Jeff probably wouldn't appear that day. They sat in the thickening twilight, inattentive to the final chirps of sleepy birds, the fading brilliance in the west and the increasing chill of the spring night, and speculated on how it would feel to be hungry—really hungry, with not a single thing to eat.

"It won't be that bad," Walter predicted. "After all, we don't have to sit here and starve when our food's gone. If he isn't here by the middle of tomorrow afternoon, I'll go out and see if I can't get us something."

"No you won't, Walter," Chris declared. "I promised Pa I'd take care of you. I'll go."

"I'll go," Joey stated gruffly. "I know the way, and you fellows don't. You'd probably get lost the first thing."

"I'd find it, all right," Walter asserted. "Besides, if I ran into the Yanks, they'd probably think I was too young to bother with. But they might take either of you prisoner."

The argument trailed along inconclusively until it was thoroughly dark.

Finally Walter yawned. "I reckon I'll go to sleep now,"

he said, wrapping up in his blanket. "Let's see what happens in the morning, before we decide what to do. Jeff may show up. Maybe nobody will have to go for food."

The next morning, like the one before it, was mild and sunny. After eating the last scraps of ham and corn bread for breakfast, and watering the horses, the boys were faced with a long, warm, and probably hungry day.

"Why don't we take a swim?" Joey proposed. "The water's probably warm enough. It'll be the first time I've been in this spring."

"Good idea," Chris agreed. Poised on the edge of the bank, he shouted over his shoulder, "Last one in is a Red Indian," and slid down the incline. In a moment all three of them were scrambling out of their clothes. Chris, to Walter's great glee, turned out to be the Red Indian.

The water was chilly with spring, and ran rusty from the recent rains, but the boys didn't mind. They plunged in and ducked each other, sputtering and splashing. Then they swam, their pale arms and legs tossing the drops glistening into the air. Finally, winded, they climbed out and lay panting on the edge of the stream, while the sun dried them.

They were dressing when they heard one of the horses whinny.

"Drat that racket!" Joey exclaimed anxiously. Hastily pulling his shirt over his head and jerking his belt tight, he started up the bank, the others at his heels. When his red head rose above it, and he took in what had happened, it was too late.

"Hello, Johnny Reb," the big bearded Yankee said with an unhurried grin. "Come on up." The grin fell away as Joey started to drop back. "Don't try to run," the soldier warned, shifting his rifle a little. The smile came back as the two other astonished faces, incredulous eyes wide, bobbed over the edge of the bank. "Well, well, well," he said mildly. "Get on up here, all of you."

The Lieutenant looked them over, the three young rebels.

It was impossible to refuse an invitation issued at the point of a gun, so the three rueful boys, their hair still plastered flat from their swim, scrambled up beside him. A quick glance was enough to show that there was nothing they could do. There were eight or ten of the raiders, all in faded blue uniforms that looked as if they had had long, hard service. They had saddled Bess and Turnip and Joey's team, and were standing around watching the capture with amusement.

They didn't seem very sinister fellows, Walter thought wonderingly, as he stared frankly at them. They might almost be some of their neighborhood men, needing a shave and a bath and a fresh suit. He examined their clothes. They were stained and soiled, but not in rags, like the Confederates' uniforms. Most enviable of all, their boots were whole. The young lieutenant in charge of the group had on a fresher uniform than his men. As Walter reluctantly admired his fine figure it did not occur to him that, in another ten years, he would himself put on the United States Army uniform and wear it proudly for the rest of his life. Just then he would have given a great deal to see the Confederate gray and hear the shrill Rebel yell.

Their captor was solemnly searching them. Resting his rifle in the crook of his left arm, he patted their pockets with his free hand. The three knives he took from them, he dropped into his own pocket.

"Disarmed, sir," he reported to his superior with a straight face.

The lieutenant looked them over, the three young rebels. The tallest one, who looked like a farmer, glared at him, plainly uneasy about what was coming next. The other two were examining him attentively, without friendliness and without fear.

"Is there anyone else with you?" he inquired.

Joey sullenly kicked the earth with his toe. His team, the sturdy matched grays that Pa set such store by, how would they ever get along without them? What about the spring plowing? He could feel tears of helpless anger rising to his eyes.

Chris had moved close to Walter. Now he answered for all of them, a little louder than necessary in a voice harsh with indignation. "No sir. There are only three of us." No use telling about Jeff. He hoped Jeff wouldn't pick this moment to return. When he did come and found them gone, he could at least tell their families, and they would guess what had happened.

"Yes sir. That's right," another soldier, one with pale eyes and a broken nose set in a homely, weather-beaten face, said. "That's what the hired boy said—three boys, four horses. Too bad we have to bother with the kids at all—they're no good to us."

"We can't turn them loose to warn the whole neighborhood," the lieutenant answered shortly.

"So Jeff told you where to find us!" Joey blurted, flushing angrily. "Wait till I get my hands on him—wait till Pa gets at him!"

"Take it easy, son," the man with the beard soothed him. "You'll never see that boy again. The speed he showed when we let him go, he's miles from here by now, I guess." He laughed heartily at the recollection of the flying heels.

As they picked their way single file through the woods, Walter reflected on the uneasy distinction of being taken prisoner of war. There had been nothing at all glamorous about it, as he would have supposed. No ringing demand for surrender, no parley about honorable terms, no formal exchange of courtesies between enemies who were also gentlemen. They had simply blundered into a booby trap set by an ignorant, resentful boy, and been ingloriously grabbed by some good-natured, quite dirty soldiers under the command of a very junior officer who scarcely spoke to them. It was a great disappointment, practically an insult.

Dodging the branches that swept low over the narrow path, he wondered nervously what their captors intended to do with them. Only spies were shot, he knew. But maybe they would be sent to one of the fearsome northern prisons, from which such fearful rumors of want and disease filtered back. Maybe they would be taken to Sheridan himself, and questioned, Walter thought apprehensively, recalling tales of his ruthlessness in the desolated Shenandoah Valley. It was even possible—humiliating thought—that they would be liberated as not worth bothering with, their patriotism dismissed as ineffectual. Although at first inclined to resent any such reflection, Walter realized that he would quickly reconcile himself to it, if it meant freedom.

"They can think what they like, if they only let us go," he reasonably told himself.

This was probably the last time, he realized sadly, that Chris and he would ever ride good old Bess and Turnip. He leaned over Turnip's neck and gave him an affectionate pat. Fine old horses! They had faithfully carried Pa through sun and rain and cold countless miles all over Virginia. They had pulled the buggy to church, picnics, funerals, christenings. They were essential, cherished members of the family. He hated to think that they would now strain at cannon stuck in the mud, or go under fire, ridden by some stranger. He and Chris and Joey had done all they could to save them, but it hadn't been enough.

The path widened into the wagon track, the wagon track into the highway. The little group of soldiers, breaking their file, surrounded their prisoners and trotted down the road.

It was almost dark the next evening when the two limping, weary boys approached home.

"My feet are 'most worn off," Chris sighed. "Fifteen miles!"

"And some people do it for pleasure," Walter groaned. "I'm nearly starved."

"Those sardines!"

"Whew! Maybe they wouldn't have been so bad if the soldier hadn't wrapped them in his handkerchief with his tobacco," Walter speculated.

"They were terrible anyway," Chris affirmed.

"I hope I never see another one of those slimy, smelly fish as long as I live," his brother solemnly declared.

"Do you suppose Ma and Pa heard about us?" Chris wondered.

"I'm afraid so. Mr. Samuels saw us when we passed his place. He'd have let them know if he had to walk every step of the way. I hope it didn't scare Ma to death."

But it had scared Ma almost to death. When her youngest sons actually stood before her, she was hardly able to believe it. She couldn't stop hugging them, and exclaiming, "My babies! My poor little babies! Have you really come back to me safely?"

"Oh, Ma," Chris protested, a little embarrassed at being called a baby even by her, "it wasn't so bad. They didn't hurt us. They didn't even scare us, did they, Walter? Only a little bit, anyway."

"No, really, Ma," Walter clasped her hard to reassure her. "They weren't mean to us at all. We were only scared that you and Pa would worry when you heard."

"We worried, all right," Pa said grimly. "When Mr. Samuels came with the news, I thought your Ma would faint clear away for a minute. Then she wanted to set right out for Petersburg and give General Grant and General Sheridan a piece of her mind—persecuting innocent children, she called it." He chuckled. "She would have, too, if there'd been any means of conveyance left in the county."

"How did my brave boys get away?" Ma asked fondly.

"Well, you see," Walter explained shamefacedly, "it was this way. They just turned us loose. A courier came with a message for the lieutenant, and he ordered the men to break camp, fast. Then he remembered us. He said," indignantly he repeated the young officer's slighting words, mimicking his brusque tone, " 'Free these boys. They're not big enough to do us any good, and they're too small to do any harm. Sheridan's cavalry can't be nursemaids. They can go home to their mothers.' So he just let us walk away, and Joey went to his place, and we came home." He could hardly keep his voice steady as he added, "They kept Bess and Turnip, though, Pa."

"My dearest boys!" Pa exclaimed. "*You're* what matters. We can do all right without the horses, so long as we have you back safe."

"Did they feed you properly?" Ma inquired anxiously, watching Chris down his second glass of buttermilk and reach again for the corn bread.

"Sardines," he said tersely. "Sardines for supper, sardines for breakfast."

"Sardines and tobacco," his younger brother amended. "Never again!"

CHAPTER TWO

THE CHILDHOOD climaxed by this adventure had opened thirteen years earlier in the rural peace of pre-war Virginia. Since Walter Reed's whole life was destined to be more or less nomadic, with scarcely four consecutive years spent in the same place, it was quite appropriate that he should have been born in a temporary shelter.

Shortly before Walter's birth his father, a Methodist circuit rider, was sent from Murfreesboro, North Carolina, to Belroi in Gloucester County, Virginia, to travel and preach among the churches in that neighborhood. In those days the arrival of a new minister in a country community was an event comparable only to Christmas in its importance and possibilities for pleasant excitement. The neighborhood hummed. Would the new preacher frown on dancing? What kind of sermons would he deliver? What would his wife be like? How old were his children? Would he like his new parish, would they be happy in their new home?

Suddenly and horrifyingly, it appeared that an emphatic *no* must be the answer to the last question. The parsonage burnt down. How could a family be happy without a roof over their heads, especially a family of four children, with another expected any day? The parishioners were in consternation. Their new minister was even then traveling to them, they could not possibly build a house for him by the time he arrived, and where were he and his expanding brood to lay their heads?

An answer was quickly found by Mr. Stubbs, owner of the Belroi plantation. He hastily transferred his overseer to other quarters and offered the frame cabin thus vacated for the use of the minister and his family. It was a sturdy little building, small but substantially built, with two rooms downstairs each with an immense fireplace, and an attic above. A pretty little elm tree by one corner made the gesture of sheltering it, although it was so small and slender that the gesture was a mere promise, not fulfilled for many years. The neighborhood men got together and cleaned the yard and repaired the steps and whitewashed the walls, while the women swept and scrubbed inside. In short order the overseer's cabin was prepared for the role of Walter Reed's birthplace, a role the distinction of which none of the kind neighbors, of course, could foresee.

Traveling by coach and boat, the Reeds journeyed from North Carolina to their new home. Walter, in due course, was born there. He was a good-natured baby, with straight fair hair and blue eyes, and the undistinguished chubbiness of a healthy infant. The youngest of a family of five children, he was much admired, as the youngest always is until displaced by a new baby. This was a catastrophe which did not overtake Walter: he remained the baby for many years. By the time that his father, after his mother's death, remarried, and there was a baby half-sister, Walter was a responsible young man of sixteen, entered as a student at the University of Virginia.

Naturally, Walter remembered nothing of his first home, since the family lived there only a short time, but the older members never forgot their few months in the crowded little cabin. It was, however, snug and weatherproof, and Mrs. Reed, whose talent for making a strange house into a home was well developed by life as the wife of a circuit rider, soon made this one comfortable and pleasant. It was a relief, though, to them all, except perhaps the indifferent baby, when they were able to move into the new parsonage, with its spacious upper story and detached kitchen and servants' quarters, and leave Walter's congested birthplace to its next tenants, and, later, to the favorable notice of posterity.

The first Reed to arrive in America was Christian, who came to Carolina in 1640 to see how he liked the New World. He liked it well enough to live in, but not to die in, so returned to England when he grew old. He left his son Christopher, however, one of the Councillors of the Lords Proprietors who governed the colony from the safe and irresponsible distance of England, comfortably settled at Durant's Neck, a piece of land jutting down into the north side of Albemarle Sound between the Little and the Perquimans Rivers.

In good time, Christopher died and was buried near the shore, and as the years passed his grave was all but washed into the Sound. Pious hands rescued the tombstone and placed it under a gum tree near the water, far from the scattered bones it had once covered. Later, hands somewhat less pious broke off the slab for the doorstep of a new house. Christopher's son and son's sons lived on at Durant's Neck, and planted and prospered. One of them, Joseph, married a granddaughter of George Durant, founder of the settlement.

George Durant, irked by the restraints of England's tight little island, had been drawn to the new continent in 1632. A brief pause in Virginia had convinced him that that colony was too like the land he had left for his taste. He wandered into Carolina, exploring the eastern shore and the rivers, and finally settled on the peninsula on which he conferred his name. He preferred to buy his land from the Indians, and be friends with them, rather than steal it like many other settlers and win their enmity, so he came into possession of the first land title in what is now North Carolina. The old record shows that, on the first day of March, 1661, George Durant bought from Kilcocanen, Chief of the Yeopin Indians, "a parcel of land lying on Roanoke Sound and a river by the name of Perquimans."

Other settlers, among them Christian and Christopher Reed, came to the fertile peninsula, and a substantial community of farmers and planters soon grew up. George Durant held a dominant position there. When harsh laws were imposed and an unpopular governor was appointed by the absentee Lords Proprietors, it was Durant who led the opposition and raised an armed rebellion. In the quieter years of his later life his activities were less stirring: as Justice of the Peace he applied himself to the suppression of witchcraft, sorcery and other doings frowned upon by the local gentry. But the adventurous and independent spirit of George Durant was strong in the granddaughter who married Joseph Reed, and it flowed on, sometimes more and sometimes less silently, in the veins of their descendants, to crop out again undiluted in Walter Reed.

Walter's mother, Pharaba White Reed, was, like his father, a North Carolinian of English descent. Small, witty and vivacious, she was also a woman of character and intelligence.

In those days, the wife of a Methodist circuit rider needed such qualities. A preacher's salary was small, and his reward consisted largely of the consciousness of duty sincerely done and of the respect and liking of his neighbors. He could afford no luxuries. Lemuel Reed did not own slaves; a good slave might cost as much as fifteen hundred dollars. As he pointed out to Walter,

"What would a minister of the Gospel want with a slave? He cultivates souls, not the soil, and he must do it entirely by his own labor."

Mr. Reed traveled the circuit in all weathers, sometimes on horseback and sometimes in a light carriage, preaching at his churches, baptizing babies, visiting the sick, carrying news about the countryside, performing all the dozens of extra duties that fell to the lot of a country parson. At home his wife attended to the children, supervised their lessons, managed the household and waited for his return.

*Mr. Reed traveled the circuit in all weathers,
sometimes on horseback.*

Every two years, just as they would get settled and feel
really at home, the Methodist conference regularly appointed
him to a new circuit in another part of the state. Mrs. Reed
and the two younger boys, with a few bags, would get into the
cars and ride to their destination behind the woodburning
locomotive that chugged along breathtakingly about thirty
miles an hour and scattered sparks lavishly on either side of
the right-of-way. Mr. Reed and his two older boys and their
sister would pile their household goods—chairs, lamps, bedding,
some smoked meat in the back, and Pa's Bible on the seat
beside him, where he could consult it while he thought about

his sermon—into the wagon and make the tedious trip to a new home.

The two years at Belroi were followed by two in Princess Anne County, two in Murfreesboro, North Carolina, and two in Prince Edward County. Here, at Farmville, the village on the banks of the Appomattox that was eight years later to be in the path of Lee's final retreat, the Reeds lived opposite the Presbyterian church in a story-and-a-half brick house.

Mrs. Reed, who loved flowers, laid out beds along the walk all the way to the front gate and planted them with roses, cornflowers, larkspur and other plants that grew well in the rich red soil. Walter, who shared his mother's love of gardening even as a little boy, would follow her around, digging, planting, pruning, cutting, in vigorous imitation. Sometimes his dog, Taffy, whom Nature had sketched freehand in a moment of reckless experimentation, would do a little planting himself, and dig a hole in a flower bed to bury his bone. Walter, who thought Taffy the finest dog in the world, would reproach him, but not hard enough to hurt his feelings. He was sensitive to other people's feelings, and Taffy, in his opinion, had the same standing in the family, and title to gentle treatment, as any other member of it.

It was at Farmville, when he was six years old, that Walter Reed performed his first experiment. It was not his own idea, but it had seemed like a good one at the time. He knew better, however, after the first few puffs on the homemade "cigar," made of tobacco leaves which he and Chris and a couple of their friends had picked up at a neighboring warehouse and rolled in newspaper. Convulsed with nausea, he thought he was surely dying. His frightened friends shared his alarm.

"Please, please don't die, Walter," implored the scared little boy who had suggested smoking. "Promise you won't tell who you were with when this happened? Pa'd 'most kill me if he knew it was my fault."

"I promise. I won't tell. It wasn't your fault." Walter managed a feeble smile. "Get me home, Chris. I feel so awful. I'm 'most dead now! I want Ma, quick!"

The next day Walter, still feeble but no longer in fear of death, had an interview with his father. The minister, pulling on his full mustache, covered a smile with his hand.

"So you promised not to tell who got you into this scrape, Walter? Well, then you mustn't tell. You were foolish, not naughty, and I'm not going to punish you. I think you've learned your lesson."

"Yes I have, Pa. I'll never touch the stuff again," Walter promised earnestly.

Mr. Reed smiled at his son and ruffled his sun-bleached hair.

"As a matter of fact, you probably won't," he told him. "The same thing happened to your Pa thirty years ago. To this day I can't touch tobacco."

Walter never smoked again.

Life for a small boy in rural Virginia in the 1850's was fun, especially with three older brothers, Jim and Tom and Chris, and a big sister, Laura, to play with. They made up all sorts of exciting games. As wild Indians they would lurk behind the big wood pile, a feature of every country home in those days, and fall with terrifying whoops on their parents, who always made very satisfactory victims, giving a convincing display of surprise and terror. Or they would be highwaymen and hold up the stage, or Indian scouts and crawl on their stomachs through the corn and tobacco, cautiously reconnoitering the movements of the wily redskins, and taking care not to put themselves in the way of punishment by flattening the stalks. When they played at being a pioneer family, Walter, to his disgust, had to be the baby. When he protested that he was a big boy now, almost big enough to go to school, Tom settled the matter by saying with authority,

"All pioneer families have babies. You're the youngest, so you've got to be the baby if you want to play with us."

There was no answer to that, obviously, so Walter got his nose wiped and his face washed, and was scalped, lugged around and spanked a great deal. He took it with good nature, since he had a happy disposition, but promised himself that when he got a little older he wasn't going to play any old baby any more.

Laura, as the oldest and the only girl in a family of boys, was in a privileged position. She always got to play mother, and did so with great zest, scolding and protecting her family, cooking for them when they returned from the plains with a bison, and mourning their untimely demise when the Indians murdered them. She took care, too, not to let the older boys "baby" their youngest brother with too much realism.

Probably the best fun, though, was the wrestling game with Pa.

"Let's see if you fellows are strong enough to hold down your aged, feeble Pa," Mr. Reed would challenge them. The boys would fall on him with a shout. Pa would get down on his back on the floor, creakingly and with many ostentatious groans, and Jim, the oldest boy, would issue orders.

"Walter, you hold his left arm. Tom, take his right—hold them out, straight out! Get on his legs, Chris. Wait, I'll help you. No fair starting yet, Pa. All right, now! Let's see you get away this time, Pa!"

The ensuing struggles were terrific. Pa and the boys rolled and scrambled and shouted with laughter, while Ma and Laura fluttered on the outskirts of the mêlée and moved furniture out of the way. Heads, elbows and shins got banged, but nobody minded. The game always ended the same way: the boys, exhausted and laughing, lay scattered about the room, while

Pa rose agilely to his feet and dusted himself off, saying triumphantly,

"There! Maybe the next time you'll think twice before you get rough with your poor old Pa."

"Really, Pa," Mrs. Reed smilingly protested, "one would think you were ten yourself, the way you act."

"Keeps me young, my dear," he answered, slipping one arm around her and the other around Laura. "Aren't they fine fellows, though," he exclaimed proudly, smiling at his four boys as they picked themselves up from the floor.

"Ma, when can I go to school?" Walter demanded of his mother soon after their arrival at Farmville. "I'm six, and I can read and spell and do sums almost as well as Chris."

Mrs. Reed glanced at him startled. How quickly they grew! Her youngest almost six! She put aside the bolt of cotton cloth from which she was cutting shirts for the boys and their father—the spinning wheel and loom had fallen into disuse in most of the homes of Virginia since cotton goods could be manufactured so cheaply in the north—and examined her youngest son. His hair, tow-colored from the hot Virginia sun, was darkening a little as he grew older. The blue eyes showed his father's frank intelligence. Behind the youthful softness of the alert face, with its straight nose and slightly outthrust lower lip, the maternal eye recognized character and determination.

"When, Ma?" the little boy persisted, leaning against her.

"I think you can go this next term, son," she answered slowly. "I'll ask your Pa to speak to Mrs. Booker about it as soon as he gets back."

Mrs. Reed's scissors lay idle on the table as she stared out the window. How fast, how terribly fast time went! Was it possibly six years since that night in the overseer's tiny cabin when Walter, red and wrinkled and weakly squall' confronted his family and the world? Pa had been then; he was an elder now. It was hard to believe that their baby would go to school with Chris, and under the efficient ministration of Mrs. Booker learn reading and moral tales from Professor McGuffey's readers, Latin from Professor Gildersleeve's grammar, and mathematics and geography from the appropriate texts. Then he would go to Mr. Jefferson's University at Charlottesville; and, finally, entering on the broader stage of life as a man of sound education, he would become—a minister like his father? a doctor? a soldier? a lawyer? In any case, a worthy gentleman and, God willing, a man of distinction.

Walter, unconscious of the high hopes centered on him, was at that moment telling his brother Tom where to get off. He had found Jim and Tom chopping a fallen apple tree into fireplace lengths, and lost no time in making his announcement.

"Ma says I can go to school next term, Tom, and I'm not going to play baby any more."

"Good for you, Walter," Tom said mildly. "That's fine news. I'll give you my little penknife, so you can keep your pencils sharp."

Jim smiled. "I guess you're a big fellow now, all right," he admitted. Well past the age of make-believe games himself, he still remembered with amused sympathy Walter's fruitless protests at the indignity of his role in the family dramas.

Attendance at the one-room village school was an exciting novelty at first, then settled into a routine which Walter never found monotonous. The students, about twenty boys and girls, some of them sixteen and seventeen years old, sat in rows at desks. Mrs. Booker faced them from her own on a raised platform, a blackboard behind her and a large globe beside her.

She had never been known to use the ruler, suggestive of discipline and smarting palms, which lay in front of her, for anything except pointing.

In the country about Farmville there were a number of gold mines, which had been extensively worked before the rush to California in 1849. One of them, Booker's Mine, cast an atmosphere of glamor about the teacher for the younger Reed boys, although they never found out whether it was hers or not. They used to discuss the question lengthily, until practical Chris settled it finally to his own satisfaction.

"Of course she doesn't own a gold mine. Why would she work for a living teaching school if she did?" he wanted to know.

That seemed like good sense to Walter, but it was a disappointment. It was exciting to think that your teacher could get all the gold she wanted just by taking it out of her own mine—it was almost as exciting as if she had owned a candy store. The son of the poor country minister was dazzled by the mere idea of such resources.

While one class recited, the other prepared its lessons. Walter kept his nose buried in McGuffey's tale of the honest little chimney sweep who was to occupy the next recitation period, but read, fascinated, the big flat book he had cautiously opened on his knees. The Rocky Mountains, the Colorado River, the buffalo and the Indians, the wild, adventurous west—how exciting it seemed by contrast to the well-ordered domestic scene! Someday, when he was big, he would go there himself—maybe on one of the new railroads that were even then slowly, certainly, probing their way across the wide continent, spanning rivers, crawling across plains, connecting remote villages with the outside world, binding east to west, north to south, with tough steel bonds.

The cool, crisp voice caught him off-guard. "Walter Reed, bring me the book you are hiding under your desk."

It was before the age of dime novels, but the popularity among her pupils of lurid adventure yarns about the gold rush, cattle thieves and other western topics, was well known to Mrs. Booker. Blushing, Walter stood up. Every eye in the room fastened on him. He walked slowly toward the desk, holding the suspicious volume behind him, a small, tow-headed figure in neat cotton shirt and pants. A subdued expression of humor, Mrs. Booker noted, belied the penitent droop of his bearing. He stood meekly before her, his eye on the ruler. His teacher extended her hand for the offending book.

"What is this book, Walter?" she demanded with a sternness that covered up a faint misgiving. The boy was almost smiling!

"Just my geography, ma'am," he answered.

CHAPTER THREE

THE SHADOW of the approaching catastrophe had lain, at first, but lightly over the younger members of the Reed household. The threatening atmosphere, growing more electric with every year, had seemed, in fact, a natural element to the two boys who grew up into it and were unacquainted with the bland airs of peace. If Mr. Reed's habitually calm expression took on additional gravity when he discussed the possibility of war between the states with his wife, and if Mrs. Reed, looking at her older boys, could not always keep a trace of apprehension out of her expressive eyes, Chris and Walter probably did not notice, or, if they did, merely thought that being grown up was in some mysterious way a grave affair.

1859 and 1860 saw the Reeds settled at Liberty, now called Bedford, in Bedford County, near the foothills of the Blue Ridge Mountains. After two years of duty there, discharged with the usual unselfish devotion that made the Methodist circuit riders beloved and admired wherever they went, Mr. Reed was shifted to Blackstone, in Nottingham County, then an important railway center and nearer the scene of the tragic action of the next four years.

The long dissension had been steadily sharpening between the manufacturing North and the farming South. The North wanted slavery barred from the United States territories, and the South, whose whole economy was based on slave labor, knew that its voice in the council of states would be diminished and finally strangled should slavery be kept out of the territories. Sectional bitterness was violent, and the struggle between the two societies was close to exploding into open

32

conflict. Congressmen went armed with pistols, and Senator Jefferson Davis of Mississippi sadly reported that the Congress appeared to be composed of the representatives of warring states, rather than of men assembled for the common good.

Abraham Lincoln, unalterably opposed to the extension of slavery into the territories, but no abolitionist, was elected President in November, 1860. The following month, South Carolina, traditionally prone to secession, by the decision of a popular convention in holiday spirits withdrew from the Union. Some southern states followed; others, Virginia among them, hesitated. In February Jefferson Davis was inaugurated President of the Confederate States before an excited throng in Montgomery, Alabama. Still, Lincoln solemnly assured his "dissatisfied fellow countrymen" that, while there would be no secession, neither would there be a war unless they started it. And to show his conciliatory spirit, he backed an amendment to the Constitution which passed both houses of Congress preventing the Federal government for all future time from interfering with slavery in any state in which it was already established. Almost, it appeared that war might at the last moment be staved off.

Then, on April 12, 1861, southern guns fired on Federal-held Fort Sumter in Charleston Harbor, and the hope of peace vanished with the puff of powder smoke in the damp spring air.

The antagonists quickly fell into line. Virginia reluctantly decided to join the seceding states rather than yield to the Federal government's demand for troops to discipline them. In the end, eleven southern states faced twenty-three northern ones; nine million people, more than a third of them slaves, pitted themselves against the strength of twenty-two million free men. The North had almost all the clothing, munitions and metal industries in the country, and a large proportion of the nation's banking capital. Moreover, most of the foreign goods imported for southern use passed through northern warehouses.

The South had little but cotton—cotton and courage. But they believed that Cotton was King, in the popular phrase of the day, and they had yet to learn that brave hearts are no more bulletproof than trembling ones.

Having voted to secede, Virginia, as everyone had foreseen, was immediately invaded. The war was on now, in earnest.

Daylight was fading, and Laura moved closer to the window to make the most of it. Her eyes smarted and her throat burned with the tears she painfully restrained. There was no good in crying. It would only upset the younger children, and distress Ma—brave Ma, whose air of cheerfulness deceived no one. In the dimming light she bent closer over Jim's shirt.

When Jim had returned suddenly from college at Randolph-Macon and announced that he was enlisting, there had been a heavy silence. Ma's hands, busy with a piece of sewing, had dropped in her lap and she stared at him speechless, her eyes slowly filling with tears. Her first son, only eighteen, going to the war! Fearfully she thought, "Thank heaven, the others are too young!"

Mr. Reed had been the first to speak. He pushed aside the sheets of paper on which he was writing his sermon, and said sadly, "It is your plain duty, son. Your mother and I could not wish you to act otherwise."

Tom got up from his chair and came to his father's side.

"Pa, I . . ." he began.

"No!" his father interrupted him almost harshly. "Our cause is not so desperate that a sixteen-year-old boy must fight." He took the edge off his words by putting his arm around Tom's shoulders. "Just wait," he advised a little grimly. "Your turn may come yet."

"Why, Pa!" Jim exclaimed. "The war will be over in a few

months. We can whip those Yanks easily. I expect to enter the University at Charlottesville this fall."

"I'm afraid your expectations will have to be put aside, Jim," the minister observed. "You underestimate the resources of our opponents. Not only are we vastly outnumbered, but all the tools of war are made in the North. We have almost none of the necessary industries. Even the clothes we wear, made of the cotton we grow, have to be manufactured up there."

"But Pa, that's just it," Jim pointed out. "We'll stop delivering cotton. If the cotton mills go under, the whole industrial system of the North will be shaken."

"Theirs will be shaken," his father conceded, "but ours will be destroyed. Ours is a farming economy, and cotton is our main crop. If we can't trade it for war materials—and you may rely on it that they won't trade us the guns to shoot them with, and that they'll do everything they can to keep England from doing so—we'll simply choke to death on it. We can't eat it, we can't shoot with it, we can't pay our soldiers with it, and we can't even wear it until it's been converted by northern mills. No, Jim, the South depends more on the North than it realizes, and the North is more independent of us than we suppose." He paused a moment and his family looked at him, troubled. "It will certainly be a desperate war, and probably a long one," he added.

"Then do you think it's hopeless, Pa?" Tom inquired anxiously.

The minister's answer rang with confidence. "No cause is hopeless when it is just, and when brave men defend it!"

"Pa, will it last long enough for Chris and me to go?" Walter inquired hopefully. "We're almost big enough for drummers now."

"Indeed not!" his mother answered fervently. "Will it, Pa?"

"God forbid!" Mr. Reed exclaimed.

Laura's practical mind had run in advance of the discussion.

Jimmy was going to the war; what could be done to make him comfortable?

"Jim, what can I do to help you to get ready?"

"Make me some shirts, sis. Most of mine are wearing out."

"Tomorrow. I'll start to make you half a dozen."

"No, no! Two is enough. A good campaigner doesn't carry a lot of extra clothes around with him." He smiled and took her hand. He and his sister, only two years apart, had always been particularly close friends. "One to wear while the other is drying, you know."

"Oh, Jim! I'll make you the best shirts you've ever had in your life."

"Fine! Not that I deserve it, but nothing's too good to fight for your country in," he said lightly.

And nothing's too good to die for your country in, he had not added. But the thought had leaped to everyone's mind.

Thinking of the unsaid words, Laura stitched faster, with a sort of panicky urgency. Nothing must happen to Jim—not to Jim, who was tall, and strong, and kind, whom everyone loved, who was just becoming a man, with perhaps half a century of usefulness and life ahead of him. The silent tears suddenly overflowed and slipped down her face. Pressing the almost finished shirt against her eyes, she thought desperately, "Not Jimmy! No, no, not Jimmy!"

CHAPTER FOUR

JIM WAS GONE, and the unhappy gap he left in the family circle forecast a changed manner of life that was to last for four dreary years.

When fall came, Chris and Walter and Tom went back to school as usual, now to the Union Academy where the school-masters, two severe gentlemen named Crenshaw and Hardy, taught the classical curriculum of the day and relied heavily on the hickory stick as an aid to learning. The Reed boys learned easily and were too interested in their studies to need such stimulus, but many of their friends were less fortunate. Several of the less scholarly often sought their help with their Greek and Latin, in exchange for rides on their ponies, use of their marbles and similar inducements. It was an arrangement satisfactory to everyone, and sanctioned by long use.

Although school changed little, life outside it was very different. Abandoning cowboy-and-Indian as outmoded, Walter and Chris now played that they were daring Confederate soldiers, and uttered the hair-raising Rebel yell instead of the Indian war whoop. But Tom rarely joined their games any more. He was too old to *play* at war, he told them, with an impatience that covered his increasing restlessness.

Ma and Laura were continually sewing. They gathered at the church with other neighborhood women, to make clothes for the soldiers. Cotton cloth was running out, and it was not long before spinning wheels and looms were brought down from attics and homespun garments began to appear again.

How to help the men in the army was the thought upper-most in every patriotic mind. Pies, cakes, hams and other things to eat were prepared and sent to the troops. It was not long, however, before Virginians began to feel the pinch as the food shortage set in. Desserts disappeared, luxuries went out of common use; all good things available were saved for the "boys." As the grip of the blockade established by the North gradually and surely tightened, even such necessities as salt and coffee became increasingly scarce.

Mr. Reed, taking his first taste of adulterated coffee, choked into his napkin and glared at his wife.

"What is this stuff, Ma?" he demanded.

"It is dreadful, isn't it?" Ma agreed. "I made it out of parched corn and dried sweet potatoes, and just the least pinch of coffee, for flavor. Mrs. Sydnor told me about it. She thinks sweet potato's better than rye. Our coffee is almost gone, and it's the last we'll be able to get."

Mr. Reed poured into the despised brew a liberal amount of "long sweetening," the sorghum which was replacing sugar, and stirred it with a resigned expression.

"Well, we shall have to accustom ourselves to it. I suppose we may even get to like it when we're used to it," he observed.

"Like tobacco, Pa?" Walter inquired smiling.

His father laughed, something he rarely did now. "I hope it won't be that hard, son!" He added, "Even so, we're much better off here than they are in Richmond and Petersburg, where only corn bread and peas and sorghum are really plentiful. No one except the blockade runners has any of the luxuries —we used to consider them the necessities—of food and clothing."

"And our poor soldiers," Mrs. Reed sighed, thinking of Jim with Lee's Army of Northern Virginia. His letters were infrequent, brief and cheerful. He had escaped the measles epidemic; the Yanks hadn't shot him—yet; the life was hard, the food rough and scanty; General Lee, adored by his men, shared their hardships, accepted few privileges, and called the

Yankees "those people," never "the enemy"; a soldier's life left little time for writing letters and he still hoped to enter the University, if not this fall, the one after.

The deferment of Jim's plans was significant of the altered attitude of the South. The Confederates were beginning to grasp the length of the odds against them. The northern campaign to capture Richmond in the spring of 1862 came dangerously close to success. Later in the year, the southern invasion of Maryland ended in failure at Antietam, the bloodiest battle of the entire war. For the Reeds this last engagement fought on the fabled Indian battleground was not only a serious reverse to their cause, but a personal grief as well. Jim was wounded, his left arm shot away by a cannon ball.

The war might disrupt the state and the nation, but the southern Methodist Church continued to operate on schedule. At the close of his two years at Blackstone, Mr. Reed in 1863 was transferred to a new circuit, this time to Lawrenceville, in Brunswick County, a few miles from the southern border of the state and a little farther from the front.

But near or far, there was no escaping the war. No matter where the fighting lines were, it was in their homes. Tom had received his father's consent and joined the army. The blockade was being more keenly felt. Food shortages amounted to acute hardships and the prices of all commodities, calculated in the almost worthless Confederate money, were fantastic. Increasingly urgent appeals flooded the countryside from Petersburg, where the big military hospitals, kept going largely by voluntary contributions, were in desperate need of food, clothing and, above all, medicine and surgical supplies.

On January 1, 1863, President Lincoln had proclaimed those slaves within the enemy lines free. The Mississippi, back door of the Confederacy's foreign trade, had been effectively stoppered, and seaport after seaport was falling into the hands of the superior Yankee fleet. The incomparable Stonewall Jackson, idol of his men and right hand of Lee, was accidentally killed by his own sentries after the battle of Chancellorsville, another of those southern victories which served only to stave off the end. (It was God's purpose, a southern minister said later, that the South should be defeated, but, he added quite without impiety, He first had to get rid of Stonewall before He could accomplish His will.) Early in July Vicksburg, sole remaining southern port on the Mississippi, succumbed to siege. At the same time Lee, reminding his troops that vengeance was the Lord's, and not theirs, to execute, tried again to carry the war into enemy territory and was defeated at Gettysburg. The tide had already set against the South; now it was running strong.

"Pa, you can stop worrying about your ink," Walter, running to meet his father in the yard, shouted to him. "We've made you some. It's fine stuff."

Mr. Reed, returning from a call on a sick parishioner, dismounted from Bess and hoisted his son into the saddle.

"How did you manage it, son?" he asked. It had become impossible to buy ink, and to a man who wrote as much as he, this was as great a hardship as the lack of tea and coffee.

"Ma thought of it," Walter told him, "and Chris and I worked on it." Riding the horse to the barn, with his father walking beside him, Walter explained about the elderberry wine and soot. They had made several small batches, to work out the right proportions, and finally produced a satisfactory ink, smooth and glossy.

Pa was pleased. As he congratulated his wife on her ingenuity, he was glad to observe that her cheerfulness seemed less forced than it had for some time. Her determined vivacity had not concealed from him the effort behind it.

"It was quite simple," she assured him. "The boys did all

the work, anyway. Really, Pa, it's wonderful how independent of foreign aid we are becoming."

"We're doing splendidly," he agreed heartily. His conscience compelled him to add, "It's fortunate for us that there is this lull now, since the defeat at Gettysburg and Lee's offer to resign his command. It gives us a breathing space." A breathing space for what? he could not help wondering.

"That was good blacking we made, too. Remember, Ma?" Chris chimed in.

"It was indeed. I shouldn't wonder if we were quite self-sufficient in another year," his mother answered hopefully.

All at once, in the face of this courageous, pathetic optimism, the minister found himself unable to evade his fears any longer. The blockade was all but impenetrable, their money worthless, medicine unobtainable, food scarce, their resources of materials and man power approaching exhaustion. How could they go on? He dropped into his chair, grasping its familiar arms for assurance in the whirling world.

"Really, my dear, let us not deceive ourselves any longer," he said with sudden, utter weariness. "We are doing remarkably well, but not well enough. Under the circumstances, no people could do better. But it won't do. The war is already lost; soon it will be over. I am glad," he added, taking Chris and Walter by the hand, "that you two boys have been spared the worst of it. When it is all over, then we will need men as never before."

But the sinking Confederacy, like a mortally ill man who by sheer will prolongs his life for a few more hours, would not die yet.

The fall and winter of 1863 and 1864 dragged past in comparative quiet in Virginia. By the middle of January, 1864, there were only three ports still open to blockade runners on the entire southern coastline, and with the return of spring the pressure on land began again. The Yankees were swarming irresistibly, in heartbreaking numbers, all over northern Virginia. Richmond, the precariously held capital, was continually shaken by alarming rumors and the "croakers" mournfully predicted surrender at any moment. The rich Shenandoah Valley, a farm region vital to the half-starved Confederacy, was pillaged bare. Sherman made his desolating march from Atlanta to the sea, breaking the South in half. Lee, holed up in Petersburg, stood off Grant's advance against Richmond for nine months, while the Union foragers plucked the country clean for miles around. Confederate strength was almost spent.

Even while the handful of Sheridan's raiders were capturing the minister's sons and the farmer's boy and appropriating their horses on the bank of the Meherrin, southern resistance was melting.

On the night of April 9, 1865, the cannon boomed one hundred times in the capital of the Confederacy, but it was several days before the news of Lee's surrender was confirmed in the evacuated city.

The government had fled south a week before, and President Lincoln had entered Richmond, while General Lee, rallying his thirty-five thousand "Miserables" for the last time, retreated westward. Only eight thousand of his starved and tattered army remained when he reached Appomattox; the rest, scattered, captured, demoralized, had melted away on the march. Lee, as serene in defeat as in victory, surrendered, and accepted General Grant's terms, offered with soldierly generosity.

"Our past is a memory," Pa said sadly to his sons when the bitter news of defeat reached them, "but there is still the future. It is up to you, and to boys and young men like you, to make something of it."

CHAPTER FIVE

NOW THAT THE WAR was over, young Lieutenant William Richardson Abbot thought, he could get on with his work. His father had been a scholar, a gentleman and a schoolmaster; he, he trusted, would be another.

Educated at his father's academy near Washington, and at Georgetown College and Military Academy, young Abbot had attended the University of Virginia, where for his brilliance he had been given an honorary master's degree on his graduation in 1857. Three pleasant years of teaching ended with the outbreak of the Civil War and the young schoolmaster took a job in the Treasury Department at Richmond. Irked by the safety of his work, he later enlisted for active service, and was assigned to the First Regiment Engineers. His engineers—it was a source of undying pride to him—had fired the last volley at Appomattox; then they had surrendered and he, like the other officers, had been paroled.

Soldiering had been his duty, not his choice, and he was glad to get back to his business. The South might be defeated, but there were always children to educate, boys of whom to make men. So in the fall of 1865 Mr. Abbot opened, with Major Horace Jones, a day school for boys at Charlottesville, the Charlottesville Institute.

Mr. Reed had been worrying about his sons' education.

"I'm a poor man, Ma," he had said. "I don't see how I'm to give those boys the education they should have."

"Everybody's poor now," his wife had reminded him. "I hope we can manage to send them to the University, too, but if we can't I shan't be too distressed. There's no finer man in the whole world than their Pa," she told him proudly, "and he didn't go to college."

"Hush, Ma," Pa said, smiling, "you'll turn my head. But," he continued, "if we could live at Charlottesville, half our problem would be solved. Then the boys could live at home instead of boarding at the University."

"Why don't you talk to the bishop about it? It's time for us to move on, anyway."

Lemuel Reed was a modest man. He did not feel that he deserved any special consideration from his church, nor did he want it. But four boys, every one of them a fine fellow and deserving the best education available! Finally and with reluctance he told the bishop that, should there be an opening in a town having good educational facilities, he would appreciate being considered for it, for the sake of his sons. He was overjoyed when he was appointed Presiding Elder of the Charlottesville district.

So it happened that, when Mr. Abbot opened his school, young Walter Reed was one of some thirty boys who attended it.

A mile or so of red mud separated the Charlottesville Institute from the University of Virginia, but the path led straight from the one to the other. Indeed, it was the single aim of all the classical schools in the state at that time to fit boys to pursue advanced studies at Mr. Jefferson's celebrated University. The courses of study at these schools were almost identical: Latin, Greek, mathematics, history, a modern language, and often a science course taught from a textbook, without laboratory work.

Walter by now was an excellent linguist, well advanced in the classical languages; strangely, however, considering his later choice of medicine as a profession, he had no particular interest in science. But perhaps it was not so strange that the future doctor, whose consuming desire was to relieve suffering wherever he found it, was unmoved by scientific study, drily presented between cardboard covers and applying, so far as he could see, only indirectly to human problems.

The schoolmaster immediately liked his young pupil. The boy, he found, had a sound, keen mind, and enthusiasm for learning. Moreover, he had a gracious and winning personality: gaiety without frivolity, and the unfailing, unstudied courtesy that springs from a warm and considerate nature.

Walter, in turn, was deeply impressed by this man with the erect bearing and vigorous intellect, whose formality was tempered with friendliness. All the boys were impressed by him, and imitated him in little ways. They cultivated his manner of speaking, tried to copy his incisive handwriting, and laboriously trained their hair to fall, like his unmanageable forelock, over their foreheads.

A teacher, in Mr. Abbot's opinion, should have a wide and thorough training to be worthy of his calling. But enthusiasm was the first essential. He had a way of expressing himself in telling aphorisms. "Who was ever convinced," Walter remembered his saying, "by one who did not feel the truth? What mind was ever lighted up or warmed by that which was dark and cold?"

Under the Virginia schoolmaster Walter learned his lessons well; he learned also principles of teaching which, thirty years later, were to come back to him in all their force and make him a teacher worthy of his old preceptor.

Metropolitan Charlottesville, with its five thousand inhabitants, half-dozen churches, stores, daily paper, Court House and cobbled streets, amazed the boy from the slow-paced rural tobacco towns of mid-Virginia; but it did not distract him from his object. He was anxious to get to the University and begin his professional training, in what field he had not yet decided. He owed it to Pa and Ma to become self-supporting as soon as possible; and his wish to do something that would "help people," as he had hesitantly expressed it to Joey, made him want to get out into the world without waste of time.

In the roomy brick house in Charlottesville life shifted back to its pleasant pre-war routine, a routine which Walter had almost forgotten. He worked hard for Mr. Abbot, and stood close to the head of his class; he listened tirelessly to his elder brothers' accounts of that Mecca of all Virginia students, the University; sometimes he made short trips with Pa, or tramped with Chris over the rolling green hills surrounding Charlottesville.

The pleasant, profitable fall gave way to winter, and the time passed rapidly—almost like a happy dream, Walter thought, looking backward sorrowfully, shaken by his first major grief. Early in February, 1866, Mrs. Reed died, leaving her family, in their first shock, unable to see how they would get along without her. Ma, with her sympathy and humor, her inexhaustible energy and patience and enterprise, had more than anyone else made the family a closely united one.

Her death brought home to Walter jarringly the realization that the span of a life is relatively short. If he was to accomplish anything worth while in the world in which so much needed to be done, he had no time to lose.

He worked with extra diligence the rest of that session, and again the following. At the end of the second he was ready to enter the University—except for one thing, and that was beyond his control. He was under the required age. He decided, however, to try. The authorities were doubtful. They conceded that there was nothing wrong with his scholarship or preparation. After all, had he not been in the hands of their own Mr. Abbot? But, they thought, it was unwise to accept so young a student, a mere boy. Finally, perhaps on his schoolmaster's recommendation, they consented to admit him.

In the fall of 1867, Walter Reed, barely sixteen, entered the University of Virginia.

The benign shade of Thomas Jefferson still lingered almost visibly over the University he had founded nearly half a century earlier. Although for more than forty years he had been lying in the family burial plot on the shaggy Virginia hillside crowned by his beloved home, Monticello, professors and students respectfully alluded to "Mr. Jefferson" almost as though he might any day ride in again, as he had on his last visit, to consult with Mr. William Wertenbaker, the librarian, about cataloguing some new books.

The University was peculiarly the product of his versatile genius. Not only had he planned its first curriculum, engaged its original faculty and shaped its policies, but also he had designed and erected its buildings. The Rotunda, adapted from the Roman Pantheon, and the flanking pavilions, modeled after Roman temples and baths, suggested the great democrat's admiration for the sturdy, uncorrupted republic of Rome.

A strong unanimity of feeling existed among both students and professors. They were united not so much by their lost cause—that was history now—as by the resolution to do everything in their power to restore the prostrated South to economic and political health. During the war many of its most promising boys and valuable professional men had been killed. Those who were left had much to do. The student body was more than usually serious, too, for another reason: all of them had grown up among the sobering hardships of the war, and a number, especially in the professional schools, were young men in their middle twenties who had interrupted their training to fight through the four years. A few, like Jim, had a missing arm or leg, a limp or a patch over the eye, to testify to their service.

The faculty were worthy successors to those men whom Mr.

Jefferson had picked to conform to his exacting ideal of the good teacher. Walter now studied Greek with Dr. Basil Lanneau Gildersleeve, considered the finest Greek scholar in the country, and author of the Latin grammar he had used as a child. Dr. Gildersleeve's cutaway and silk hat, his full black beard and mustache, his limp from a battle wound—he had taught during the sessions, fought through the vacations—made him one of the most distinguished figures at the University, while his erudition and good-humored witticisms made him a popular teacher. The unimposing appearance of Walter's professor of history and literature, Dr. George Frederick Holmes, did little to suggest his scholarship and ability. Habitually garbed in an ill-fitting cutaway and shapeless pantaloons, with his neck in the grip of a badly knotted cravat, he always conveyed the impression of being in a great hurry, as he strode along, gray whiskers flying and gold-rimmed spectacles glittering.

Dr. William Elisha Peters, with whom Walter studied Latin, was a small, mild man, plain in his dress but vastly proud of his dainty feet, which he never disfigured, even in the worst weather, with overshoes. No one laughed at his little vanity. He was a man of character, and entitled to his foibles. As a colonel in the Confederate army, it was said, he had refused the order of his superior officer to burn Chambersburg with the retort, "I am not in the war to burn the homes of helpless women and children"—a piece of insubordination which General Lee later approved.

There were other celebrated characters, too, at the University whom Walter frequently saw. William Holmes McGuffey, from whose readers he and countless other children had learned reading and morality, both similarly adjusted to their years, taught Moral Philosophy. A small, beardless, bright-eyed man, he was pointed out to Walter as he trotted along the arcade, carrying a cane and dressed with old-fashioned conservatism in a long, black, full-skirted coat, a high collar and stock and a tall silk hat.

Another figure having a distinction all his own was Mr. Wertenbaker, almost the last man left at the University who had known the great founder personally. Small and infirm, with a wrinkled face topped by thin gray hair, he was looked on with general affection by the boys. He handled the University's printing, made up the annual catalogue, kept the library open at specified hours every day, filled in and signed diplomas, and played chess tirelessly in his spare time in the back room of Dr. Michie's drugstore. More than anything else he loved to recall the early days of the University, when Mr. Jefferson was Rector, Mr. Madison and Mr. Monroe were on the Board of Visitors, and Mr. Poe was a student.

The only other relic of Mr. Jefferson's day then remaining was Henry Martin, the ancient and respected Negro who had been brought from Monticello in the year of his master's death. A tall, stalwart old man, with thick black hair, almost straight, a long, thin goatee and remarkable gray-blue eyes, he rang the bell hourly for classes, kept the fires going in the Rotunda and classrooms and took care of the buildings. Perhaps his most impressive attribute was his ability to call every student by name, not only during his years of residence at the University, but long after.

No time was wasted at the University. Classes began early in the morning, the school year was nine months long, and no vacations broke it. The faculty thought long holidays were demoralizing; even Christmas was observed with but a single day's freedom.

Walter quickly felt at home attending lectures or working in the library in the Rotunda, walking to class through the arcades formed by the classical porticoes of the pavilions, or strolling with one of his brothers down the avenues of trees on the Lawn. It was a congenial and stimulating atmosphere for the boy whose youthful face was already beginning to assume the expression of intentness that later characterized the doctor.

At home life was much happier than it had been at any time since Ma's death. Pa had married again, Mrs. Mary Byrd Kyle of Harrisonburg, Virginia, and although no one could replace Ma, the boys soon became fond of their stepmother. Laura had married J. W. Blincoe and gone to Ashland to live, and they had missed having a woman in the family. When a baby half-sister, Annie, was born, they all felt that their shattered family was, in a sense, restored.

Walter was charmed by Annie. She seemed to like him, too, or at least to think he was funny, and laughed and clucked at him as she clung to his extended finger.

"Do you remember when Walter was born, Jim?" Tom asked at supper one evening. "What a terrible little pest you and I thought he was!"

"Do I! He couldn't do a thing for himself except yell."

"We'd just about reconciled ourselves to Chris, and then there was this new baby. But we finally got kind of used to him, too," Tom added, grinning at his youngest brother.

"Walter, as I remember him, was much squallier than Annie," Pa joined in the teasing. "I think babies have improved a lot in the last sixteen years."

"Well, Pa," Walter answered good-humoredly, "I hope I've improved in the last sixteen years, too, although I know I still can't compete with the young lady."

"I don't see how any of you could improve any more," Mrs. Reed confessed, smiling around happily at them. "You'd be too good to be true."

At the University Walter was working very hard. He had a plan in the back of his head. It might take persuasion to put it across; certainly it would take hard work, and he would need the highest marks he could get. He intended to ask for his bachelor's degree at the end of his first year because he realized that it was too hard for Pa to keep three boys in the University at once. The University sometimes certified students whose records were very good, and he was out to make the best one possible.

He still found time, however, to stop occasionally for a chat with Mr. Wertenbaker when he climbed to the library by the narrow, steep stairs which, built into the wall and hidden from sight, were the only kind Mr. Jefferson could tolerate. Sometimes the old gentleman would show him a cherished book, its fly leaf endorsed in the founder's fine, legible hand, or read him a page from Jefferson's memoir and correspondence, edited by Thomas Jefferson Randolph, Mr. Jefferson's devoted grandson. Once he showed him a framed letter from Mr. Jefferson to young Mr. Kean,* appointing him student assistant in the library in the first year of the University's existence.

"He was a fine young gentleman," the old librarian reminisced. "His son was a student here, too. He married a Miss Randolph, daughter of Mr. Jefferson's grandson, and now he has a fine little boy, must be six or seven years old by this time. He'll come here too, like his pa and his grandpa." He was off now on a complicated genealogical discourse to which Walter, smiling, only half listened. He did not foresee that this little boy, in whose existence he was now barely interested, would in thirty years be his colleague and dear friend.

Once in a while, as long as the ice held, Walter would go skating with Chris or Tom or some of the other students on the University ice pond, or on Cochran's pond beyond Charlottesville. As spring came on the boys took long rambles in the hills around the city, and once had a picnic at Monticello.

The beautiful home of Thomas Jefferson, the site of which

* Pronounced *Kane.*

he had selected in his youth and which he had spent some thirty
years in building, was in ruins. The roof was decayed and
the rooms were dust covered and moldering, with cracked
walls and fallen ceilings. Windows and shutters, skillfully designed by their architect to give the impression of a one-story
rather than a two-story house, were broken and unhinged.
The slates of the porch were overgrown with moss, and visitors
had disfigured with their names and their sentiments the front
door and the columns of the portico. The aged overseer
always welcomed students and let them roam freely. After all,
what more harm could they do than his own goats and chickens,
innocent creatures that wandered at liberty through all the
rooms?

Even in its decay, the building impressed Walter with its
simple grandeur and dignity. The hens scattered ahead of the
boys as they came into the spacious entrance hall, covered with
the second parquet floor ever seen in the country—the first
had been in the palace of the colonial governors at Williams-
burg, and Mr. Jefferson, during his residence there, had admired it. Set above the front door, the ingenious two-faced
clock of his own design, which had once told for the benefit
of the absent-minded the day of the week as well as the hour,
looked blind and broken with its inner face on the desolate
elegance of the big hall, while its outer one gazed blankly
over the weedy lawn and the wooded hill. A skinny goat stared
back at them, curiosity in its mild eyes, from the room in
which the great man had worked on the plans for the University. In an upper room, reached by the narrow, typically Jef-
fersonian stairs, they found the coach in which the Marquis
de Lafayette had ridden on one of his visits to the University,
stored there for a reason long since forgotten by someone
equally lost to memory.

The ruin of the beautiful house, which had been its architect's beloved home for fifty years, distressed Walter. But Mr.

Jefferson, Walter reflected, had left behind him, in the Declaration, in the University, in all his other varied achievements, more lasting memorials. Let his home, let every physical reminder of him crumble; he would still be remembered because he did work worth doing, and did it well. That was better than a monument.

It was the last week of the term. Walter waited for a quarter of an hour in the hall, then came out on the steps of the Rotunda and stood looking down the Lawn. A slender boy of medium height and erect carriage, he had a determined, almost stubborn, mouth, and his blue eyes were clear and pleasant. Straight brown hair was brushed neatly across his forehead, which he patted with a clean white handkerchief. It was warm now, mid-June, but not warm enough to account for the prickle between his shoulder blades, or the dampness of his palms. He ran his finger around his collar, which felt too tight, then hoped that he hadn't disarranged the cravat his stepmother had carefully knotted for him.

"I want you to look your very best, Walter, when you go before the faculty," she had said. "A neat appearance always helps. Pa's so proud of you. I do hope your application will be successful. Such a shame you haven't a beard," she added, touching his smooth cheek.

"A long, woolly beard at sixteen, ma'am?" he teased her. "I'd be a freak."

"Not a long one—just enough to shave, so you'd look older," she explained. They had both laughed.

Walter felt very little like laughing now, as he leaned against the column and waited to be summoned before the faculty for their decision. He had made his request to be certified for a bachelor's degree without completing the academic course, and he was to receive his answer today. Although such exceptions were occasionally made, he feared that his youth would prevent it in this case. If they refused him—well, then he had another proposition to make to them.

Behind him he heard a door open, and turned. Dr. Holmes was peering up and down the hall.

"Ah, Reed, there you are. Will you come in now?"

Walter followed him into the lecture room. Ten or a dozen professors were standing around talking to each other. He recognized, besides those under whom he studied, Dr. Socrates Maupin, chairman of the faculty and professor of chemistry and pharmacy; Dr. James C. Cabell, one of a family famous in Virginia history; and Dr. John Staige Davis, the professor of anatomy. Dr. James Harrison, teacher of legal medicine and obstetrics, was raptly following a play by play account of one of Lee's victories given by Colonel Venable, who had been a staff officer of the general's.

"Come in, Mr. Reed," Dr. Maupin greeted him. "Gentlemen, shall we continue our business?"

They all resumed their seats, and in the brief silence that followed Walter could hear his heart thump.

Dr. Maupin, clearing his throat, looked around him and then at Walter.

"Mr. Reed," he said, "I am very sorry to disappoint you. It is, however, the decision of this faculty that we cannot waive the regulations to certify you for a degree."

"I see, sir," Walter answered slowly, fighting back his disappointment. "My work has not been up to the required standard?"

"On the contrary, my boy. Your record is excellent, excellent. Your age is the obstacle. A graduate at sixteen is almost unheard of, and as a matter of long-range policy we do not care to set such a precedent, however worthy your case may be. We made, you will recall, an exception to let you into the University. It would really be too much to have to make another to let you out."

The gentlemen were glancing doubtfully at each other.

Walter could not help smiling, Dr. Maupin had put it so neatly.

"Very well, sir. I must bow to your judgment," he agreed. "But may I make another request?" The chairman assented. "Will you give me a medical degree next year, if I pass the examination?"

Dr. Cabell, whose chin had been sunk up to the fringe of his side whiskers in his stiff collar, straightened and looked sharply at the slim, beardless young man. The medical school, one of the best in the country, would give a degree to any student, regardless of the length of his attendance, who could pass the rigorous examination. It was rare for anyone to take it in less than two years; some needed more. If the boy wanted to get his degree the hard way, let him try it, Dr. Cabell thought, and shrugged. If he hadn't the brain or the stamina, and it would take plenty of both, he wouldn't last long.

Walter was waiting for an answer. For a moment there was none. The gentlemen were glancing doubtfully at each other, with expressions which held a trace of amused pity for this overconfident boy.

To clinch matters, Walter added, with a deferential little bow toward the anatomy teacher,

"Where Dr. Davis has blazed the trail, perhaps it will not be impossible for others to follow."

Dr. Davis, who had received his own medical degree from the University when he was seventeen, smiled broadly at the adroit and flattering invocation of precedent. Consulting the other doctors with a glance, he nodded to Walter. Walter drew his first deep breath that afternoon.

"Thank you, sir," he said warmly. "Dr. Maupin, you have witnessed these gentlemen's consent. Will you see that I get my medical degree if I meet the required standard?"

"You shall have it, if you pass the examinations," Dr. Maupin promised him.

"Then, gentlemen," Walter turned to the faculty, "I shall hold you to your word." He bowed to them and left the room.

Alone in the hall, he leaned against the wall, his knees suddenly limp. Pulling his handkerchief out, he patted his forehead and wiped his damp palms.

"Thank heaven," he thought fervently, "my voice didn't break."

Another year, and what a year it would be, what a mountain of work in it! But at the end of it, a profession to practice, and beyond, the world and the future! Elated, he set off as fast as he could walk to tell Pa and the family.

Back in the lecture room, Dr. Harrison was shaking his head.

"I'm doubtful about it," he said. "It's a dreadful grind for one year. Few have tried it, and fewer have come through it."

"I think he may make it," Dr. Gildersleeve observed. "He's an excellent student, quick and sound. Look at his record."

"I scarcely anticipate that he will win his degree in a year," someone else remarked, "and I am even more doubtful of the wisdom of giving it to him if he does. A boy of that age lacks balance, experience."

"There I can't agree with you, sir," Dr. Davis came to the defense. "He appears to be a very competent young man. He behaved like a reasonable adult, respectful, no show of disappointment; and his reminder that he had precedent on his side was most tactfully put. And," he added with a smile, "he kept his wits about him—no loose ends. He left us no way out. He exacted our word, and we will have to give him the degree if he passes. It was a very smooth performance for a youngster. I have an idea that we may make a fine doctor of that young fellow."

CHAPTER SIX

THE OIL in his lamp was almost gone, Walter noticed. Turning the flame low, he pushed back his book and got up from the desk. His legs were stiff from long sitting, and he had a crick in his neck. Stretching, he went to the window. The silence lay softly over the dark city. He liked the feeling of having the world all to himself that came when everyone else was in bed. Then he had elbow room to think and study; the dark and the silence quenched all distractions.

The door opened softly. It was Pa, dressed, like most of the male population of the country at this hour, in the classic white nightshirt.

"My dear boy!" he exclaimed. "Aren't you ever going to bed? It's after three."

"Come in, Pa. I'm going soon. We're having a chemistry quiz tomorrow, and I wanted to brush up a bit."

"Another? You had one a couple of weeks ago."

"I know. We have them all the time. In everything. It keeps your knowledge in circulation. You don't have a chance to forget what you've learned."

"It's a good system," his father agreed. "But I'm worried about you, Walter. I don't think you've had more than four or five hours sleep a night for weeks."

"I'm trying to do two years' work in one, Pa," Walter reminded him. "I'm not brilliant, so I can't learn without working, but I can work hard. It isn't doing me any harm. I have no fear of the consequences."

"Well, I have," Pa said with emphasis. "You'll make yourself sick."

"I don't think so. I feel fine. In any case, I have no choice.

It was Pa, dressed in the classic white nightshirt.

I got into medicine by accident, but I can't stay in it that way. I'll have to work my hardest, especially if I'm to get my degree by the end of this session. Getting a medical education isn't the easy thing it used to be, you know."

"Walter, the best assets you'll ever have in your life are your health and your wits. Keeping hours like this will ruin one and addle the other. Now get on to bed, like a good fellow," Pa said authoritatively. "You can resume your education in the morning," he added drily.

"All right, Pa," Walter yielded with a smile. "I'll go now. But please stop worrying about me." Picking up the lamp, he followed Pa into the hall. At the door of the room he and Chris shared he whispered good night to his father. Then, blowing out the lamp, he quietly opened the door and slipped noiselessly into the dark room, so as not to disturb his sleeping brother.

Walter was right when he said that a medical education was not the easy thing to acquire that it had been; certainly it was not if you went to the University of Virginia for it.

During most of the eighteenth century there had been no medical schools at all in America. Very few men went abroad to study. A young man who wanted to be a doctor apprenticed himself to a physician for a period of from three to eight years, accompanied him on his calls and helped him compound his medicines. Then, having learned as much as his native ability permitted through observation, trial and error, he went into practice for himself.

In the decade before the Revolutionary War two medical schools had been founded: the Medical College of Philadelphia, which later became a part of the University of Pennsylvania, and the medical school of King's College, afterward Columbia University's College of Physicians and Surgeons. Before the end of the century, both Harvard and Dartmouth had established medical schools. Then a mushroom growth of them set in. A large proportion, staffed by incompetents and quacks and run for private profit only, graduated "doctors" after only a few months of haphazard training. In spite of the work of the few good schools, by the middle of the nineteenth century the reputation of American medical education was so scandalous, and its results were so dire, that a group of reputable physicians formed the American Medical Association, with the primary purpose of forcing certain uniform, minimum requirements on both schools and students. Their progress was slow and often discouraging, but the association did, gradually, cause a great improvement in medical education.

The medical training offered by the University of Virginia, however, had never caused the educational reformers a moment's distress. Its term of study was considerably longer, and its requirements for the degree were far more exacting than those of the general run of medical colleges. It ranked with the best schools of the time. Although it had no hospital attached to it then, and hence few facilities for clinical instruction, its theoretical teaching was unexcelled, as its founder, himself a more skilled and learned practitioner than most doctors of his day, had intended it should be. In Walter's time, those who intended to go into practice usually went to Philadelphia or New York after their graduation, where they got their clinical experience and took another medical degree at a college connected with a hospital.

The current state of medical knowledge was reflected in the school's curriculum. When Walter studied there he took just four courses: chemistry and pharmacy under Dr. Maupin; medicine, which included legal medicine and obstetrics, with Dr. Harrison; physiology and surgery with Dr. Cabell; and anatomy and *materia medica* with Dr. Davis. That session, for the first time, Dr. John William Mallet was offering his optional course in clinical microscopy, but there is no record to show that Walter took it.

Acceptance in America of the discoveries of Pasteur, which were to revolutionize both the theory and practice of the science of healing, was still years in the future. No one in this country conceived of the role of bacteria in disease and infection. Preventive medicine and sanitation were practically unexplored fields, although it was realized that there was some connection between cleanliness and good health. Epidemic fevers were still attributed variously to filth, the night air, "miasmas" and the wrath of God.

Although the discovery some twenty years earlier of anaesthesia, the greatest single medical advance of the century up to that time, had given surgery a great impetus, Lister's recently demonstrated antiseptic technique had as yet gained no followers in this country. Wounds either healed "by first intention"—that is, immediately and without complication—or something mysteriously went wrong and infection set in. When Walter was studying, even the most scrupulous surgeon would have dismissed as ridiculous the notion that he might be carrying with him, from one of his patients to another, infection and even death on his bright instruments and his bare hands.

The sum total of medical knowledge, however, had increased vastly over the preceding century. Much more was known of the functions of the body and its organs, and of the cellular structure of bone and tissue. Diseases were more accurately classified and identified, and symptoms were differentiated from diseases themselves. Typhus and typhoid were no longer confused; measles, scarlatina, smallpox and chickenpox were clearly distinguished. The "bilious remittent fevers" were now separated into yellow fever, dengue, typhoid and malaria. Kidney diseases had been recognized and described, heart and lung and other diseases of organs identified. Medical knowledge was constantly on the march, a march no less significant for being overshadowed by the tremendous burst of progress shortly to follow.

The tools physicians worked with had improved, too. The stethoscope had been in use for about fifty years, enabling doctors better to diagnose valvular diseases of the heart. The clinical thermometer, an unwieldly instrument almost a foot long, was just coming into general use, and could reveal to a physician in five minutes whether his patient had a fever or not. The hypodermic syringe was beginning to be used, as were various instruments useful in examination and diagnosis. The greatly improved microscope made possible the study of cellular structure.

At the University of Virginia most of the medical lectures

were given in the upstairs room of the small square brick building to the west of the other University buildings. Five years
before, Henry Scharf had completed his beautiful series of
colored plates, considered at the time the finest anatomical
pictures in the country, for the use of the physiology and
anatomy classes; and although the practice of working on
cadavers and, later, on laboratory animals, was to make them
outmoded in time, they were in constant use in Walter's day,
when it was still difficult to obtain corpses for medical students
to dissect.

The University's medical course had provided for dissection
from its beginning, but it was not until 1884 that the state
recognized the need for legal provisions governing the supply
of anatomical material. Until then, all medical schools in Virginia had to obtain bodies by such devices as grave-robbing and
bribing dishonest undertakers to bury coffins heavy not with
the remains of the dear departed, but with weights. Executed
criminals and paupers buried in the potter's field were fair game
for the resurrectionists, as the grave-robbers were called.

The operations of the resurrectionists provoked a certain
ghoulish humor, as the following jingle, popular among medical students of the time, suggests:

> "The body-snatchers, they have come,
>   And made a snatch at me.
> It's very hard them kind of men
>   Won't let a body be!
>
> Don't go and weep upon my grave
>   And think that there I be.
> They haven't left an atom there
>   Of my anatomy!"

At the University of Virginia the problem of getting cadavers was left to one of the janitors—not to Old Henry, who

was too dignified to be cast in the horrid role of body-snatcher, but to another less venerable. Only a real love of science got most of the students through the anatomy course. The cadavers, few in number and ill preserved, gave many of the boys a life-long distaste for dead bodies—not a bad thing, after all, in a doctor.

Sometimes, looking back on his days as a medical student, Walter wondered how he could have handled so much work. Day after day, he spent hours in the dissecting room, working on the corpse of some pauper or criminal who was rendering this final, involuntary service to society; hours working in the chemistry laboratory; hours examining and copying Scharf's anatomical plates, until he had fixed in his mind forever the position of every muscle and organ, the course of every vein and artery; more hours at home, and these regularly carried him into early morning, studying his textbooks and preparing for the frequent quizzes.

He was young and healthy and strong, so the grind, as he insisted, did him no harm. Above all, he was single-minded; and that, more than anything else, enabled him to drive steadily ahead, working night and day as though his life depended on it, and ignoring fatigue when he could no longer deny it.

Chris and he had definitely decided to go to New York, Chris to practice law and Walter to work at Bellevue Hospital Medical College.

"If you're going to be a lawyer," Chris theorized one night when they were studying together after the rest of the household had gone to bed, "you might just as well be one in a place where you won't ever run out of clients. Even if there are a lot of lawyers in New York, I reckon there still are enough disputes to go 'round among them."

"It's as good a place as there is in the country for a young doctor to train, too," Walter observed, "and it certainly has some of the finest hospitals. I'm glad you're going, too. Won't we have fun exploring the city together!"

"Just think! Nearly a million people all at once! Remember how Joey Rogers wouldn't believe us when we told him? It's almost impossible to imagine, isn't it?"

"Charlottesville, times two hundred," Walter suggested. "Just suppose that, for every person you see here, you were seeing two hundred. Does that help?"

"Help!" Chris groaned. "How does it make you feel to imagine four hundred people working at this desk right now? It makes me feel so terrible," he closed his book with a grin, "that I'm going to bed. You'd better come, too."

"Pretty soon," Walter promised him. "Mind you don't wake Pa, the way you did last night. It wasn't twelve yet, and he made me go to bed."

"Pretty soon" was two hours later, but when he finally followed Chris to bed, Walter felt that he could face Dr. Cabell's test the next day with confidence.

Belching threateningly, the steam engine gathered its energies for the start. Its bell tolled loudly. Smoke, shot through with sparks, puffed faster from its flaring stack. The high, heavy wheels, which the engineer had tapped while the train waited, began to turn. Slowly the old one-story brick station moved backward, taking with it the platform along which stood a line of ancient hacks and Negro drivers equally aged. Mrs. Reed waved her damp handkerchief again as she receded. Pa, remaining stationary amid the sliding scene by walking as fast as his long legs could take him, shouted some final word lost in the clamor, and dropped back waving his hat.

The train went faster. The scenery began to flow. Chris, who had been staring out the window for a last look at familiar things, sat back in his seat and regarded his brother.

"Well, Dr. Reed," he said almost with awe, "we're on our own now."

As the train pounded over the long bridge across the Rivanna River, both young men gazed out the window for a final sight of Monticello, which, its decay softened by distance, watched the valley from the crown of its flat-topped hill.

"Dr. Reed!" Walter repeated. "I can still hardly believe it."

Commencement, preceded by the festivities of the various fraternities and clubs, the parade through the arcades with Chinese lanterns, the open house receptions of convivial professors, the sermons and the speeches, was past. On the first of July, 1869, Dr. Maupin, true to his word, had given Walter his medical degree. He was, the chairman told him, the youngest man ever to earn one from the University of Virginia. Walter was less impressed by the luster of that distinction than by the responsibility it laid on him.

Through cuts, up and down inclines, the little engine roared and strained along the road over the rugged, hilly country to Gordonsville. It paused, blowing hard, at the tiny town with the big whitewashed hotel, handful of stores and small white houses, and let Chris and Walter, with the other Washington-bound passengers, change to the Orange and Alexandria line.

"Walter, aren't you excited?" Chris demanded, after they had disposed their baggage and lunch boxes about them for the second time. "I feel as though I could hardly breathe."

Walter turned shining eyes on his brother. "You know," he said, "I feel as if we were just about to step into the future."

"Yes, we are about to step into the future," Chris agreed soberly. "And to step out of the past, too," he added. "All this . . ." he waved his hand, glancing out the window at the liquid landscape streaming past. The train was passing out of the gradually subsiding hills, covered with pine and oak and infrequently broken by scrubby farms in cleared patches, into the rolling farmlands beyond. An occasional leveled farmhouse among blackened trees, a trench and breastworks on a bit of rising ground, a plow abandoned in an uncultivated field, were all embraced in the past that Chris's gesture implied.

"It's still very much the present for most southerners," Walter said sadly. In the peaceful countryside, so lately ravaged and bloodstained, and in the towns poverty-stricken by defeat, partisan feeling was as bitter as ever, and the war was still the one absorbing topic among people burningly resentful under the savage reprisals of the Reconstruction.

As the train rocked and jolted over the irregular and neglected roadbed through the wide battlefield of northern Virginia, the two young men saw everywhere reminders of the war. In the country, neglected farms and buildings falling into disrepair testified that the slaves, who had carried the South's whole farming system on their broad shoulders, were now free men, most of whom would bear no burden for a long time but their own tragic bewilderment. Skinny steers hitched to rickety carts indicated that the ruined farmers still had neither the draft animals to plant and reap crops, nor adequate crops to feed to or trade for draft animals. In the towns, worn uniform jackets and trousers, the newest and most substantial clothing their impoverished wearers could muster even now, were liberally sprinkled through the groups waiting on station platforms to see the Washington train go by. Neatly kept military cemeteries, with row after row of small white markers watching over the last sleep of the Confederate dead, were to be seen at almost every stop.

Not the least cogent reminder of the war's destruction was the railroad itself, its roadbed even now in its wartime condition. The light rails, repeatedly torn up and replaced, according to the strategic necessities of retreating and advancing armies, were loose and irregular. Rickety bridges sometimes collapsed, or cars screeching around a curve left the track and plowed up the sagging roadbed. Occasionally an exhausted engine would explode, or the train would be delayed by running into cattle wandering in fatal innocence along the unguarded right-of-way and nibbling the grass that grew unhindered between the rails. The railroads' disrepair all over the former Confederacy was dangerous, but the economy of the South, shattered by the war and saddled with the ironic burden of paying for its own defeat, was unequal to rebuilding them.

At Culpeper, from which Grant had launched his costly Wilderness campaign, Negroes balancing trays on their heads passed up and down the platform under the car windows, selling fried chicken, hard-boiled eggs, sandwiches, cakes and apples.

"Albemarle Pippins!" Walter exclaimed, "Chris, we must have some! This will be our last chance to have a home-grown apple for a long time."

Leaning out the window to attract the attention of the vendor, the young doctor and the young lawyer could see the well-groomed burial ground of the Union dead, a reminder of Grant's operations in the vicinity.

Walter wiped his apple thoughtfully and took a bite before he spoke. "I wonder how it's going to be up there, Chris. Is the war still as hot an issue as it is in the South?"

"I doubt it. Nobody can forget it here, where it still shows so much—the cemeteries, and the cripples, and the uniforms, and the poverty, and all the Reconstruction. Up there, they're probably already forgetting; they have less to remind them."

"Of course, you and I have put it pretty well behind us, but we're a little unusual. We were young when it ended, and we've been too busy getting our professional training to think much about it since. And Jim and Tom, who actually fought, are such kindly fellows that they've let it go past, too. But most southerners remember bitterly."

"The losers always remember longer than the winners. Victors are always glad to forget," Chris pointed out.

"Well, the country's at peace again, and we're a new generation," Walter said. "We didn't make the war, and we didn't fight it—although we did want to be drummers, remember?" He smiled. "It seems to me that the best thing we can do is try to forget our grievances, and look to the future instead."

Cinders were flying through the open window. Chris blew some off his apple before taking another bite.

"Of course," he assented. "It's the hard thing to do, but it's the right one. And in a country the size of this one, there is room and work for everyone. You know, that reminds me—I rather like your idea of going west some time. With the railroad clear across the continent now, it isn't a bad trip at all any more."

Walter laughed. "What a restless fellow you are, Chris! We haven't even reached New York yet, and you're already talking about going on."

"You're the one who's restless," Chris reminded him. "You've been talking about going west ever since you were big enough to read your geography."

"Well, one thing at a time," Walter decided. He tossed his apple core out the window and watched it roll down the cindered embankment. "We're on the brink of a new world. We both have work to do in it, and there's no telling where it may take us."

Falling silent, he gazed, his clear blue eyes fixed in his characteristically intent expression, at the speeding landscape as it poured by, giving the illusion of pivoting on a point somewhere beyond the horizon.

CHAPTER SEVEN

DR. REED, with cold politeness, finished questioning his well-dressed visitor, whose heavy gold watch chain, spanning his comfortably curved front, loudly proclaimed the successful professional man. The tall hat was tilted back on the fringed dome, and the off-hand manner pointedly condescended to the youthful Health Inspector.

"From your lucid description of the symptoms, sir," the younger man summed up, carefully keeping sarcasm out of his voice, "I should conclude that the unfortunate child was a victim of lymphadenoma." And of a conscienceless quack, he added bitterly to himself.

The older man assumed a judicious air. "Hmmmm, possibly," he conceded, stroking his full beard thoughtfully. "A rare case, of course. Don't recall seeing one quite like it in my experience—wide experience," he stressed the last phrase suggestively. "The symptoms do suggest it, however." He shrugged. "You might as well enter the cause of death as lymphadoma."

The miscalled medical name jarred on Reed only a little less than the tone of dismissal, a tone that implied that there were, still, a great many children in the world.

"Very bright of you to think of it, I'm sure," the stout doctor added patronizingly, drawing on his yellow kid gloves.

"Not at all," Dr. Reed answered drily. He showed his visitor to the door of the office, but did not offer to shake hands. Outside he caught sight of the doctor's carriage, with a pair of handsome bays, waiting in the street. He watched while the coachman held the door and the doctor's portly person disappeared within.

"Very bright of you to think of it, I'm sure," the stout doctor
added patronizingly.

Walter Reed's mouth was set sternly as he seated himself at his desk and jotted down a report on the case. The doctor who had come to notify him, as one of the Brooklyn Health Inspectors, of the death was locally prominent. Yet he was so ignorant that he was unable to use medical terminology correctly, or even to state symptoms accurately. Lymphadenoma was not a rare disease, but he had failed to recognize a well-marked case. In the days before medical education was strictly regulated such men were, unfortunately, not unusual.

"The poor little girl!" Reed muttered aloud, then finished writing and read over his report. "The poor little thing!" he repeated resentfully.

Death was very familiar to the young doctor now. He had met it countless times—the corpses brought to the narrow white room of the Bellevue dead-house, the quiet, sheet-covered forms on the hospital beds, the pitiful figures dead of filth and neglect and sometimes violence in the swarming tenement houses—but he could never see it with indifference. Sensitive and imaginative, he always felt the pathos of each individual. It was never a "case" that he treated; it was always a person.

His zeal for his profession was keen; his enthusiasm for the immense city, however, he realized, had changed in the four years he had spent in it. During his first year, when his principal work had been to attend lectures and go to clinics and autopsies, he had found time to be delighted with New York's endless variety.

He had occasionally gone to the theaters—to the stock company on fashionable Madison Square, or to the Italian opera at the Academy of Music—and dropped in afterwards at the Fifth Avenue Hotel, where gay young men and stylish women came for after-theater suppers. On hot summer evenings he had listened to the concerts in Central Park, and admired the brisk carriage horses, handled by liveried coachmen, as they trotted along the winding drives.

The big new buildings, springing out of the earth everywhere, had interested him, too. The Grand Central Station
which, wonderfully, had two acres of glass in its roof, was
almost finished then, and the splendid St. Patrick's Cathedral,
begun a dozen years before, was slowly toiling upward. He
had been fascinated by the waterfront, through which flowed
some sixty percent of the country's foreign trade, with its
ocean-going steamers, and tugs and ferries and sailing craft;
and by the ambitious beginnings of the new Brooklyn Bridge,
to be the longest suspension bridge in the world and the first
to link Brooklyn to New York across the swift current of the
East River.

In Mott Street he had seen his first Chinese, some of the
bland and industrious hundreds who crowded in the rotting
tenements of Chinatown. On almost any street corner he could
encounter Italians, Germans, Irish or French, and hear them
speaking their own tongue. On his walks uptown he used
sometimes to come upon old farmhouses, relics of the colonial past, tucked here and there about the city and hemmed
in by factories and slaughterhouses.

The contrasts and the bustle, the feeling of drive and power
in the big city, the sense of the new boisterously displacing the
old and of life expanding at breakneck speed into vistas of
boundless hope and wonder, had intoxicated the young man
from the country. Home had been nothing like this.

Gradually, however, his viewpoint had changed, adjusting
and sobering. Interrupting his course at Bellevue at the end of
the 1870-1871 term to work in various of the city's hospitals,
he had come into close contact for the first time with the
misery of the submerged half of the city's population. Then
he had taken his Bellevue medical degree in 1872, and from
that time on his services had been, for the most part, devoted
to the very poor who lived in the tenements that huddled in

side streets toward the rivers and downtown in the older parts of the city. In tottering buildings, without sanitary facilities, ventilation or privacy, half a million people, half the population of the richest and largest city in the country, lived neglected in a squalor that he would have found unimaginable a few years earlier, and which he could now believe only because he actually saw it.

It was a period of unrestricted immigration. The poor of all countries were swarming hopefully to the United States to work in the coal mines and oil fields and factories, and to take up claims on the free lands of the west. Steamship companies, cutting their rates to attract trade, crowded the immigrants like cattle into hold and steerage, where epidemics inevitably took root among them. Pouring into New York, they spread their diseases through the miserable tenements and the poverty-ridden neighborhoods. Immigrants and native poor had an appalling rate of sickness and death. Even those not actively sick with something worse suffered from "the tenant-house rot," grim blanket term for rickets, scurvy, outright starvation and a dozen other ills.

When Walter Reed had begun his hospital work in New York, the situation had been slowly improving. Sanitary legislation had been passed and the Metropolitan Board of Health established in 1866, after years of agitation by medical men and public-minded citizens. The Board, set up by the state legislature and thus free from the grasp of the Tweed Ring, a gang of criminal politicians who were just then ruling and robbing New York City with brazen greed, had sweeping powers not only over the city proper but over Brooklyn and widely outlying districts.

The Board worked through Health Inspectors, most of them young doctors recently out of medical school, who, among their other duties, saw to it that cases of contagious diseases were isolated or removed to the proper hospitals, and that tenement house owners kept their property up to the requirements of the Board of Health.

The young doctor, while interning at the King's County Hospital, had attracted the notice of Dr. Joseph C. Hutchison, then a leading doctor and surgeon in Brooklyn and a member of the Board of Health. Dr. Hutchison had taken a liking to the pleasant, competent young man, whose skill in surgery and in the treatment of children's diseases was already marked. Perhaps, too, he remembered his own struggles twenty years earlier when, like Walter Reed, he had come from the country to establish a practice in the toughest city in the nation. In any case, Dr. Hutchison had had Walter Reed appointed a Health Inspector.

The modest salary attached to this post was very welcome to the young man just starting out in practice, and the experience that the duties involved was welcome. New York's million population furnished a huge and interesting variety of medical and surgical cases which came to the hospitals where Reed, both as student and practitioner, had the opportunity to see them. Cholera, diphtheria, typhoid and erysipelas were among the diseases which, we may assume from his later work, particularly interested him at this time.

Perhaps, however, as early as 1871, the eruption of the scandals about the Tweed Ring suggested to the young man from the country that there was something rotten in the glamorous metropolis. Later, increasing familiarity with the submerged and shameful side of the city had disenchanted him completely. Now this episode of the arrogant, ignorant doctor, prospering on the miseries of people whom he did nothing to relieve, seemed the last straw.

He told Chris who, now launched on a successful legal career, lived with him and shared many of his experiences. Noticing his dejected air when he came in after his office hours, Chris asked, "What's the matter, Walter? Did you have a hard day?"

"No, not particularly." Walter walked to the window of their room and stood looking out over the busy harbor and at the low jumble of the Manhattan sky line beyond it. He noticed an ocean steamer being warped to the pier, a steamer which, he supposed from his experience, would debark not only its passengers but a cargo of disease as well.

"Not particularly," he repeated, "but I am so disgusted that I should almost like to give up my profession!"

"Walter!"

"No, no. Don't look so alarmed, Chris. You know nothing would induce me to. But do you know what happened to me today? I'll tell you."

Speaking of the doctor's patronizing air, he could smile. But he did not smile when he told of his ignorance and callousness. Those, he declared, could work tragedy, and heaven knew how many times they already had. "And yet that man, a first-rate quack, has the leading practice in that part of Brooklyn. It makes one ashamed of the profession."

"But how *can* such a man become eminent, if he has no qualifications?" Chris wanted to know.

"Oh, he has 'qualifications' all right, but they're not medical ones. He's independently wealthy, for one thing, and puts up a good front. He married a society woman, too. And he has all sorts of political connections. It all adds up to a big practice. It's very hard for a young man to have to compete with pull and front."

"It is discouraging," Chris assented.

"And my age, too," Walter went on, listing his difficulties. "It's funny, but a doctor's success for the first decade depends more on his beard than his brains. I entered my profession three or four years earlier than most men do, and I look young. There's a tendency not to take a young man as seriously as an older man, or to have as much confidence in him. On top of that, this work as Health Inspector is keeping me so busy that I haven't time to build up a private practice. I'm thinking more and more definitely of leaving New York. Maybe I'll go to some smaller city, where I can get a faster start."

Chris had been listening with a smile. Now he inquired, "Haven't you rather—ah, glided—over another motive for leaving?"

At Walter's expression he broke into a laugh. Walter joined in.

"Well," he answered a little sheepishly, "what better motive could I have?"

"None," Chris agreed unhesitatingly. "You've been almost bubbling ever since you visited Pa in Murfreesboro in June," he teased. "And you should see your face when you find a letter waiting for you. A blind man could tell what's the matter with you."

"You may call it something the 'matter' with me," Walter said cheerfully, "but I like it. But I haven't asked her yet—I don't see how I can until I have an assured income. That's another reason I'm so anxious to get established in a hurry. I've been thinking about entering the Army—that's a modest, steady salary, and I'd like nothing better for a few years than moving about and seeing the country. Torney's been talking it up to me, too."

"George Torney? The fellow you were in the University with? I thought he was a Navy doctor."

"He's changing," Walter grinned. "Dry land may not be as exciting, but at least it doesn't roll. He suffers from invincible seasickness. Every time he sets foot on a boat he's the sickest man aboard."

"Poor fellow," Chris laughed. "It does seem rather a good idea for you, Walter, and an answer to your problem. Who would ever have thought, though, ten years ago, that one of us would want to wear the Army blue?"

"No one, I guess. It would have been scandalously disloyal even to dream of such a thing. However, I haven't decided yet. I want to ask Pa's advice. Let's go out to dinner now. I have a lot of calls to make this evening."

In mid-July he confided his plan to the girl whom he had met on his visit to his father. In his clear, even writing he wrote to Emilie Lawrence,

"I have been recently contemplating a departure from Brooklyn. . . . I have about made up my mind to make a strenuous effort to enter the Medical Corps of the United States Army." He went on to explain his reasons, and added that he would want to remain in the Army for just a few years. "If at the end of that time (3 or 4 years hence) I could find some fair damsel who was foolish enough to trust me," he suggested hopefully, "I think I would get—married, and settle down to sober work for the rest of my days in some small city where one could enjoy the advantages of a city and at the same time not feel as if lost."

The onset of love had been sudden and hard. He had known the girl to whom he was writing just a month. She, for her part, was already taken with the decisive young man who had fallen so impetuously in love with her.

The Examining Board of the Army Medical Corps, which examined applicants for the service, met in New York on August 4, 1874. Walter Reed, taking a few hours off from his duties, went over to see its Recorder, and was dismayed to learn that candidates were examined not only in medical subjects, but in Latin, Greek, mathematics and history. "Horror of Horrors!" he lamented to Miss Lawrence when he wrote her a week later. "Imagine me conjugating an irregular verb, or telling what x + y equals, or what year Rome was founded, or the battle of Marathon fought. Why, the thing is impossible, I shall utterly fail. Add to this that each applicant is examined five hours each day for six successive days—thirty hours' questioning—and, to cap the climax, there are more than 500 applicants for less than 30 vacancies! The very thought of it makes me dizzy. Think of my condition and pity me, for I need all the sympathy of all my friends."

Dizzy or not, the young doctor must have had higher hopes of success than he betrayed. Having a naturally cheerful disposition, he always approached undertakings with an optimism that gave him a good running start. He surrounded himself with textbooks and set to work with the same industry that had carried him through the University medical school in a year.

Unfortunately, he worked so hard that he made himself sick in a fortnight. It had been years since he had had any sort of illness, but now he was prostrated for three weeks.

"I remember the time when I could safely study as much as 20 hours uninterruptedly day after day, and not experience any bad effect from it, but I presume that time shall return no more." Thus he mourned his lost youth to the young lady who would, he hoped, share his rapidly advancing years.

The approach of the examination and the difficulty of refreshing his knowledge of so many forgotten things threw him into a panic. He worked desperately, late into each night. When he was exhausted he would lay aside the book and try to rest. But, as he wrote his sympathetic confidante, "the thought flashes through my mind that there are a thousand things in that cast-aside volume of which I am ignorant, a thousand unanswerable questions that may rise up against me in the day of my examination, to humble and mortify me. Racked with a thousand fears, I tear open the book and eagerly scan its pages, determined to exhaust every effort, and, if need be, to suffer death rather than defeat."

The mental strain that fathered this somewhat extravagant resolution subsided as the rest enforced by illness began to take effect. The examination, too, was deferred, and deeply relieved, he determined to treat himself with more discretion now that he had until the middle of January to prepare for it.

His good intentions to the contrary, he made himself ill again by the beginning of November, but with the unpretentious determination characteristic of him, he wrote Emilie Lawrence, "Still I believe that when a person determines to accomplish an end, that he should put forth all honest effort, nor turn aside, unless for the best of reasons; and if he meets with defeat let him accept it like a man, remembering that many better men have found themselves in a like situation. At all events I shall pursue my course until every prop is knocked away from under me."

By January improved health had cheered him to the point where he could write hopefully of the impending examination. It was postponed again, this time for a month.

Finally, one February day, Walter Reed entered the shabby building in downtown New York where the Examining Board met to face the week-long inquisition. At its close, he jubilantly wrote Miss Lawrence that he had passed with conspicuous success.

She was as elated as he. But his letter was not satisfactory, she complained. He must come down and tell her in person. The happy young man hurried south with the details of his good news. Bemused with joy, he lost his bag in Norfolk and arrived in Murfreesboro, barely disconcerted, to greet his beloved in travel-stained linen. Her brother equipped him with fresh clothes, and, restored to his customary cleanliness, he proceeded to deal with the matter most pressingly on his mind. Miss Lawrence saw eye to eye with him on it. Family blessings were obtained, and their engagement promptly followed.

CHAPTER EIGHT

ON JUNE 26, 1875, Walter Reed was appointed an assistant surgeon in the Medical Corps of the United States Army with the rank of first lieutenant. His oath of office reached him a few days later in Harrisonburg, Virginia, where he was visiting his father, who was still moving about the state on behalf of his church as briskly as in his younger days.

"I, Walter Reed," the oath read, "having been appointed an Assistant Surgeon in the Military Service of the United States, do solemnly swear that I have never voluntarily borne arms against the United States since I have become a citizen thereof; that I have voluntarily given no aid, countenance, counsel or encouragement to persons engaged in armed hostility thereto; that I have neither sought nor accepted nor attempted to exercise the functions of any office whatever, under any authority or pretended authority, in hostility to the United States; that I have not yielded a voluntary support to any pretended government, authority, power or constitution within the United States hostile or inimical thereto. And I do further swear that, to the best of my knowledge and ability, I will support and defend the Constitution of the United States against all enemies, foreign and domestic; that I will bear true faith and allegiance to the same; that I take this obligation freely, without any mental reservation or purpose of evasion; and that I will well and faithfully discharge the duties of the office on which I am about to enter. So help me God."

Walter Reed, a youthful rebel a dozen years before against the authority of the United States, unhesitatingly signed the oath with his clear, bold signature. He had no doubts about the wisdom of his choice. Then he went to Murfreesboro to visit the Lawrences and wait for his orders.

On July 23rd he was ordered to the Army post at Willets Point, Long Island. Between the novelty of his new life and happy musing over the future, he forgot his birthday.

"Would you, could you believe that I would allow my twenty-fifth birthday to pass without so much as thinking of it during the whole day," he inquired of his fiancée. "The very day on which I wrote you last I was twenty-four years old (just think of it), and yet I was totally ignorant of it. Of course, I felt the weight of years more than usual on that day, but I could not account for it. Suddenly on Tuesday the 14, it occurred to me that I was one year older and immediately the cause of my fatigue flashed across my mind." Becoming serious, he asked himself what he had to show for his years. "What good deeds have I done that merit approbation! How negligent and wayward have I been! What golden moments of opportunity have come and gone, all unheeded! As I look back over my past life tonight, but few thoughts occur to me such as cause my bosom to swell with honest pride." Thus the twenty-four-year-old doctor, who had entered his medical career at an age when most boys were preparing for college and who already had years of practice behind him, upbraided himself for his "squandered youth."

To him the serious side of life was always uppermost, but his cheerful disposition usually prevented him from lapsing into melancholy. His more characteristic attitude was resolution, as appears from a letter to his future wife about this time on the death of her little nephew.

"Alas, while I prayed that his life might be prolonged to many years of usefulness, he had already departed for a better and a brighter home. . . . When I see the little lambs hastening home, I would not call them back, for though I have scarcely begun life, I have known what sorrow is and felt the weight of care. Do not think that I shrink from meeting life's realities. No, no. That would display a lack of courage and a want of faith. Nor that I would not wish to live many years yet. It may be that God in his all-wise Providence has some wise purpose for me, humble as I am, to fulfill, and shall I," questioned the minister's son, "shrink from it?"

Had he had certain knowledge of his own future, he could not have written more prophetically.

That future almost got off to a bad start. Just before his wedding, which was to take place in the spring of 1876, the new lieutenant was ordered to Arizona. He was stunned. It was unthinkable to drag a new wife into the unknown and distant west, equally unthinkable to postpone his marriage. His feelings toward Uncle Sam, to whom he usually referred as "a good-natured old chap," must have been, for the moment at least, mixed.

The young officer conceived the idea of going to Washington to discuss his orders with the Surgeon General. Surely General Barnes, remote and godlike though he was, would understand how pressing his problem was and suggest a solution. So Lieutenant Reed went to Washington.

Although he was preoccupied with his mission, he was not indifferent to the appearance of the capital city, with which he had already formed a slight acquaintance on several previous trips. Since he had first passed through it half a dozen years before, the city had changed vastly. He observed that paved streets and sidewalks had replaced the dusty roads. Street lights had been erected, whose flickering gas glow made the passage along them less hazardous after dark. Sewers had been installed, parks laid out and thousands of trees planted along the avenues, to the mounting outcries from taxpayers against "squandering the public funds" to convert the seat of government from a wasteland to a suitable capital.

Congress was again discussing resumption of work on the Washington Monument, whose abandoned base, desolate and shabby, stood on the Mall, less a reminder of the father of his country than of public parsimony and Congressional indifference. Even now, as he approached the Surgeon General's office, Reed could glimpse, farther along Pennsylvania Avenue beyond the White House, the partially finished State, War and Navy Building, an extraordinary granite confection adorned with a cascade of small columns that made the critical eye reel.

The short trip from the station, however, dislodged his problem from his mind only for a few minutes. With sinking heart he entered the old bank building on Pennsylvania Avenue opposite the Treasury, where General Joseph K. Barnes and his small staff had their modest offices. Smoothing his hair, straightening his uniform jacket and hoping that his appearance would pass muster, he asked for the Surgeon General. Barnes, a gruff old gentleman with side whiskers, who had been head of the Medical Corps since the later years of the Civil War, glanced up from his desk as Reed was announced.

"Sit down," the general ordered the lieutenant without ceremony.

The young man obeyed.

"Now, sir," the general demanded abruptly, "what do you want?"

Lieutenant Reed was glad, since his interview was plainly to be without social trimmings, that he had a faculty for concise statement.

"I should like to know, sir," he answered, "if I can get leave while I am stationed in the west. I am engaged to be married, and shall want to return for my wedding."

His throat was dry when he finished speaking, and he observed the clouding of his chief's brow with apprehension.

"Young man, if you don't like your orders, leave the service," the general snapped.

His caller heard him with utter astonishment that instantly gave way to indignation. He had asked a simple question, irregular perhaps but innocent, and he had too keen a sense of his own rights and dignity to lie down under this undeserved rebuff. His nervousness replaced by his sense of outrage, he retorted,

"General Barnes, I did not labor with all my will for my commission just to toss it away lightly. Neither can I be deprived of it except for unworthy conduct!"

The older man took another look at his subordinate. He remarked the erect military posture, the unsmiling, almost stubborn mouth, the keen blue eyes that did not waver from his own. Here was a man, it occurred to him, who was the kind of material they needed in the Medical Corps. His officers were too often treated with scant regard by the line officers, and a man who expected respect, who could stand up for himself with firmness and courtesy even against a superior, would be a good thing for the service. A good boy, Barnes thought approvingly. His scowl faded.

"Have a cigar, Dr. Reed," he suggested mildly, "and let's talk this thing over."

When Walter Reed left his chief some half-hour later, he was puzzled and thoughtful. It had again been impressed on him that a man always had to make his important decisions for himself. Some officer stationed in the west, the general had said, would "probably" become insane "in a few months." He should postpone his marriage, go to Arizona, and take a chance on being designated to escort this problematical poor fellow to St. Elizabeth's, the Federal asylum at Washington. There would be the opportunity for his wedding, Barnes had pointed out. What a prospect to offer a young man in love! Aside from that, the idea of gambling on the misfortune of a fellow officer repelled him. What a solution for a general to suggest! A first

He felt solemn and slightly incredulous with happiness:
he was a Married Man!

lieutenant should be able to think of something better than that. Walter Reed did.

The next few weeks passed so rapidly, in such a blur of happiness and haste, that it was not until he was on the train, making the long trip from New York to the coast with the recruits that he was escorting to California, that he was able to assemble his recollections and sensations. His dominant feeling was a solemn and slightly incredulous happiness: he was a Married Man. Whatever shocks or disappointments the future could contrive for him, he could face them with calmness now, with Emilie to share them and encourage him. He felt steeped in well-being and confidence.

The wedding had been held rather suddenly, on April 25, 1876, at Murfreesboro. Then Reed had taken his wife to his father's home at Harrisonburg, in the Shenandoah Valley, and for several happy weeks they had been together. They had gone for long walks through the countryside, just stirring with spring; and sitting with their backs against a battle-scarred tree they had discussed and planned the future. They had played with his half-sister Annie, no longer the baby he had left behind when he went to New York, but a big girl nine years old, who was disappointed that she had missed the wedding. The happy bridegroom had had his picture taken in uniform, arms folded across his chest, a confident, grave-looking young man of twenty-five, with straight eyebrows, direct glance and slightly outthrust lower lip.

Then his leave was up almost as soon as it began, it seemed to them both, and he had to leave Emilie with Pa and his family while he went to the frontier post where she would join him in the fall, when travel was more comfortable and after he had made arrangements for her comfort. As he jiggled over the endless miles of track, he sometimes caught himself wondering if it all actually had happened. Nothing seemed outwardly changed; inside, however, he felt a different man, transformed by this new feeling of pride and responsibility and happiness.

The trip from New York to San Francisco took eight days and nights. The recruits were bored, played cards and occasionally quarreled, but their escorting officer, with his unflagging enthusiasm for new experiences, was delighted with every moment of it. The great west had captured his fancy when he was a tow-headed little boy studying his first geography lessons at Mrs. Booker's school. The idea of seeing it had teased him ever since, becoming more insistent as a result of his depression with the city and the persuasions of his friend Torney. Now he was actually penetrating into it, rolling jouncingly along the thin gleaming rails that railroad pioneers had adventurously, doggedly, and in an atmosphere of resounding financial scandal, stretched all the way to the Pacific Ocean.

Beyond Omaha, where the famous Union Pacific began, the train toiled through Nebraska and Wyoming, over whose plains the bison, which a decade earlier had wandered by the millions, now wandered by the thousands, and left their whitening bones as a memorial to the white man's wasteful slaughter. The vast expanse of this country astonished the young man used to the domesticated nature and the shrunken distances of the settled east. Confined in the cramped railway carriage, covered with soot and sometimes smothered with alkaline dust, he wrote long letters to his wife, telling her that he missed her, and that he was enthusiastic about this wild immensity. He mailed them at the wayside stops where, in those days before dining cars, the passengers debarked to fight with swarms of flies for the greasy, ill-cooked food served at long tables in public dining rooms close to the station.

Arriving tired and dirty and still enthusiastic in San Francisco, whose old frame houses and wooden sidewalks teetered on the steeply pitched hillsides, he took the little coastwise steamer *Orizaba* to San Diego, and fully appreciated, for the first time, George Torney's preference for dry land. Probably he began to question it, however, on the wearisome overland route across the coastal range to Fort Yuma, where he arrived about the first of June, in time to savor at its height the famous climate with which, according to garrison tradition, hell itself compared favorably.

His two months at this hottest of all Army posts, where the thermometer day after scorching day mounted to a hundred and fifteen degrees in the blistering shade, was not enough to accustom him to the routine and monotony of post life. His most vivid recollection of this short tour of duty centered on the infantry captain with whom he shared one of the cramped, bare quarters reserved for the bachelor officers. This officer, whose imposing bulk amounted to some two hundred and fifty pounds, always appeared at dinner in his underwear for maximum relief from the heat, equipped with a fan and a towel to wipe his face. Seated opposite his sweltering and fully clothed junior, he would politely serve him with a slice or two from the substantial roast of range beef before him, then fanning and mopping heartily he would consume the rest of it to the last scrap, emptying a large pitcher of water between mouthfuls. Walter Reed's amazement at this gastronomic stunt was equaled only by his respect for the digestive apparatus that could absorb such punishment.

He was snatched from admiration of this wonder in early August, 1876, by orders to proceed to Fort Lowell, near Tucson, Arizona.

CHAPTER NINE

MRS. REED, muffled to shapelessness in her waterproof and two Army overcoats, asked, with just the trace of a quaver in her tone, "How much farther is it now, do you suppose?"

"It can't be far," her husband answered cheerfully, straining his eyes into the moonless night for the glimmer of light that would mark their overnight stop. She was holding his hand tightly under the robe, and he gave hers an encouraging squeeze.

The doherty wagon, a primitive ancestor of the station wagon, with seats that could be converted into beds at night and canvas sides that rolled down, lurched and bounced behind its four-mule team, which felt their way at a gingerly walk over the rutted, stony road. The driver, constrained by the presence of a lady, did not swear aloud. Silently, however, with hair-raising oaths, he cursed the mules, the darkness, the frightful road, the missing station, and the day he joined the Army. Having left San Diego, where Dr. Reed had gone to meet his wife, at two in the afternoon of November 15, 1876, the party expected to pass the first night at Jamul (pronounced, Mrs. Reed learned with interest, Ha-mool), a tiny roadside station seventeen miles inland; but the road had turned out to be so rough that any progress faster than a walk threatened to shake both the ambulance (as the doherty wagon was also called) and its occupants apart. They had passed their baggage wagon, which was making even worse headway, some miles back. The sun had gone down about five; by seven it had become cold and they had begun to worry about missing the station in the dark, and by nine, as they still lumbered hesitantly through the almost tangible blackness, even the doctor's cheerfulness had worn a little thin.

Holding his wife's hand and bracing her against the shattering jolts of the wagon, he peered intently ahead.

"There! There!" he exclaimed suddenly, relief escaping into his voice. "That must be it."

A light shone some distance ahead, a stationary, unblinking light that must come from a house.

"Oh, I *am* so glad. A fire, and something hot to drink!"

"Poor darling, you've had a dreadful time," her husband sympathized. "A train collision, a blizzard in Wyoming, and now this awful ride. And all," he added in a whisper, "for a worthless fellow who adores you." It was too dark to distinguish expressions, but he knew she was smiling now.

The light gradually drew nearer. Misgivings sprang to Reed's mind—surely it was on the wrong side of the road for the Jamul station! Ordering the driver to stop as close to it as possible, he sent him in to inquire. In a few minutes he was back. It was not the station.

"The man hopes the doctor and the lady will stay overnight with him anyway," he reported, addressing Reed in the third person that soldiers always used to officers. He added, "However, if the doctor doesn't think the station is too far away. . . ."

"Why?"

"He has no hay or grain for the mules, sir, and," he continued, "he hasn't a bed, either. He says he and his old lady had a little—'family jar' he called it—today, and she walked out and took the bed and covers with her."

Reed's laugh ended in a sigh. "Well, let's get on. He's a very kind gentleman, I'm sure, but we'd better wait for a more favorable time to accept his hospitality."

The driver climbed aboard and shouted at the mules, and the ambulance again bumped off behind its reluctant team. The road got worse. The soldier sitting beside the driver had to get down several times to see where it was. The driver was now earnestly cursing not only the day he joined the Army but the day he was born. Ten o'clock passed. After an endless length of time, Reed again looked at his watch. Only eleven. Emilie, uncomfortably dozing against his shoulder, opened her eyes.

"What's that?" she demanded, as they rounded a bend.

It was a smoldering campfire, its dim glow just enough to outline two wagons and two men wrapped in blankets sleeping beside it. The doctor sprang out of the ambulance. He shook one of the sleepers, a brawny, bearded fellow, who sat up abruptly and reached for his rifle in the same movement. Reed hastily stepped back so that the dim firelight fell on his uniform and asked how far they were from the station.

"Two miles," the teamster answered, his voice a sleepy rumble, "over the worst road in California. Last mile," he informed them gloomily, "through a canyon a coyote can't hardly cross in broad daylight."

"Thanks. Sorry I had to disturb you."

"That's all right," the man growled, lying down again and pulling his blankets around him. Dr. Reed heard him remark to his companion who had awakened and raised up on one elbow, "Young Army fellow wants to get to Jamul. He'll never get through that canyon tonight."

"Oh, won't I?" the young Army fellow said to himself grimly. "Go ahead," he told the driver. "Only two miles more."

After another mile the road dipped into the mouth of the canyon and lost itself completely in the jumble of boulders. The tree-covered walls rose up steeply on either side, multiplying the darkness. The mules, unable to feel anything but stones under their hoofs, balked, while the driver cracked his whip over them in vain.

The young officer took a lantern, and the soldier a bit of

candle, and, getting out of the wagon, they clambered over the rocks to the head of the team. Now stumbling and now sinking to their knees in the soft sand, they kept just ahead of the mules and called directions to the driver, who was by this time too preoccupied with trying to get out of this boulder-strewn waste without breaking an axle to remember his grudge against Providence. Their slow, jolting progress, halted every few yards by a sizable boulder against a wheel, made them feel that the preceding hours had been passed on a race track. Emilie, clinging to the pitching, straining wagon, could see the flickering light up ahead, and kept calling anxiously, "Where are you, Dr. Reed?"—she could never get used to calling him anything else. "Please come back and let the soldier carry the lantern!"

After an hour of calling directions, digging, shoving and hoisting, the dreadful canyon was behind them. Ahead, again, was a light. This time it was really the station. It was nothing but a one-room shack of plain board, about ten feet square, and a stable, but never before had a human habitation looked so inviting to the young doctor or his wife.

Lieutenant Reed aroused the station keeper, a frontiersman of forbidding appearance, who came out to the wagon with the officer.

"A lady!" he exclaimed, astounded, when he detected Emilie shivering in the body of the ambulance. A few minutes before she had been sure that nothing could ever make her smile again, not at least until she had had something hot to drink and a good night's rest, but his complete astonishment was so comic that a wavering little smile came of itself to her face.

"You must be right tired, ma'am," he said, as he helped her down, "but we'll have you comfortable in no time at all."

When they entered the barren shack, with its dirt floor and tiny window, which was really unnecessary since the wind poured unhindered through wide cracks between the boards,

Emilie wondered how he could ever make her or himself or anyone else comfortable in it. It was furnished with a stool and a broken chair, an unpainted pine table, a cooking stove and a bed which was nothing more than a frame with a piece of canvas stretched over it. She sank stiffly onto the stool.

Their host wasted no time. He started a roaring fire in the stove, and made them some tea which he served in cracked cups without saucers. Then he asserted with awkward gallantry that the lady should have the bed—he would do all right with the mules—and withdrew to the stable for the night.

Dr. and Mrs. Reed agreed that he was a dear man, toasted him in scalding strong tea, and enthusiastically ate the lunch they had carried along in the wagon. Both of them forgot that they had been cold and tired and discouraged so short a time before.

"I wouldn't have missed this for anything on earth," Emilie exclaimed.

"Darling," her husband said, "I hope you'll always be able to say as much. You're in the Army now, you know."

"This is the place, but that's not the man," Dr. Reed observed late the next day, as the wagon halted on the barren hillside. The mules, blowing, hung their heads and let their long ears flop. The fading sunlight glinted coldly off the barrel of the Winchester rifle that leaned against the wall of the hut. The tall man in ragged pants and deerskin jacket slouching against the door straightened and came toward them. He was plainly not Jackson, the station keeper whom Reed had seen on his way to the coast.

"Howdy," he drawled amiably to Reed. "Howdy, ma'am," to Mrs. Reed, touching his cap.

"Howdy," Dr. Reed answered him. "Jackson here?"

"Was that the pore fellow's name?" the stranger inquired. "No, he ain't here. He won't be here no more. He's dead."

They had little choice but to accept the invitation.

"Dead!" the doctor exclaimed. "What happened to him? There didn't seem to be anything the matter when I saw him on my way through."

"It wasn't nothing lingering," the hunter said drily. "I found him four-five days ago with a bullet through his head. Coyotes didn't leave nothing but bones, polished him clean. I buried him up yonder," he jerked his thumb vaguely over his shoulder. "I been camping in his cabin."

The doctor was shocked. "Haven't you any idea who killed him?"

"Some varmint. Indians, mebbe." He dismissed the speculation with a shrug. Lonely frontiersmen were always getting killed. It was one of the chances they took. "You all better stop here. It's 'most sundown, and no place to stop farther on. The lady can have the cabin. It ain't much, but it's shelter."

They had little choice but to accept the invitation.

The frontiersman helped the soldiers put up the mules and prepare the dinner. Emilie, suspecting him of having done away with the cabin's previous occupant, followed his every movement with wide eyes. She was less impressed with his sinewy agility than with his possible wickedness. Would he, perhaps, dare to sneak softly up on them in the night, and . . . she shuddered, unable to finish the thought. Her husband, guessing her uneasiness, reassured her.

"I don't think he did it. He hasn't even protested his innocence. He takes it for granted that *we'll* take it for granted. Anyway, a murderer doesn't go around telling strangers that he's found the body of his victim. If he hadn't told us, we'd never have known that Jackson was killed."

"Maybe," Emilie agreed reluctantly, "but I don't like this place. It gives me the creeps."

After dinner their host indicated the rough bed under the cabin's single window. "Guess you'll want to turn in early," he suggested. "I'll get the window open for you—it's mighty stiff."

He gave it a vigorous jerk, and it screeched up. Reaching behind the bed, he pulled out something with which to prop it open. Reed could not smother an exclamation.

"My dear man! *What* have you got there?"

"This?" the frontiersman inquired with mild surprise. "It's right handy to hold this here window up."

It was the upper arm bone of the deceased Jackson.

The wagon road wound across the coastal range, dipped over its crest and snaked down its eastern side. Far ahead, they could sometimes glimpse stretches of the Arizona desert, threaded by the trickle of the Gila River. The days were cool and pleasant in mid-November, the nights cold.

Following the stage road, the party crossed the Colorado River a dozen miles below Yuma on a small barge, attached to a rope stretched across the river, which was pulled along by a couple of husky Indians. The road then followed the Gila River for more than a hundred miles, before leaving it to strike off into the desert toward Tucson. The region was still wild, and trouble with the Indians common, but the frontier was yielding to the penetration of ranchers and miners, and the country was opening up to travel.

The length of each day's march was determined principally by the distance of water holes from each other. Travel by wagon was slow; since the mules were not changed at frequent relays, as stage horses were, they could not be driven too fast. It took Dr. Reed and his party about three weeks to cover the five hundred miles of mountain, valley and desert between San Diego and Tucson, where Camp Lowell was situated. They arrived at the post the first week in December, 1876, and Army life, as they were both to know it for the next fourteen years, began for them.

It was a life distinguished principally by its narrowness. The United States Army in the late 1870's and for many years thereafter was an organization of about twenty-five thousand men, scattered in small groups all over the country. Existence, particularly at the distant western posts, was very monotonous. Pay for both officers and men was meager; patriotism was its own reward, in the opinion of the country that, confident it would never have to fight another war, took little interest in the upkeep of its fighting force. There were, in any case, few places to spend money, since most of the western posts were planted miles from centers of population offering any diversion but saloons.

The life was, by modern standards, a hard one. The officers' quarters, built of unpainted board, adobe or logs, were small, ugly and barren, and entirely innocent of such comforts as central heating, running water and bathrooms. Water was hauled in wagons from the nearest well or creek, and stored in barrels behind the houses. The Commanding Officer usually had a fairly large dwelling, but a lieutenant was lucky to get three or four rooms. Enlisted men lived in ill-ventilated, ill-heated barracks, often with dirt floors, where it took enterprise and ingenuity to achieve even minimum personal cleanliness.

Time was heavy on the hands of men and officers alike in between the occasional Indian disturbances. The routine of inspection, drill, guard and other duties neither filled their time nor taxed their energies. The soldiers got up baseball games, held running, jumping and boxing matches and other contests. On their days off, they went hunting, fishing, or riding about the countryside on visits. And, always, they spent an uncommon amount of time devising practical jokes on each other, and, in general, found ways of disturbing the local peace.

The officers and their families did the best they could with their meager entertainment opportunities. The men hunted and rode and fished, and the more intelligent among them developed hobbies that could be indulged locally, like geology or botany. There were frequent picnics, dinners, improvised theatricals—gay entertainment, if repetitious. The women called on each other, had tea parties, made over their dresses, and eagerly attended the auctions of the household goods of departing officers.

Tucson was unlike any town Mrs. Reed had known before. In one respect it did not even seem American. Spanish was the language you most commonly heard spoken as you drove down its single dusty street, or stepped over a dozing Papago Indian on your way into the general store; the sprinkling of Americans had adapted themselves to the usage of the over-whelmingly Mexican population. The San Diego-El Paso stage regularly rolled through the street, raising a cloud of dust. An occasional prospector, plodding along with his flop-eared donkey, passed through on his way to the mountains on the eternal search for gold and silver. Otherwise there was little travel. Buchalew Block, a row of one-story adobe houses, symbolized modern progress, and the number of saloons suggested that it was a country to build a man's thirst. The sun-baked town, it seemed to Mrs. Reed, looked as though it had sprung up out of the arid soil overnight, complete with basking population and dusty main street. Nothing could have been less like the civilized, gracious South in which she had grown up, with its great shade trees and softly weathered homes set in green lawns. But if she missed home, she did not complain, and settled into the monotonous life of the "Army wife" with the same kind of enthusiasm and interest as Reed.

Where there was so little variety, amusement tended to fall into a routine, but life was not without its unexpected humor. The Reeds never forgot the post chaplain and his pet. He came to call on them one evening, a diffident and serious man nearing middle age, plainly excited and a little shaken. Greetings were hardly over when his story came out: he had found a Gila monster, the large, ugly venomous lizard native to the arid part of Arizona, in his kitchen. He had captured it in a potato sack.

"What are you going to do with the horrid thing?" Mrs. Reed asked, shuddering.

"I am not quite sure. I wondered," the minister speculated, "if it might not respond to kindness. I believe that I shall try to make a pet of it."

Dr. Reed smiled. "You're a brave man, chaplain. They're ill-natured things, and their bite's poisonous."

The chaplain nodded absently. He was already laying plans to win the heart of his lizard.

He named it Sally Anne, for two officers' wives who were his most faithful parishioners—the compliment was wasted on them since neither cared greatly for Gila monsters—and spent a great deal of time catching it insects for food. When the Reeds left the post a few months later, the chaplain was still industriously trying to rouse a spark of affection in its reptilian bosom.

CHAPTER TEN

"SO SOON?" Mrs. Reed inquired in a stricken tone, glancing around the ugly square room with the worn furniture that had seen service with so many officers' families. There was little beautiful about it, or even attractive, she admitted to herself, but it had the well-lived-in look that rooms acquire when people have been comfortable and happy in them. They were leaving their first home, she thought with a small pang. "But we've hardly been here any time at all."

"That's Army life for you," her husband said philosophically. "The Army's quite a lot like the Methodist Church—it doesn't give you a chance to stagnate in one spot. My childhood training in frequent moves will come in handy. Personally, I'll be glad to miss the rest of the August heat here. It's cooler at Camp Apache, and wilder country, too, in that part of Arizona."

"Wilder? What about the Indians?"

"I don't think we need worry about Indians. All the Apaches in the state except the scouts enlisted in the Army and a few outlaws are at San Carlos Reservation now, and behaving themselves. It was the tribes under Geronimo and Victorio who were making most of the trouble, and now that Clum's got them on the reservation they'll probably be good." No point to alarming Emilie with the information that the young civilian Indian agent, John Clum, who had made a model reservation of San Carlos, had just resigned his post in protest because troops had been stationed there. Already, Dr. Reed had been told, the fierce and crafty Geronimo, whom Clum and his Apache police had captured and imprisoned, after the Army had several times failed to catch him, had been liberated and given the run of the reservation.

On August 11, 1877, Dr. Reed and his wife were ready to set off on their second major expedition, to proceed "by the shortest usually traveled route," as the Army orders of that day always expressed it, to Camp Apache, north of Tucson in the White Mountains. The baggage wagon, loaded with such household furnishings as could withstand the rough two-hundred-mile trip, had started the previous morning, and at nine o'clock the doherty wagon, painted white to turn a little of the burning heat, waited outside their quarters for the doctor and his wife.

"You're sure you haven't forgotten anything, Dr. Reed?" Mrs. Reed questioned anxiously as she hurried out of the house. Her little dog, Undina, wedged tightly under her arm, began to sniff with excitement.

"If I have, I really don't know where we would put it now," her husband observed, watching her expression with amusement as she surveyed the ambulance. He, the driver, and the strapping corporal who sat up front with the driver had packed it to the brim.

Only the back seat, on which he and Mrs. Reed and the dog were to sit, was vacant. Beneath it was an emergency kit of medicines, a large lunch box, a pair of the doctor's boots and a bulging bag which rattled with coffee pot, frying pan and sauce pans. A couple of folding chairs, a valise, blankets, a bundle of shawls, a work basket, a feather pillow and some light reading crowded the front seat, while under it were packed a mess chest containing tableware for the journey, a box of provisions and a clothes basket holding an assortment of necessaries. Two hats, Dr. Reed's sword, an umbrella, fire-arms, a pair of shoes and two canteens full of water swung from the roof. Outside, underneath the front seat, the doctor had stowed his heavy instrument case beside a sack of grain and the driver's ten days' rations. His trunk, and a mattress and bedding tied in a canvas cover, were securely strapped on behind.

"A very stylish equipage, don't you think, my dear?" he inquired smilingly. "At last I feel completely at home in the Army. The only difference is that Pa didn't arm to the teeth when he traveled. Hop in and let's be off. We've a forty-mile run ahead of us today."

Seasoned travelers by now, the Reeds enjoyed the ten-day trip through the almost uninhabited Apache domain. Hazards and hardships were, at their best, fun; at their worst, merely routine.

A leading item on the fun side of the ledger was Undina's behavior. Unsubdued by a temperature of a hundred and ten degrees, she barked at the top of her lungs the whole first day out, and jumped tirelessly back and forth across the seats. Having made herself too hoarse even to yelp, she thereafter behaved with more composure.

Under routine hazards came anxiety about hostile Indians. Dr. Reed, recalling that they sometimes frequented a spot called the Lime Kilns which his party was to pass on the second day, kept his weapons loaded and close at hand, and avoided the topic of Indians, in which his wife was showing an untimely interest. The wagon, however, rattled unmolested along the hot road past the danger spot, between the innocent grease-wood and mesquite bushes which concealed nothing more alarming than an occasional reptile.

The road skirted the southern edge of the mountain range that lay between Tucson and Camp Apache. Bending north off the stage route to cross the plain, it left to the right the Dragoon Mountains, still infested with outlaw Indians, where a stage driver had been murdered only a week before. It led then through the green Aravaipa Valley to Camp Thomas, where they spent a night with Lieutenant Powell, an acquaintance of Dr. Reed's. Mrs. Reed was the first woman

It gave Mrs. Reed quite a turn when an Apache came into the camp.

who had ever been on the post, and a small dog, catching sight of her, ran away yelping with alarm.

From then on, they had to camp out, sleeping in the doherty wagon, with Undina, who demanded all the comforts of home, on the bed at their feet. There were no way stations or even houses along the trail which ran through the San Carlos Reservation, which they had now entered, but there were Indians. It gave Mrs. Reed rather a turn when, at their first halt in the open, an Apache came into the camp. He laid down his rifle, sat beside the doctor, and explained with unsmiling friendliness that he was on his way to Camp Apache and would like something to eat. When he had devoured a loaf of bread, he said "Adios" and walked away.

The fishing expedition Dr. Reed took one afternoon was a complete failure. They had reached camp—that is, the nearest water—early that day, and Reed spent an hour dangling his line in Ash Creek. His only bite was a turtle, and after spending another hour trying to get it off his hook, he gave up. A sudden downpour that evening, just at dinner time, flooded the oven, ruined the bread and depressed the spirits of their soldier-cook without dampening the Reeds' at all. Bad weather, they agreed, was part of the fun—if you could stay in the doherty wagon.

The way then gradually ascended into the White Mountains, and the trail became almost impassable, even to stout hearts and Army mules. How to get up and down hills where the track was only a steep jumble of barrel-sized rocks became the major problem. Leaving the baggage wagon stuck on a tremendous hill with the soldiers who were to unload it and bring it up empty the next morning, the Reeds one evening pushed ahead with the ambulance. Again those bugaboos, bears and Indians, so potent a fiction in the safe nurseries of the east and so real a danger in the lonely reaches of the far west, haunted Mrs. Reed. The sight, however, of the blazing fire under the tall pines and of her husband preparing supper for them reminded her that life in the open made her even more hungry than nervous.

Heroic measures—in trying to keep the wagon from going over a steep bump with a fatal smash, the doctor was jerked along behind it with such violence that the soles were ripped from his shoes—brought them safe and whole, in body and baggage, over the last lap and into Camp Apache. They were to live at this post, one of the most inaccessible in all this wild and inaccessible region, for the next three years.

It was the last month of 1877. The year, so eventful and so crowded with new experiences for Walter and Emilie Lawrence Reed, still had one major novelty in store for them. On December 4th their first child was born.

The new father knocked very softly at the door, and bent his brown head attentively toward it.

"Come in," his wife called. "I'm not asleep."

He entered and closed the door quietly.

"The future President is, though," she greeted him.

"He's nice, isn't he," Reed said, bending over to look at the tiny baby. "He already looks just like you. I feel unreasonably proud of him."

The baby opened his eyes and stared unwinkingly at his father. Dr. Reed picked him up gently and looked at him with a combination of fatherly tenderness and professional interest.

"A sound specimen, doctor?" Mrs. Reed asked with a smile.

"A fine specimen, ma'am," he assured her, "and a credit to his parents."

She laughed and reached out for the baby. Her husband carefully laid him beside her and pulled a chair up to the bedside.

"Hadn't we better give him a name pretty soon?" he suggested. "We've had him now for a week, and it isn't very convenient just to call him 'he' all the time."

"I want him named after his father," Mrs. Reed asserted. "And I want him to grow up like him, too," she added positively.

"We can easily arrange for your first request, anyway," Reed agreed, "but the other will have to wait for a while. I want him named after you, though, but I'll compromise. Let's name him Walter Lawrence, and call him Lawrence."

Mrs. Reed thought that a splendid solution. The object of the discussion, however, was not interested. He had gone back to sleep.

CHAPTER ELEVEN

THE DOCTOR looked more disheveled than his wife had ever seen him before, even on camping trips. Amusement and desperation mingled in his expression. She did not need to ask what was wrong.

"The cook has left!" she exclaimed.

"Yes! How did you know?"

"By your face." She could not help laughing.

Her husband sighed. "He's gone, all right. Out the window, too. After I found him drunk last night, I made him go to bed and locked his door and pocketed the key."

"Oh dear! And after he *promised* you to keep sober until I was up again."

"Twice he promised me: when I hired him, and when the baby was born," Dr. Reed said bleakly. "And you should see the kitchen this morning, too—all yesterday's dirty dishes. What would you suggest?" he asked helplessly.

Mrs. Reed lay back on her pillow and smiled sweetly at her husband. "There's only one thing I can think of," she said. "I'm surprised it hasn't occurred to you."

"It has. But I was hoping for something better from your ingenuity, my dear." He grinned ruefully and went over to the bureau. "Where do you keep your aprons?"

Mrs. Reed could follow his progress from the noises downstairs. She heard him shake the stove; next came the slam of the door as he stepped into the lean-to shed for wood; the clank of the stove lid and the thump of wood being tossed in followed, and the slosh of water ladled into the tea-kettle. After a bit came the clatter of dishes inexpertly washed and dried.

She slipped off to sleep again to the sound of pots being impatiently banged on the stove, and to the rising smell of fresh hot coffee.

When her husband came upstairs again, carrying a tray, she woke up. His face was flushed, and her apron was knotted around his middle in a most unmilitary manner.

"I'm all worn out from hanging over the hot stove," he grumbled in comic imitation of a disgruntled housewife, setting the tray on the bedside table. Whisking the napkin off, he exposed bread, butter, coffee and boiled eggs.

"If you were getting this superb breakfast in a city hotel," he pointed out to his hungry wife, "it would be listed on the menu as *pan frésco, mantéca, café caliente y huevos asados.* But it wouldn't taste a bit better." He served her and began to eat with enjoyment. "I don't know what we want with a cook when I do so nicely."

"How did you like the dishes?"

"Well, that's something else. I suppose I shall have to be severe with Private Anmach when he comes back. In fact, I feel like being severe," he added grimly.

"Oh, the poor man," Mrs. Reed protested. "He must have such a dull life. Anyway, Christmas comes only once a year."

"A good thing, too. We couldn't afford to have our cook disappear much more often. He's eccentric, but as soldier-cooks go, he's pretty good."

Private James Anmach had agreed to cook for the Reeds on the first of December. Although officers could not have enlisted men as cooks in more civilized stations, wherever it was impossible to get civilian help they were permitted to engage a soldier, if the soldier was willing. Anmach, when approached by Dr. Reed with the suggestion, had been willing. He had been at one time or another a plasterer, painter, carpenter, tinner, plumber and farmer. He wouldn't mind learning to cook, he said; it might come in handy some time.

His cooking, under the doctor's direction, had developed well; but he had original ideas about serving. His favorite crockery was soup plates. Steak, chicken, vegetables, flannel cakes, everything, appeared on the table in soup plates. His employer was expected to eat from a soup plate, too. Thankful that his wife was upstairs in bed, beyond the reach of such barbarism, the doctor remonstrated mildly that soup plates were for soup. Whether the explanation offended Anmach, or merely baffled him, Reed never knew. But the next day at dinner he found potatoes in the soup tureen, and pickles in the gravy boat. He wisely refrained from further comment.

It became a point of honor with him not to betray surprise at Anmach's ingenious flouting of table convention. When a boiled potato rolled out of the water pitcher and plunked into his glass, the doctor blandly speared it onto his plate, like a man accustomed all his life to having boiled potatoes served in water pitchers. Anmach's little game was harmless, his victim thought with amusement, and since he took a great deal of pains with the cooking, he was willing to indulge him.

Then Anmach, carried away by the holiday spirit, disappeared Christmas night, leaving behind him the day's dirty dishes. For three days Reed saw nothing of him. And for three days he did the cooking and housework. By his own account, the dishes he prepared were barely fit to eat. Sympathetic ladies at the post sent Mrs. Reed her meals. Distrust of the culinary prowess of husbands was general among them.

On the morning of the fourth day, while Dr. Reed was starting the fire in the stove, he heard a meek rap at the door. He opened it to Anmach, a penitent Anmach who asserted that he was a "dog" and reproached himself so movingly for his base conduct that the doctor did not have the heart to add reproaches of his own. Besides, he was too happy to see him again to think of any. That night, as he warily reconnoitered his dinner, which Anmach had served with his usual talent for surprise, he was conscious only of gratitude: he would not have to wash the dishes. His troubles were over.

So he thought. But he had reckoned without his wife's feeling for the fitness of things. Eating from soup plates and finding dumplings in the cream pitcher did not conform to it. By the middle of January she was up again, and having her meals with her husband. Disregarding his urgent advice, she protested to the soldier-cook. Anmach, offended, disappeared again; and Dr. Reed, for another five days, took over the kitchen department, since Mrs. Reed was not yet well enough. Finally he found another private as cook.

Powers, Mrs. Reed reported, was a jewel. He was sober, pleasant, took suggestions kindly and outraged no conventions. Her satisfaction was so great that she did not conceal it. Powers' renown came to the ears of the Commanding Officer, whose cook had lately deserted the stove for the bottle. The Commanding Officer, therefore, found himself under the "painful necessity," as he regretfully put it, of taking Powers to cook for his household. The "painful necessity" was neither painful nor necessary, his junior well knew, but what could a lieutenant do when the CO coveted his cook? He could look around for another cook, that was all.

He engaged Private Howard, who had the reputation of being a good one. The reputation was undeserved. His cooking was deplorable, his disposition worse. Mrs. Reed hotly insisted that he be discharged. But her husband, remembering those mornings when he had shiveringly come down to the icy kitchen to start the fire and make the breakfast, begged her to be patient. Tapping her foot, she replied that she could be patient with that impudent lazy-bones only so long. Howard relieved the situation by asserting that he was being overworked, and asked to be sent back to his company. His disgusted employer paid him off and tried to find another cook. It seemed impossible.

"I simply don't know what to do about it," he lamented the next evening. Mrs. Reed was preparing the dinner, and he had just finished setting the table. The despair in his voice was only half comic.

She took the roast out of the oven and put it on the platter—not a soup plate.

"That gives me the most wonderful idea!" she exclaimed suddenly. "Why shouldn't we get Anmach to come back?"

Her husband looked at her with admiration. "Why shouldn't we, indeed? I can't think of any reason on earth. My dear, you *are* wonderful!"

So Anmach came back. The doctor, cannily determined to avoid shoals this time, drew up a contract: Private James Anmach agreed to cook, to do general work such as milking and gardening, and to serve food in the traditional vessels; and Dr. Walter Reed agreed that Private Anmach should have a week's bender after every pay day, or once every two months.

Dr. Walter Reed knew how to compromise.

He summed up his experience in a quotation from Edward Lytton's "Lucile" which he sent to his wife's sister.

"We may live without poetry, music and art;
  We may live without conscience and live without heart;
  We may live without friends; we may live without books;
  But civilized man cannot live without cooks."

This was the lighter side of post life, but there was more to it than comedy. There was, for instance, nothing funny about the Indians.

"There are no good Indians but dead Indians," General Philip Sheridan had sweepingly declared in a callous epigram that was widely taken for truth.

The majority of the settlers and soldiers in the far west

knew little about the rights and wrongs of white and Indian affairs. All they knew was that they were trying to open up the country and make it safe, and that the Apaches would sweep down without warning, burn and kill and capture, and then dissolve into the mountains or across the Mexican border. It would probably have surprised them to know President Hayes' opinion: "Many, if not most, of our Indian wars have had their origin in broken promises and acts of injustice on our part."

By the time that Walter Reed was stationed in Arizona, however, most of the Apaches, submitting to the pressure of the inevitable, had given up the unequal war against the white men and were living as government wards at San Carlos Indian Reservation. But Geronimo, an outlaw, was irreconcilable. When John Clum gave up his post as Indian agent, the war chief, crafty and vengeful, was set at liberty again. He spent the winter of 1877-1878 at the reservation, living at government expense in more ease and comfort than he could otherwise have enjoyed; but when spring came, and the snow began to melt from the mountains and game was easier to find, he and his followers slipped away from the reservation and headed south toward Mexico's Sierra Madre range, the "Mother Mountains" of the Apaches, raiding on the way.

The Camp Apache cavalry was sent in pursuit, with the friendly Coyotero Apaches who had enlisted in the Army acting as scouts. They followed Geronimo's trail, but were unable to catch him. The Apaches, when pursued, usually broke up into small bands of two and three and escaped separately, to reunite later at some prearranged safe place.

Dr. Reed, who had not been ordered to accompany the expedition, was awakened before dawn one morning by persistent knocking on his door. When he stepped out on the porch, he could distinguish by the starlight two enlisted men standing there, one of them with a bundle in his arms. Before anyone

Before anyone could speak, the bundle whimpered.

could speak, the bundle whimpered. The doctor stepped sharply forward and demanded,

"What's this?"

"A child, sir," the soldier holding the bundle answered. "A little Indian girl, badly burned. Two days ago our force came into a camp that Geronimo had just left, and found her there. They'd left her to die, so we volunteered to bring her back. We'd have got here quicker, but the captain ordered us to travel only at night, because of hostile Indians."

"Good men," Reed approved them. "Carry her to the hospital and have the steward stir up the fire and put water on to heat. I'll join you right away."

He dressed hastily and hurried over to the rough log hospital. A wood fire was roaring in the stove, and the water was already heating. The child lay in the middle of the single ward on the pine table that served as operating table. Dexterously the doctor snipped away the makeshift bandages from her burned side. A youthful cavalryman with a broken leg woke up and, raising himself on his elbow, watched from his bed. He admired the young doctor's skill and gentleness—he had recently experienced them himself—and noticed that his slight frown of concentration did not at all detract from the kindliness of his expression. As his skillful hands moved, Dr. Reed spoke once or twice. "Closer," he said, to the soldier holding the candle which flickered in the cold air seeping through chinks in the logs, and "Water, now," to the steward. The boy drifted off to sleep again. When he opened his eyes the sun was rising. The doctor was rolling down his sleeves and advising one of the soldiers, who was looking very green and miserable, to go over to his quarters and ask Anmach for some coffee: that would put him back on his feet after his hard night. The child had stopped moaning and was sleeping under an opiate. Reed smoothed the straight black hair off her low forehead and lightly patted the round cheek.

"She'll come through, all right," he said confidently.

Funny, the young soldier thought, an educated man like the doctor taking so much trouble just for an Indian kid.

Dr. Reed walked briskly out, whistling softly between his teeth, to get his breakfast and tell his wife about the little Indian girl whom he hoped to save.

He thought live Indians were good, too.

CHAPTER TWELVE

THE PRACTICE of an Army doctor in those days was much like that of his civilian confreres. He treated wounds, injuries, frostbite and any illness that occurred among the healthy young men of his post, and cared for the officers' wives and children. Because he was often the only doctor for miles around, he also attended anyone in the surrounding region who sent for him. His practice was a general one. Specialization was just a word to him, one, indeed, that he rarely heard.

His life was not easy. The Army was neglected by the country that thought it was through with wars, and the Medical Corps was the stepchild of the Army. In posts such as Apache the hospital was usually a crude building erected by the troops. It was built to last ten years on the theory, possible only in an age that knew nothing about bacteriology, that it would by then be too "saturated with hospital infection" for further use and should be torn down. An office, a dispensary, a storeroom and a kitchen were usually partitioned off in the four corners, and the rest of the room served as a ward. It was heated by wood-burning stoves and lighted by candles or coal oil lamps. Such necessities of a modern hospital as a laboratory, an operating room and running water were undreamed of.

There were no nurses, and the Hospital Corps had not yet been formed. The sick were cared for by hospital stewards, many of them men of education and training who were attached to the Medical Corps as non-commissioned officers; and by privates, detailed by their company commanders to hospital duty, and not greatly interested in the work beyond the extra-duty pay.

Dr. Reed got along well with the men working under him, and succeeded in inspiring them with a little of his own devotion to the art and, as he saw it, the privilege of healing. Order and cleanliness were strict rules with him. Lenient with his cook's lapses from sobriety, he would not tolerate drinking by hospital attendants: the welfare of his patients was at stake.

Usually gracious and pliable, he could be rigid when his authority was slighted. There was a tendency at that time among the line officers—the fighting men—to pay scant attention to the advice of the Army doctors. The medical officer was in the unhappy position of being able only to advise on health and sanitary matters; he had no enforcement power at all. The Commanding Officer of his post could ignore even his most urgent recommendations. It was a galling situation, and one which Dr. Reed met with his customary directness.

On one occasion a soldier still on sick list who was taking a walk was ordered to active duty by the Commanding Officer at Apache, who remarked that if he was well enough to be strolling about he was well enough to work. Reed did not waste his time or temper in a protest to his superior. Instead he sent a letter through him to headquarters asking if such interference with medical treatment was allowed. The answer, filtering back through official channels, upheld him. The Commanding Officer, who received it first, read it and sighed as he handed it to his adjutant for delivery to Dr. Reed. "Ah, those doctors, Mr. Adjutant," he said. "We can never get ahead of them."

He could snare the doctor's cook away from him, but he knew better now than to interfere with his patients! Surgeon General Barnes had been right when he recognized the young lieutenant as a man who would defend the dignity of his Corps.

The duty of safeguarding the health of his handful of patients left Reed time for his favorite hobby, gardening, which he and his wife enjoyed together. She grew flowers; he, vegetables. The Army, in the days when little was known about the importance of fresh vegetables in the diet, made no provision for them in the daily ration. Even if it had, there would have been no way to obtain them at posts like Apache, except by growing them on the spot. A soldier threatened with scurvy —a disease caused by lack of fresh vegetables and fruit—was ordered to go to the commissary and get canned tomatoes; and this food at many posts took the place of fresh vegetables. The doctor could not grow enough in his garden for the whole post, but he did provide the hospital.

Nobody worried much about hostile Indians at the post. The few Coyotero Apaches who, with their women and children, lived there were peaceable folk, and most of their men were enlisted in the Army. As long as Geronimo was at large the danger from hostile Indians was real, but it was chiefly confined to the southern parts of Arizona and New Mexico from which retreat across the border, out of reach of the United States troops, was easy. And even that danger abated for the time when, in October, 1879, Geronimo, seeing a cold hard winter ahead, proclaimed that he was tired of the warpath and wanted to return to San Carlos—where the government would take care of his food, clothing and shelter.

The post Indians were fond of games, and the men, in their free time, could often be found squatting in the shade playing cards, each with his little scrap of red flannel, which all Apaches wore for good luck, stuck in hat or belt or buttonhole. The cards, homemade from horsehide, were marked with crude sketches of men and animals, and with dots and Apache signs; stakes were a bit of tobacco, small coins, a knife, or perhaps a pair of canvas pants.

They were a sturdy people, of great endurance and strength, who had little sickness. When an Apache became ill the medicine man, hideously painted, with chanting, incantations and dancing would set to work to drive out the evil spirit. The Indians at Camp Apache, when an illness did not immediately yield to this treatment, got in the habit of sending for the white medicine man.

They liked him and looked on him as a friend. He had saved the life of the little Indian girl, they knew, had named her Susie and was bringing her up in his own household; and he was never too busy or tired to come to them when they asked for him. Dr. Reed, on his part, treated them faithfully and was never discouraged by the almost certain knowledge that, the moment his back was turned, the witch doctor, shaking his gourd rattle and whooping frightfully, would resume his effort to scare the devil out of the sufferer—who probably needed quiet more than anything else. That they appreciated his efforts for them, whether or not they thought them as effective as those of their own medicine man, they made plain by bringing him presents—a haunch of venison, or a wild turkey, or a few quail. If no one was in the house to receive it, they would slip inside and, removing a picture from the wall, hang the game in its place, or perhaps lay it on Mrs. Reed's dressing table.

It was, in some respects, an ideal life, active, healthful and busy, and free of financial strain; but it had drawbacks, too, distressing to Reed's scholarly temperament. In this remote Army post, seven hundred miles from the nearest railway and six weeks by mail from the east, he was shut off from the distractions of the world, but also from its problems and ideas. Medical knowledge, he knew, was not static; it was continually pressing against its frontiers and forcing them back as surely as the ranchers and miners and farmers were forcing back those of the west. It was a slow process, but a continuing one, one with which it was hard to keep up from an isolated garrison in the Arizona mountains.

Revolutionary new theories were seeping into the medical journals. Some European doctors were saying that "germs," tiny living organisms that could be seen only through a microscope, were the causes of certain diseases and of the infections that made even the simplest surgical operation dangerous. Lister himself had addressed a skeptical audience on antiseptic surgery at the International Medical Congress at the Philadelphia Centennial in 1876. A brother officer, Captain A. C. Girard of the Medical Corps, had been abroad in 1877 and, convinced of the value of Lister's technique, had sent the Surgeon General a full report of it. Barnes, somewhat impressed, had published it to the Corps in August, 1877, and more than a year later had made available to any post surgeons who asked for it "Weir's Antiseptic Spray Apparatus," with antiseptic dressings. The new scientific medicine was barely launched, but it was beginning to make headway.

Walter Reed, scanning the few and belated medical journals that penetrated his wilderness, noticed and wondered about the daring new theories. Meanwhile, he faithfully attended to his post duties—sick call, inspection, hospital calls, professional visits outside—practiced with increasing skill and knowledge, and cultivated his garden.

Modestly, because there was a lady present, the corporal stepped behind one of the supply wagons to take off his red flannel undershirt. He emerged in a moment holding it in his hand, his uniform jacket buttoned over his bare chest.

"Now," Dr. Reed directed him, "cut off a limb and tie your shirt to it by the arms. As soon as the train comes in sight, start waving it." The corporal saluted and withdrew.

The paired steel ribbons before him stretched two thousand miles eastward, a thousand westward. Behind lay more than seven hundred miles of the roughest and loneliest country left in the United States. Walter Reed, his three years of frontier

They hung the game in its place.

duty finished, had been ordered to travel north from Camp
Apache until he picked up the Union Pacific tracks west of
Cheyenne. He was to flag the first train and identify himself to
the engineer. The engineer on his next trip would bring out
the doctor who was to return to Camp Apache in Reed's place
with the wagon train; and the Reeds, in the expensive discom-
fort that distinguished railway travel in the early days, would
return to civilization.

It sounded easy, but they had been twenty-seven days on
their way—twenty-seven days over trackless territory un-
marked by a single settlement. The ambulance and the four
escort wagons—one with feed for the mules, one with the soldiers' baggage and provisions, two with the furniture they
were able to bring out—had had to break their own trail. It was
like all the rest of his wagon trips, only longer and tougher.
Just as well that Lawrence, now a robust two-year-old, was a
good soldier like his mother, the doctor thought.

Lawrence's mother stepped out of the doherty wagon to
join her husband who was thoughtfully heating a cup of shav-
ing water by the camp fire.

"Lawrence is asleep, I'm glad to say," she reported, "and
so is Susie." They were bringing the Indian girl back to civilization with them to train her, on government orders, as a
household servant.

The doctor turned to her with a rapt expression. His blue
eyes had the look of one who sees a lovely vision. "A hot bath,"
he said reverently. "Just think! A hot bath all over!"

The soldier by the track shouted and began to wave his
improvised flag in wide arcs.

CHAPTER THIRTEEN

BY 1881 WALTER REED was a captain and had a mustache. He had been in the United States Army for six years. He did not know when his original idea of leaving it had faded from his mind, but it was gone.

He had begun his Army career with a dutiful regard for the good name of the Medical Corps. That sentiment had expanded quietly into complete devotion to the service which, struggling against disadvantages, rose constantly above its limitations.

There were never enough medical officers to go around, so that civilian doctors had to be hired under contract to fill even the peacetime needs. Overworked hospital stewards and bored privates continued to care for the sick. Post hospitals still were unequipped with modern facilities. Hidebound officers sneered at bacteriology and antisepsis. The prospective retirement of Surgeon General Barnes had brought about an undignified scramble among the higher ranking men who hoped to succeed him.

There were, however, certain heartening advances. The use of antisepsis in surgical operations by post surgeons was no longer infrequent, although Lister was still being ridiculed in London. Some of the more alert officers had become interested in bacteriology and modern hygiene. In George Miller Sternberg the Medical Corps had an officer who was a scientist of real distinction, one of the earliest and foremost bacteriologists in the country. There might be much to deplore in the Corps, but there were also many things to be proud of, and these sprang from the initiative and enterprise of men like Walter

Reed, who, by no means blind to its faults, were proud of its progress and eager for its improvement.

On his return from Arizona, he had been appointed a captain in June, 1880. After three months' leave of absence, which he spent in Virginia, he had been stationed that fall with the infantry at Fort Ontario, at Oswego, New York. The next March and April found him on duty at Fort McHenry, in the vicinity of Baltimore—and, incidentally, of Johns Hopkins University.

This university, operating on a principle new in American education, had been established in 1876. It was not, like most American colleges, a school for the general education of undergraduates, but a center of learning, like the European universities, where advanced students trained for work in their chosen fields. Thomas Huxley, the famous English biologist and exponent of evolution, which was then widely regarded as a theory that could not be reconciled with religion, had spoken on biological research at the inaugural exercises, which had been held without the customary prayers and hymns. The incident had provoked a storm. "It was bad enough to have asked Huxley. It were better to have asked God to be there. It would have been absurd to ask them both," wrote an indignant minister. The incident had also served notice that the new university was backing modern science.

During those two months early in 1881 Reed was briefly introduced, at first hand, to modern medicine. Dr. Newell Martin, formerly an assistant of Huxley's, was the professor of physiology, and had established the first biological laboratory in the United States. Special students, not enrolled in courses, were sometimes given the privilege of attending lectures at the university, and it appears that the still young Dr. Reed took advantage of this opportunity to hear Martin lecture. There were not yet, in 1881, courses in pathology and bacteriology—they were to wait four years for the coming of Dr. William Henry

Welch, whose student and friend Reed was to become—but interest in both subjects was already keen. Conservative medical journals might still make game of Pasteur for seeing germs everywhere, but modern medicine had enthusiastic converts at the new university. It quickly made another of the young Army doctor who had been for the last five years almost entirely out of touch with scientific developments.

The time at Fort McHenry passed with exasperating quickness for the eager medical officer who was barely given time to glimpse the new scientific world opening before the explorations of research men. At the end of two months Capt. Reed was ordered to duty at the coast artillery post, Washington Barracks, at Washington, D. C. He must have felt like a starving man jerked unceremoniously away from an irresistibly appetizing meal.

The Reeds, however, found Washington an agreeable change from the lonely years on the frontier. They could go to the theater, make short trips into Virginia and North Carolina to see their families or, on more limited excursions, walk about the city without sinking, as they once would have done, in mud to the ankle. "Electric speaking telephones," although still rarities, had been in use for several years. The first electric light had just appeared in the city. Work was continuing on the huge and fussy pile of the State, War and Navy Building. The Washington Monument was deliberately laboring upward. The city everywhere proudly flaunted signs of its progress, progress which was exciting to the officer and his wife so recently arrived from the west. Their most vivid memory of Washington, however, had nothing to do with its growth and the changing scene. It centered on July 2, 1881.

It was hot that morning, hot and clear. Dr. Reed, glancing through the newspaper at breakfast, scanned the big headlines proclaiming Yale's crew had defeated Harvard's and noticed with more interest the statement in smaller type that the President's wife, Mrs. Garfield, was rapidly improving in health and strength. Mrs. Reed remarked that weather like this made one appreciate Arizona, and Lawrence upset his glass of milk across the table.

At his mother's reproachful exclamation his lower lip turned out ominously, and his blue eyes floated in tears.

"There, there, old man," Reed consoled him, hastily righting the glass and sopping up the flood with his napkin, "this is one thing we never cry over. Come on, smile now for Father, like a good fellow. Smile?" Lawrence smiled, a little uncertainly, then laughed at the funny face his father made for him.

"Really, Dr. Reed, you'll spoil him to death," Mrs. Reed said smilingly and without conviction.

"He's like his mother. He won't spoil," her husband said and went back to his paper.

"'President Garfield will probably not take action on the expected retirement of Surgeon General Barnes and Paymaster General Brown until Congress meets,'" he read aloud. "Barnes is a fine old gentleman," he commented, "but it would be the best thing in the world for the Corps to have a man with modern training at its head."

"Who do you think will be the next Surgeon General?" Mrs. Reed wanted to know.

"Oh, probably one of the old timers. Crane, maybe. He's been Barnes' office assistant for years."

"You'd like to see Dr. Sternberg get it, wouldn't you?"

"Indeed I would! Professionally he's the most eminent man in the Corps. But it's out of the question; too many outrank him. Think what a clanking of brass hats there would be! Did I tell you that Sternberg has set up a biological laboratory at his own expense at Fort Mason?"

Mrs. Reed sighed. She suspected that her husband, after his brief Johns Hopkins experience, would like to do something of the sort himself. But it was one of the things—there were a great many—that you couldn't do on a captain's pay.

The doctor folded the paper and took a final swallow of coffee.

"Well," he remarked, getting up, "I can't sit here and gossip with my charming wife and interesting son all morning. I work for a living, you know." A warm, quick smile that made his blue eyes sparkle, and he was gone.

Mrs. Reed did not see him again until evening. By that time neither the newspapers nor anyone else cared about the crew races or the Surgeon General. The shattering news of the attempt on the President's life had crowded all other matters from everyone's mind. He had been shot and gravely wounded in the Baltimore and Potomac Railroad station as he was about to depart for New York. His assailant had immediately been caught, and troops had been ordered from the barracks to keep order.

Reed, when he returned, was tired and depressed. He had guarded the man, he said, at Police Headquarters before he was transferred to the greater safety of the District Jail.

"And the President?" Mrs. Reed questioned.

"It's a bad wound, so I was told," her husband answered. "He may well die of it."

"Who could have done such a senseless, wicked thing!"

"A crack-pot. His name's Charles Guiteau. He's a little man with thin brown hair and sunken cheeks and gray eyes. When we got to Police Headquarters, he was boasting that he had done it on inspiration from God for the good of the Republican party. He'd been trying to get some political appointment, and had been snubbed. He said the blood of French Revolutionaries ran in his veins, and made a number of other irresponsible remarks. He's simply unbalanced. He's afraid," Reed smiled faintly, "that Nast"—the popular cartoonist who had launched the Tweed Ring exposé—"won't make a good likeness of him."

"To think that the President of the United States may die because a crank imagined a grievance against him!"

"It's frightful," the doctor agreed wearily. He raised himself stiffly out of his chair and went to the door. "I'll have to look in at the hospital for a few minutes. I haven't been there since early morning, and there are a couple of men I want to see again. Don't wait up for me."

The President lingered manfully. General Sherman, granting an interview in his garden, tried to allay public anxiety. He expected the President to recover; his face didn't have "a certain death-like look." Everyone hoped the Civil War hero knew what he was talking about. Certainly he had seen enough dead men. Ungrammatical with emotion, he had added, "The dreadful act was committed by a fool—he don't even rise to the dignity of a crazy man."

For more than two months Washington lived in a crescendo of muted anxiety. Then the President was moved to the seaside. Two weeks later he was dead. Chester A. Arthur took the oath of office as President of the United States, and life in the capital returned to normal.

CHAPTER FOURTEEN

SO THIS TIME it was Nebraska. You could never tell where they'd send you next. I've never been to the northwest, Walter Reed thought, and my southern blood chills at the idea of going there in mid-winter. It was November, 1882.

Omaha for a month, and then Fort Omaha, the infantry post near the city. A daughter, Emilie Lawrence Reed, was born there on July 12, 1883.

"She looks like a little angel," the doctor exclaimed, touching the light down on her head with a finger that almost hesitated.

"Dr. Reed! how you exaggerate!" his wife teased him. "Angel, indeed. She looks more like a little lobster."

"Angel, lobster—it's all the same thing," he said cheerfully. "I'm so glad it was a girl! I think I'm going to like her a lot."

"Do you really think so? She is rather sweet, at that," Mrs. Reed said complacently.

And then, in October, 1883, to Fort Sidney, an infantry post on the Union Pacific, over toward the western border of the state.

It wasn't long before the settlers for miles around found out: you could always call on the post doctor; he never failed the sick or distressed. He had been known to come out on a pressing call—these lonely people rarely sent for the doctor until it was an emergency—when he was so ill himself that he had to lie down on arriving and rest before seeing the patient. He made a sick person feel better the moment he came in the room. He joked and played with the children. The women, drab and stringy from overwork, were touched as much by the hint of chivalry in his manner toward them as by his painstaking care. A man might, at first sight, underestimate him for his thin mustache, his quick, slender figure and his quiet manner, but only at first glance. There was an endurance and courage in the Army doctor of which the toughest settler might have been proud.

The sturdy post horse wanted to turn his tail to the wind, heavy with biting snow, that whipped in his face, but his rider forced him on. Snorting protest, he plodded ahead.

Capt. Reed was glad of the buffalo overcoat, and the cap with muskrat ear-flaps. A man could freeze solid in this sub-zero weather before he realized it, if he weren't well protected. The boy who had come on snowshoes to fetch him had cheeks and nose badly frostbitten. He had been most of the day covering the dozen miles that took only a couple of hours in less dreadful weather. He had begged to be allowed to start back with the doctor, but Reed had made him go to bed in the post hospital.

"I've made a call on your mother before," he assured him. "I know the way, and I'll take a steward with me."

The fearful cold, and the sparkling white loneliness out here did something to people. The boy had been almost hysterical as well as exhausted when he floundered into the post. He'd be all right with a little rest, but sometimes, after a more severe ordeal by snow and silence, a man would come out crazy as —they had a word for it here—as a shitepoke, the big awkward heron that seemed to have no sense at all.

The doctor and the steward pushed on through the whirling whiteness that muffled their vision. They had been out several hours, and it was getting dark. Both were anxious to reach the sick woman; their own safety was involved, too. People who got lost in a plains blizzard were usually found

The doctor and the steward pushed on through the whirling whiteness.

the next spring—when the circling buzzards drew attention to them. Reed recognized the danger, but did not dwell on it: it was just one of the chances you had to take.

This snowstorm reminded him of the toy that the major's wife had brought back to little Emilie from the east. It was a hollow glass ball, holding a miniature snow-covered landscape, across which three tiny figures made their way toward a little church with a pointed steeple. When you shook the ball the snow flew up and whirled about, obscuring for a few moments the people and the church, and then settled down leaving the little scene clear and serene again. The doctor felt that he and the steward, like the little people at the center of the glass ball, were plodding through the whirling snowflakes at the heart of a shut-off world exclusively their own.

Then, thank heaven, they were no longer in a private world!

There, peering dimly through the growing darkness, was a light!

"Ma's mighty bad," the settler said in a hoarse whisper as he helped the cold, stiff doctor out of his overcoat, "and fretting something terrible about Tom, gone to get you in this blizzard."

The steward, who had carried in the saddle-bags full of instruments and medicines, was gathering pans full of snow to heat on the rickety stove.

Reed washed his hands and stepped over to the bed. Ma was, as her husband had said, mighty bad. Her face was gray, but she had made a pathetic effort to fix her hair, which was damp with sweat.

"Your Tom's a fine boy," the doctor cheered her. "He came through like a soldier, and he's snug in bed now. He certainly thinks the world of his mother."

She smiled wanly. "Now," Dr. Reed took her wrist and lightly felt the pulse, "let's have a look at you."

Hours later, numb with fatigue, he sat in a chair by the stove. The steward was asleep on the floor and the settler, haggard from another sleepless night, was making coffee. Ma was resting comfortably, and the baby had an excellent chance to survive his hectic entrance into the world. One of the hardest deliveries I've ever handled, and I was fortunate to pull them both through, the tired doctor thought gratefully. It wasn't just skill, either. That's never enough, by itself. It takes something extra. Some call it luck. Maybe, the minister's son speculated, God's help is a better name for it.

Drowsily he watched the settler pour the coffee. The steward smelt it and sat up. How on earth do these people stand the racking, nerve-splitting loneliness of these winters? Reed wondered. It had stopped snowing, and out the window through which the lantern had shone, the view was an unbroken white monotony. Inside, the only reading matter he could see was a few well-worn government pamphlets on agriculture. Although tired to the point of exhaustion, he was burning to get back to the post—the post with its noisy young soldiers, the military band, the railroad station, his family and his journals—to escape the crushing white silence that lay like death all around this speck of a house.

The settler handed him his coffee and gave some to the soldier. This skinny young doctor was a real man, tough as a whip and not scared of weather. His wife was going to be all right, and he had a new son. He was feeling better now.

"Doctor," he said sociably, "we sure do feel sorry for you young fellows shut up on the post all winter. It must get powerful lonely sometimes."

The soldier spluttered into his cup. Dr. Reed was not too tired to smile.

In August, 1884, they packed up again, furniture, dogs, two children and the Indian girl Susie, and traveled in a wagon train four days across Nebraska's panhandle to Fort Robinson.

It was toward sundown one day that fall that a wagon, moving at a cautious walk, pulled into the post. Swooning and swearing, the disheveled invalid with the fierce eyes was helped out by the driver and his companion and carried into the log hospital. Dr. Reed examined the crushed ankle, horribly discolored and swollen, and whistled softly.

"This injury has been neglected so long," he said, "I'm very much afraid you will have to lose your foot."

The settler, his mind filmed with pain and opiates, clung savagely to consciousness long enough to promise the doctor in profane and broken English that he would kill him if he amputated. Reed believed him; those burning eyes didn't lie.

If he wanted to take a chance on dying with his foot on, rather than make sure of recovering with it off, Reed told him calmly, no one would interfere with his choice. He might even get well. The patient, dimly impressed by the quiet officer who yielded to his wish in ignoring his threat, went under the ether without further protest. The doctor operated, removing the dead flesh and loose bone fragments. He put a drain through the joint, dressed the wound antiseptically and put it in a plaster of Paris splint. The hospital was full, so he had his patient settled comfortably in a tent.

Later the same evening, Sturgeon and Scribner, who had driven the injured man the seventy-five miles from his claim on Mirage Flats on the Niobrara River to the Army post, dropped in to see how their friend Jules Sandoz had stood the operation. Bathed, shaved and clothed in a clean nightshirt, he was a very different-looking person from the ragged and semi-delirious wild man they had carried in earlier. The doctor, who was with him, beckoned them outside. Their friend, he told them, was tough. He would probably recover, but he would be lame. He listened while they explained that Jules had been injured in a fall down a forty-foot well almost two weeks before. He was a stubborn fellow who had had part of a medical education before emigrating from Switzerland; he had thought he could take care of the injury himself. They had tried to nurse him, then persuaded him to let them bring him to the post doctor. They had been two days on the road, walking the team every step of the way.

Then they said good night to the doctor. Afterwards, half-way home, they wished that they had thought to ask him his name.

Jules, soon transferred to the post hospital, turned out to be a bright spot in the post doctor's winter. When he had time after dressing the ankle, he would stay with his patient to discuss politics, science, the shortcomings of American medical education and the possibilities and promise of this harsh and fertile territory about which Jules was enthusiastic.

Only the most tenacious, like this Swiss immigrant, were

equal to its challenge. Storms and blizzards swept fiercely over it. The sun, blazing like an evil eye, glared unwinkingly for weeks, and the rain, when it came, came too late and in floods. Prairie fires swept the earth clean of pasturage and game. Horse-thieves and highwaymen hid in the broken hills to the north. Cattlemen tore up the government section markers, cut the settlers' fences, even shot the settlers. The law was not highly regarded; nearly everyone adjusted his grievances personally. The ground, however, was fertile and the home-steaders were determined. Fighting the cattlemen, the elements and the land itself, men like Jules were settling the country. The young medical officer, too, saw a future in the forbidding country and remarkably, because an Army captain rarely had spare cash, invested in a town lot in Crawford, the settlement rising near the post.

Under the doctor's careful treatment the infection in Jules' crushed ankle slowly drained away, and by spring the settler was well enough to return to his deserted dugout on his claim at Mirage Flats. He was permanently lamed, but he knew enough medicine to realize that the post doctor had worked what was almost a miracle in saving his mangled foot.

Walter Reed had been right when he thought he was going to like his new daughter. He adored her. They became inseparable companions. The dignified young doctor played games with her on the floor, held her on his lap to tell her stories and recite Mother Goose rhymes, gravely attended her kittens in their make-believe illnesses and took unfailing interest in her small world. "Little daughter," he always called her. She had a different name for herself.

"What's your name, little girl?" an officer, seeing the doctor's small daughter playing in the yard, had asked her.

Twiddling a mangled flower, she had looked at him without shyness, and he noticed how like her father's her eyes were.

"Blossom," she informed him. The direct glance stopped him on the point of protesting that he knew better.

"Well!" he said helplessly. "Blossom—that's a pretty name."

Reed thought it was a pretty name, too. From that time on she was never called anything else.

The doctor who succeeded Walter Reed at Fort Robinson in July, 1887, heard much about him from the soldiers and settlers. His warm smile, his blue eyes, his fine brown hair, his skill and kindness and studious habits, all became familiar by hearsay to Jefferson Randolph Kean. The little boy whom the librarian, Mr. Wertenbaker, had mentioned to Walter Reed while he was still a student at the University of Virginia had followed him, at a decade's distance, through the same school, like him had entered the Army and now was hearing, for the first time, of the man with whom he was to become so closely associated.

The Alabama summers were hot, the winters mild, and spring came in, not with the noisy bursting of ice-locked streams as in Nebraska, but easily and softly as though it had no need to force its way in this congenial climate. Many of Reed's recollections of his three years from 1887 to 1890 at Mount Vernon Barracks, a small coast artillery post fifteen miles above Mobile, were pleasant ones.

He knew that his work in Nebraska was not forgotten when Jules sent him a handsome otter pelt which he had prepared himself. Pleased at being remembered, the doctor sent the settler a small bag of tobacco with a five-dollar bill, squeezed from his slim captain's pay, tucked away in it.

He enjoyed his gardens, vegetable and flower, and especially admired the splendid avenue of magnolia trees on which the line of officers' quarters faced. Mischievously flaunting the local belief that whoever transplanted a magnolia tree that lived would have a death in his family within the year, he dug some out of the woods and set them out in the hospital yard. The trees lived, the Reed family flourished, nor was the vitality of the tradition impaired.

The doctor was a medicine man once more, too. Geronimo and his Chiricahua Apaches, who had left San Carlos again in a flurry of murder and surrendered in the fall of 1886 to United States troops, were being held then as prisoners of war at Mount Vernon Barracks. They lived, several hundred of them, in a tepee village flanking the post. Walter Reed treated their sick—there was considerable bronchial trouble among them—and Lawrence rode his pony with the Indian boys, swam with them in the Tombigbee River three miles from the barracks, played Apache games and learned a little of their language. He even knew Geronimo and proudly pointed him out to visitors.

It was hard to believe that anyone had ever been afraid of this stolid, wrinkled old man who, on Sundays and holidays, squatted quietly near the main entrance of the little artillery station and sold curious sightseers toy bows and arrows he had made during the week, and picture post cards of himself. Not long before, his name had been enough to spread panic in the scattered ranch houses on either side of the border, but now he was through with the warpath. He was old, and he was comfortable, sitting in the sun and selling trinkets to awe-struck white men who well remembered his fearsome past.

Lawrence, ever since he had been old enough to understand, had heard of the fierce Apache war chief. Now, living within a stone's throw of him and seeing him almost daily, he felt that he was something of a historical personage himself by virtue of the contact.

His father, too, was feeling historical—unpleasantly so, as though he were a relic of a past age. Medicine was moving fast into the new era and he was being left behind. Buried in the rural Army post in the deep South, he learned through medical journals of the new discoveries which were coming faster and faster on each other's heels. Great advances were being made in the understanding of infectious diseases. The German scientist, Robert Koch, had worked out the life cycle of the bacillus causing anthrax, a cattle disease; he had identified, among other bacilli, the one causing tuberculosis; and he had introduced new methods of cultivating and studying bacteria which had made possible many more discoveries. The germs causing cholera, leprosy, pneumonia, tetanus, typhoid, malaria, diphtheria and many other human and animal diseases had been identified. Pasteur had worked out a method of immunizing animals against the bite of a mad dog. From his reading, the Army doctor was familiar with these discoveries, but he did not know how to make sections of diseased tissue for microscopic study, cultivate and stain bacteria, or identify the various bacilli. His training was outmoded and it would take time to bring it up to date.

On leave in Washington, he requested the Adjutant General on October 1, 1890, to assign him to some duty in Baltimore, where he could study at Johns Hopkins. Four days later, he was ordered there as attending surgeon and examiner of recruits. At last, as he neared forty, Walter Reed was about to enter on his career.

CHAPTER FIFTEEN

THE PATH to the future, however, was not yet clear. It must have been a deep disappointment to Reed when he was told not to spend any time on bacteriology, the promising branch of medicine that was throwing new light on the origin and spread of contagious diseases. Surgeon General Baxter had made it plain that he was permitted to study at Hopkins so that he could learn more about the treatment of sick and wounded soldiers, not so that he could fiddle with a microscope. That there was any connection between the two activities apparently did not occur to the senior officer.

Then fortune, which had been with Reed only enough to tantalize him, came over to his side wholeheartedly. The new Surgeon General, Charles Sutherland, who was appointed on Baxter's sudden death, gave him permission to do laboratory work in bacteriology under Dr. William Henry Welch.

When Reed arrived in Baltimore in October, 1890, Johns Hopkins did not have a medical school. One of the investments of the thrifty Quaker who had given the institution his name and his fortune had turned out so badly that there were no funds for it yet. Graduate doctors, however, were coming from all over the country to work in the hospital and laboratories with William Osler, Howard A. Kelly, William S. Halstead and Welch, the "Four Doctors" of John Singer Sargent's well-known painting.

Welch had established, in 1885, a laboratory which was already famous for the training it gave young men in pathology and bacteriology. Celebrated as the leading exponent of modern medicine in this country, Welch was only a year older than Reed.

He had gone about his medical education more slowly, taking his degree at the College of Physicians and Surgeons in New York in February, 1875, at the same time that Walter Reed, crammed with facts and dates, was undergoing his grilling at the hands of the Army medical examining board. While Dr. Reed was doctoring the routine ills of hardy young soldiers on frontier posts, Dr. Welch was studying the new medicine in Germany, with the men who were contributing most to its brilliant advance. On his return to the United States he gave, at Bellevue Hospital Medical College, the first laboratory course in pathology ever offered in an American medical school. His growing reputation as a scientist and teacher induced the trustees of Johns Hopkins University, who were gradually collecting a medical faculty, to invite him to teach pathology and bacteriology. Welch, who loved research and detested the prospect of practicing for a living, eagerly accepted, and began his long and influential career at Hopkins in the fall of 1885.

Plump, bright-eyed, baldish and bewhiskered, at the age of forty he was already moving in the aura of greatness that was to grow steadily stronger for the rest of his life. His students regarded him with a sort of affectionate awe, and called him Popsy behind his back. All of them, including Reed, were well fitted to his novel method of teaching which was based on the belief that medical students in this country were overtaught, directed and guided until their self-reliance was stifled. Popsy would deliver the lecture in bacteriology or pathology three times a week and demonstrate the subject of it at the microscope; or, if he felt like it, he would fail to appear and leave the session to his assistant. Students selected their own special problems for study without advice from him. With his long cigar tilted at an angle and his rounded waistcoat sprin-

*Dr. Welch—plump, bright-eyed, baldish and bewhiskered—
already moving in the aura of greatness.*

kled with ash, he would go among them at the end of the
demonstration, encouraging and suggesting, and then proceed
to his own microscope and the work that currently held his
interest.

Dr. Reed, from the first moment, loved the Pathological,
as Welch's laboratory was called. It was full of alert young
men, enthusiastically investigating problems in the new fields
of bacteriology and pathology, who discussed, experimented
and joked together endlessly. The scientific curiosity and the
friendliness that gave the atmosphere its tone made it the
most stimulating place in which he had ever worked.

The worktable in the Pathological extended under the

windows along three sides of the room. Each student had his own space on it, where he kept his microscope, slides, notebook and other materials. Reed was assigned a space at the end of the table next to a soft-spoken young doctor from Louisville, Simon Flexner. Absorbed in his work, Flexner at first scarcely noticed the Army man working next to him; the only effect of his arrival was to prevent him from spreading out as freely as he had done before. One day Reed came into the laboratory and found Flexner working at his microscope, with his materials, as usual, spilling over unnoticed into the next space.

"Well, doctor," Reed observed smilingly, as he sat down at the tiny space left, "you'll soon have me clear off the end, won't you?"

Deeply abashed, the younger man started to apologize for his thoughtlessness. "I'm so sorry," he stammered, "I hadn't realized. . . ."

Seeing the laughter in Reed's eyes, he began to smile, too. He decided he liked this friendly newcomer.

A sort of family feeling, based on enthusiasm for their work and admiration of Welch, prevailed among the laboratory workers. Reed was soon accepted cordially into the intimate circle of the students and their teacher, all of whom were quick to respond to his charm and to recognize his ability.

Welch, urbane, kindly and aloof, paid little personal attention to any student until he had given evidence of ability. It was not long, however, before he became interested in the Army doctor who, in spite of his belated introduction to pathology and bacteriology, was already showing marked aptitude for the work. Reed and Welch probably liked the same things in each other: the dignity which, while friendly and pleasant, forbade familiarity; the scholarly and inquiring attitude of mind; the scientific enthusiasm and the personal graciousness. The two doctors became cordial friends.

Reed's military duties took little time, and he worked in the laboratory early and late, searching far beyond class requirements and eagerly learning his way around the fascinating new world that had so nearly escaped him. He learned to recognize the murderers of the microscopic world: the slender motionless bacillus that causes diphtheria, the rod-shaped tubercle bacillus, the comma-shaped germ of the Asiatic cholera whose ravages he had a few times seen in New York, and the other villains invisible to the naked eye.

As soon as he became familiar with the new technical methods, he began to do independent work. Anxious to make up for his late start, he haunted autopsies to obtain pathological material to study. On these occasions he often saw Osler, and became friendly with this beloved and brilliant man who was known to the younger doctors as "The Chief."

Osler was working on malaria at the time. Welch was investigating both hog-cholera with Dr. A. W. Clement, a veterinarian, and diphtheria, the anti-toxin for which had just been discovered, with Alexander C. Abbott, one of his students. Reed followed these investigations as well as his own. During the winter, too, he probably attended the lectures in which Welch, in his logical and lucid way, covered the entire subject of diphtheria. He regularly went to the weekly meetings of the hospital medical society and to the monthly ones of its medical historical society. Reed knew his time at Hopkins was to be short, and he wanted to squeeze every possible advantage out of it.

His work was interrupted just before Christmas when he was ordered to Fort Keogh, Montana, for a short time. When he returned to Baltimore toward the end of January, he was grateful for the friendliness and co-operation of his fellow-workers: Flexner and William T. Howard, another of Welch's young men, during his absence had mounted for him pathological specimens which they thought he might want to study.

Reed usually had lunch with his new friends at the "Church" —it somehow sounded better, if you were a serious scientific man, to say you'd be at "Church" than at the hotel—across the street from the hospital. In the private dining room which the proprietor kept for the laboratory doctors they could have a lunch of wild duck, or sea food in season, or sandwiches for a quarter, and enjoy an hour's relaxation. The younger men would urge the Army doctor to tell about post life, and he would tell of his adventures as cook and medicine man, or of the hardships of travel by doherty wagon or horseback in sub-zero weather, or of the discomforts and boredom of garrison life. In the companionship of these friendly, enthusiastic young scientific workers, it all seemed very remote, so distant and so different from this congenial new life where modern medicine was taken for granted, and where the desire to study it was regarded as the mark of a reasonable being, not an eccentric.

In the late afternoon when Schutz, Welch's laboratory helper, seemed about to sweep him out, Reed would leave the laboratory and walk down the hill from the hospital to the boardinghouse where he was living with Mrs. Reed and Blossom. The apartment seemed almost empty now, with Lawrence in school at Bedford, where the doctor himself had lived as a child, and Susie gone, too. The Indian girl who had lived with them for the last dozen years, helping with the housework and sewing, had stayed with the Apaches at Mount Vernon Barracks to teach them English. (The Reeds, incidentally, never saw her again, since she went with her people to Fort Sill, Oklahoma, and died there about 1902.) Blossom was the only juvenile member of the household. "Little daughter," now seven years old, took up most of her adoring father's spare time.

In the evenings the doctor would sometimes go to a concert with his wife, or, more frequently, to one of the medical meetings. Usually, though, he looked up articles in the medical journals in the hospital library, or studied German so that he could follow the work being done by German scientists.

Although Reed did not join the younger doctors in their Saturday night poker games, he occasionally had dinner with Popsy, whose good food and good conversation were memorable. On summer afternoons he would sometimes leave his work to go with Welch or Flexner or Councilman, Welch's assistant, to the ball game. Baltimore at that time had occasion to be very proud of its Orioles, and Welch was an enthusiastic fan. Shortly before the game he was likely to appear at the laboratory door, his small bright eyes twinkling, the inevitable cigar cocked in his mouth, and coax them away from their microscopes. He rarely had to use persuasion. Few people could resist the prospect of spending the afternoon with Popsy, whether at a ball game or an autopsy.

By May, Reed knew enough to undertake his first big piece of scientific investigation. He had noticed in autopsies that victims of typhoid fever had tiny nodules, or lumps, in the lymph glands of the liver. Under Welch's supervision, he undertook to study these nodules. As he worked tirelessly over his problem, it probably never occurred to him that the few months' scientific training he was then receiving were to turn him from a competent, obscure Army doctor into a scientific investigator who would solve one of the gravest health problems that had ever bedeviled the public and baffled the medical profession. But he did know that his old sense of dissatisfaction, the feeling of being left behind, was gone for good. He had had to wait until his fortieth year, but now he was learning something beyond the mere treatment of diseases; he was beginning to understand a little about the organisms causing disease, and to think in terms of prevention rather than cure.

His summer's work was broken into several times by military duties that called him away from Baltimore. Each time he reluctantly laid aside his investigation, confident, however, that one of the other men, perhaps Welch himself, would carry on his animal experiments for him. In June he went to West Point to give physical examinations to candidates for the Military Academy and members of the graduating class. Lawrence was already talking about becoming a soldier, and his father examined the fit and intelligent boys who appeared before his board with special sympathy, for he hoped that Lawrence, too, would qualify to enter the Academy.

Then he had to go to Washington as a member of another board; and in October to New York, to sit on the board examining Medical Corps aspirants. More than sixteen years separated the young Health Inspector, anxiously approaching the fateful examination, from the medical officer in the blue dress uniform sitting in judgment on a new generation of nervous candidates, but Reed could still remember his alarm and depression. He hoped these poor fellows were not feeling like that, or, if they were, that they would be able to look back sixteen years hence and feel, like him, that it had been worth it.

In spite of interruptions, however, he managed to complete his typhoid fever study. By November, when he had to leave for his new post at Fort Snelling, Minnesota, he had produced the little lumps experimentally in laboratory animals, and had demonstrated that they originated as small groups of dead liver cells.

Walter Reed was confident now that he had found the work to which he could enthusiastically devote the rest of his life.

CHAPTER SIXTEEN

WALTER REED'S new skill had little opportunity to develop in his ten months at Fort Snelling, nor was it particularly appreciated. His Commanding Officer, in a routine report, remarked that his character and attention to duty were excellent, his scientific attainments "nothing special," and his prominent talents "none." If Reed had known, it would probably have caused him rueful amusement, and no surprise at all. How could a colonel of the line be expected to judge the scientific qualifications of his medical officers? How should he know the difference between a horse doctor and a bacteriologist?

The indifference of the line officers notwithstanding, the Medical Corps was beginning to win a little renown for the bacteriological work of some of its members. Sternberg's excellent textbook on the subject, the first ever written in the United States, appeared in 1892, reflecting credit on the service. Reed drew favorable attention in interested circles with his first paper, published in March of the same year in the Boston Medical and Surgical Journal, on the contagiousness of erysipelas. Some of the more enlightened intelligences of the line, as well as of the Medical Corps, were beginning to get the idea that, since sickness regularly took heavier toll of an army in the field than enemy action, the Medical Corps was important, especially in preventive work.

As Reed went about his old routine—sick call, visits to officers' families, hospital work—he wondered when he would be able to go back to bacteriology. As he regretfully wrote

to Sternberg, his regular duties left him time only for "dab-
bling" in his favorite field.

"If only Sternberg would be appointed to succeed Sutherland when he retires for age!" he exclaimed longingly to his
wife. "Then I'd get the opportunity to do the work I'm really
keen about."

"Maybe he will be," she encouraged him. "Let's keep our
fingers crossed."

Reed's transfer to the staff of General Wesley Merritt in
St. Paul, in August, 1892, was welcome: a city was always
better than a garrison, especially from his wife's point of view,
and they could have their son with them again. With the boy
attending St. Paul High School, Reed thought, maybe he could
keep an eye on his work, which he was inclined to neglect.

As attending surgeon and examiner of recruits on Merritt's
staff, Reed had an opportunity to appreciate the general's
advanced opinion, entirely sympathetic to his own, that one of
the Medical Corps' most important functions should be the
prevention of disease among the troops. He was reminded, as
well, how far behind him now, how almost forgotten, was the
civil conflict that had dominated his childhood and youth.
Merritt, a Union officer then, had had a share in the devasta-
tion of the Shenandoah Valley. Now the Yankee general and
the Virginia doctor, ignoring the old enmity, were loyally
serving their country together.

It was the evening of March 28, 1893. The meeting of
the Ramsey County Medical Society was breaking up, and
the young high school teacher standing on the edge of the
group around the Army doctor had a chance to get a good
look at him. He saw a man in his early forties, erect and slender
and a little above medium height. Mr. Wilson liked his quick,
animated manner, and the courteous attentiveness with which
he was listening to Dr. Millard, dean of the University of

Minnesota Medical School. His bearing suggested that, although he was known as an excellent bacteriologist and a fine doctor, he was also a modest man. He had attended the meeting as a guest speaker to talk on the cholera germ, the fatal comma-shaped bacillus which was just then savagely flourishing in Hamburg and neighboring German cities.

The medical officer, his face lighting with a quick smile, made some remark which the teacher on the edge of the circle did not catch. Laughter followed it, and as the group shifted a little Wilson moved closer and caught Dr. Millard's eye. Beckoning him forward, Millard presented him to Reed.

"Dr. Reed," he said, "I'd like you to meet Louis Wilson, one of our medical students. He teaches biology at the Central High, and has a biological laboratory there."

Reed, the smile still lingering around his blue eyes, turned eagerly to Wilson. "Young man," he exclaimed as he shook hands with him, "do you really have a laboratory?"

"Yes, sir. It's nothing elaborate, though. But for a high school lab it isn't bad."

"You should see mine—all I have is a few test tubes."

"If you'd care to come over and have a look at mine . . ." Wilson suggested diffidently.

"When may I come?" Reed asked promptly. "Tomorrow?"

When they said good night, it would have been hard to tell which was the more elated: the student at having the opportunity to work with the medical officer who knew about bacteriology, or the doctor at the prospect of again getting into a laboratory.

It was a good thing for Reed and Wilson that Central High decided to discontinue its domestic science department. They were able to salvage from it a couple of gas ovens and some boilers and make them into fairly effective bacteriological apparatus. Reed spent most of the time he could spare from his regular duties helping to fix up the laboratory and working in it.

Diphtheria had always interested him. Now he heard that a New York physician, Dr. William H. Park, had begun to diagnose it from cultures made from swabs of patients' throats. If the culture, examined under a microscope, showed the diphtheria bacillus, he at once knew that the patient had diphtheria. If the culture was free of the bacillus, he knew that he was dealing with something else. The method eliminated the danger of mistaking the serious disease for less grave types of croup which it resembled in its earlier stages. Reed and Wilson obtained from Dr. Park a sample of his apparatus, which consisted simply of a small box and two test tubes, one containing a sterile swab and the other a culture medium in which diphtheria germs would grow.

"A nice, simple little outfit," Reed observed as he examined it. "What do you think, Wilson, about getting some ourselves and asking the local doctors to send us swabs when they suspect diphtheria?"

"It's a good idea, doctor. I'm sure a number of them would do it. We can have the box factory make us up some of these little boxes. It oughtn't to cost much."

"I hope it won't. It will have to come out of our own pockets, since it's neither Army nor school work," Reed remarked.

"Let's try to squeeze out a hundred," Wilson suggested. "I'm very keen to do it. I don't suppose it's been done outside of New York, do you?"

The two men scraped the bottoms of their pockets—Reed had recently sold his lot at Crawford, Nebraska, so he had a little spare money—and ordered a hundred boxes. Together they worked over the diphtheria study off and on during most of the summer. As he instructed his first student in the elements of bacteriology, Reed felt the deep satisfaction of encouraging a promising young man in the field for which he himself felt such enthusiasm. Investigating and teaching others to investigate, that was what he would like to do, he thought. That was the really radical way to attack disease. Learn to prevent it, and you would never have to cure it.

Reed wanted to toss his hat in the air. At last, at last, it had happened! George Miller Sternberg was Surgeon General, appointed late in May, 1893, to succeed General Sutherland! It was significant of the changing atmosphere, the growing appreciation of modern scientific medicine, that President Cleveland had selected not an able executive, not a man adroit in departmental politics, not merely a good doctor, but the one man in the Corps with a distinguished reputation as a scientist. The fossil age, Reed jubilantly declared, was past.

One of the new Surgeon General's first official acts was to establish the Army Medical School, improvising it, with a wary eye on a Congress already alarmed by the current financial panic, in such a way as to add nothing to the expenses of the Army's medical department. Its classrooms were in the building which already housed the Army Medical Museum and the Surgeon General's Library, and medical officers composed the faculty. Sternberg, who admired and liked Reed, appointed him professor of clinical and sanitary microscopy and curator of the museum, which already had all the materials for bacteriological and chemical study that the new school would need. John Shaw Billings, librarian of the Surgeon General's Library and a progressive Army doctor of enormous influence in the medical world, became professor of military hygiene; and Sternberg, although not a member of the faculty, lectured on bacteriology.

Reed, summoned to Washington from St. Paul to be examined for promotion to major, appeared on September 6, 1893, at the red brick building backing on the Mall where he

Together they worked over the diphtheria study off and on during most of the summer.

was to spend most of the short remainder of his life. In response to his examiners' questions, he discussed typhoid, pneumonia, tuberculosis, gunshot wounds, antisepsis and malaria to their full satisfaction. Three days later he was pronounced "physically and professionally fit for promotion." In December, after he had returned to take up his new duties in Washington, he was advanced to the rank of major.

The Washington to which Reed and his family returned after a dozen years' absence was a city of more than two hundred thousand people. Grover Cleveland, the only Democrat to win the presidency since the Civil War, was presiding for the second time over the White House, and, somewhat more uneasily, over the national destiny. The Washington Monument, completed in 1884, was a well-established landmark. Sturdy little mules pulled the streetcars along the shaded avenues. A few of those mechanical wonders, the electric trolleys, had invaded the streets and, propelled as if by magic, suggested to the far-seeing that horse cars might be on their way out. Electric lights and telephones were almost commonplace. The State, War and Navy Building, squatting massive and ornate beside the simple presidential residence, was finished at last. The city had elegant mansions built like Italian palaces and French châteaux along its wide avenues. There were good restaurants, good hotels, and a half dozen theaters which tempted the delighted public with such stellar lures as Lillian Russell, Henry Irving, Sarah Bernhardt and Lily Langtry. The capital was taking its national dignity seriously.

Mrs. Reed unpacked their much-traveled household goods for what seemed the hundredth time, with positive elation. They were settling in Washington! No more ugly officers' quarters, no more frontier inconveniences—for a while, anyway. This was civilization. She thought she could never get enough of it.

"Dr. Reed," she threatened her husband playfully, "if you ever go west of the Mississippi again, you're going alone!"

The major laughed reassuringly. "Well, my dear, I don't think you need worry about that for a while. We'll be here for a few years. Anyway, I've just about done my share of frontier duty. That's for the younger fellows. For that matter, there's not much frontier left any more, the way the country's being settled. And travel so much easier, too."

Mrs. Reed's expression was reminiscent. "It was fun, though. Remember what wonderful roasts could be made in those little Dutch ovens that we always carried in the doherty wagons —the ones you set over coals and stacked coals on top of?"

"Mmmmmm," her husband agreed appreciatively. "Travel by doherty wagon had advantages, like game en route, but I think I prefer the iron horse now. I'm not the valiant frontiersman I was fifteen years ago. Now I'm an aging medical officer who's had his fill of the west and the Indians and the rest of the trimmings."

Mrs. Reed smiled at him. It wasn't that he was tired of adventure, she knew that. The adventurous spirit that had filtered through generations from his earliest American forebears to the little boy mooning over his geography in Mrs. Booker's one-room school was still strong in the doctor to whom "the west and the Indians and the rest of the trimmings" were now an old story. It was simply that he had discovered a new and more exciting frontier in the world of bacteriology.

CHAPTER SEVENTEEN

TIME WAS GLIDING past, Reed realized with a slight sense of surprise, and he, as he advanced into his fifth decade, was settling slowly into a middle age of inconspicuous usefulness. After twenty years of active practice, he could now devote himself to the teaching and investigating that appealed to him so strongly.

It was natural that the first thing he should do was renew his contacts with his friends at Johns Hopkins. He and his assistant, Dr. James Carroll, who had also been trained in Welch's laboratory, made frequent trips to Baltimore to keep in touch with the work carried on there, and to attend medical meetings. The long-delayed medical school had been opened in the fall of 1893 with eighteen students—three of them women, to the disquietude of the modest bachelor, Dr. Welch —and Reed followed all the affairs of the new school with interest.

Hopkins doctors often came to the capital, too, for meetings and to consult the Surgeon General's Library which, under the direction of John Shaw Billings, had already attained the position it still holds as the most complete medical library in the United States. With Sternberg, Billings, Reed and Carroll all in Washington, the link between Hopkins and the Medical Corps was close.

Reed, lecturing to the rising generation of medical officers and directing them in their laboratory work, may sometimes have thought of his old schoolmaster's query: "What mind was ever lighted up or warmed by that which was dark and cold?" He was turning out to be a teacher patterned on Mr.

Abbot's ideal, with an enthusiasm for his subject that his students found contagious, and such intimate knowledge of it that it seemed to be part of himself.

A straight man with a drooping mustache, a little heavier now but still slender, and with the slight frown of concentration habitually fixed on his face as though he were always thinking ahead of his words, he would stand before his class and discuss his complicated subject with a clarity that almost compelled understanding. Peering through a microscope, he would explain what was there to some bewildered novice and kindly, with a few words, take the trouble to dispel his discouragement. He won, quite without design, as many devotees for himself by his courteous patience as he did for bacteriology by his lucid presentations. Young Dr. Leonard Wood, arriving in Washington in 1885 after a tour of duty in the west, was one of Reed's admiring students.

His assistant, Carroll, was devoted to him, and Reed felt warm respect for the quiet, retiring man who worked with him so ably. Born in England in 1854, Carroll had come to Canada as a boy, and, at the age of twenty, enlisted in the United States Army. He became interested in medicine and while still a soldier in the newly formed Hospital Corps won his medical degree at the University of Maryland. After his work in Welch's laboratory, he was attached in 1893 to the Army Medical School as Reed's assistant. He had a wife and a family of small children. Reed could appreciate what a long, uphill grind it must have been for him to reach his modest eminence, and what sacrifice must have gone into the achievement.

Reed loved his new life. "You can accomplish so much more good for so many more people by training other men in modern medicine," he answered when Mrs. Reed asked him if he missed practicing. "And that's what counts with me. I might be able to save ten children strangling with diphtheria, but if I teach ten men to use anti-toxin, they can save a hundred."

Training his students in modern ways and converting established practitioners to new methods presented two different problems, Reed found. The use of diphtheria anti-toxin was an example. Loeffler had discovered the specific germ, and his find had been widely confirmed by independent workers. Then the French scientist Roux, like the German von Behring, had immunized horses to diphtheria toxin and produced the anti-toxin that both prevents and cures. When Roux read his paper at the International Congress on Hygiene at Budapest in 1894, the scientists listening to him in the stuffy classroom of the old university had jumped shouting on their seats and tossed their hats into the air. Hat tossing, however, was not general throughout the profession. Although laboratories all over Europe, America and Japan promptly began to produce anti-toxin, a number of doctors remained unconvinced.

When the District of Columbia Medical Society met in December, 1894, a doctor of wide reputation assailed a paper supporting the use of the anti-toxin. He was not unfriendly to the new remedy, he said, but based his criticisms on the statistics and arguments of others, not on his own experience. Reed entered the discussion. He had never regretted the long period he had spent in general practice before getting into his specialty. Now it enabled him to speak not only as a laboratory man but as a practitioner of experience.

"You are theorizing," he got to his feet and earnestly, almost sternly, addressed the other doctor. "We are dealing with facts. If another friend of anti-toxin arises and deals it such a blow, the anti-toxin serum will be murdered in the house of its friends. I myself almost feel like saying that the failure to use it in a case of human diphtheria is criminal; and I beg you," he added urgently, "that, if you have not yet done so, when you next stand by the bedside of your patient afflicted with this disease, you do not withhold this invaluable remedy."

A strong word, criminal; but his seriousness, backed by his high standing, impressed the meeting so deeply that the value of the anti-toxin was not again questioned in that society.

Sternberg's routine reports sounded nothing like the one his Commanding Officer at Fort Snelling had written in 1892. So far as the limitations of the standard government form allowed, they were glowing. In his heavy, sprawling writing, the Surgeon General yearly wrote the almost monotonous praise: excellent character and professional qualifications, excellent control over the men under him, highly skilled bacteriologist, a valuable man in his work. Sternberg, dwelling on distant official heights in the State, War and Navy Building and occupied with executive duties that left him no time for the research he loved, no doubt wistfully envied his subordinate.

There was no lack in these years of the stimulating contacts which Reed had missed on the frontier. In the spring of 1895 he was appointed a delegate from the Medical Corps to the annual meeting of the American Medical Association in Baltimore. Later the same season, Welch and Osler came to Washington for the meeting of the Association of American Physicians at which Welch, analyzing the world literature on diphtheria anti-toxin, asserted that it was "a specific curative agent for diphtheria, surpassing in its efficacy all other known methods of treatment." How it must have gratified Reed to hear him express the opinion he had so forcibly stated himself: "It is the duty of the physician to use it."

By no means through with the subject of anti-toxin now that its "friends" were no longer likely to slaughter it, Reed told the District Medical Society that its manufacture should be under municipal control to prevent the production of contaminated serum by careless or unscrupulous individuals.

He was busier than ever before in his life. Not only did he teach at the Army and Columbian (now George Washington) University Medical Schools, serve on examining boards, attend medical meetings, consult with other doctors when his specialized knowledge was needed, but he worked in his laboratory on croupous pneumonia, erysipelas, abdominal typhus, malaria and other subjects, and published his observations in scientific journals.

For a time he was even busier than necessary, trying to keep up with the overwhelming supply of white rats sent him by his nephew Walter, Tom's son. Reed had seen Walter on a visit to his sister Laura in Ashland in the summer of 1894. The enterprising boy, learning that his uncle used white rats in his experiments, undertook to supply them. He went about it with such energy that the laboratory was swamped. Reed, unable to think of enough experiments to use them up, had to write his namesake to cease shipment.

He left the house in Georgetown, at Number 5 Cooke Place, early in the morning to take the horse car to the museum. When he came back in the late afternoon Blossom would meet him at the corner where he got off. She was eleven years old now, and went to school at Gunston Hall in Washington. Lawrence was in high school. He was a tall, good-looking fellow more addicted to sports than to study, and usually was off playing ball when his father came home. If the children and their friends waylaid Dr. Reed as he came up the street, he would stand by the gate with them for a few minutes, laughing and joking. His wife, watching from the porch, thought how youthful he looked, with his thick brown hair, straight figure and quick movements. The engaging young man—sweet-natured, happy, deeply in earnest about his responsibility to the sick—with whom she had so promptly fallen in love twenty years before, existed almost unchanged—a little graver, a little more serene, perhaps—in the middle-aged doctor.

Lawrence's special admiration were the Blackford girls, three sisters who lived across the street. They had a pair of smooth-haired fox terriers with the good Virginia names of Shirley and Carter. The jaunty little dogs were favorites through the neighborhood, and it was a widely lamented calamity when Shirley, rushing to hurl insults at a passing horse car, skidded and had his left hind foot badly mangled under a wheel. His tearful mistresses hurried him to the veterinarian who amputated the crushed paw.

Dr. Reed, on his way home one afternoon, waved to Blossom and the three young girls who were approaching down the street. They crossed over to meet him with Carter jumping at their heels and Shirley hobbling behind.

"Hello, Shirley," Reed bent to pat the small, sleek head, "I haven't seen you since your operation."

"Poor darling, he's quite wretched about it still," Lily said.

Reed whistled as he caught sight of the amputation. "No wonder! Poor old fellow," he exclaimed.

"Oh dear, Major Reed, doesn't it look right?"

Reed was stooping beside the little dog who, trustful and troubled, let him examine the injury.

"It won't heal properly like this, Miss Lily," he explained. "That end of bone ought to come off." He paused a moment, rubbing the dog's ear and thinking: the examining board in the morning, laboratory all afternoon—Carroll can take care of that for a while—I can manage it. "I'll tell you what you do—bring him to me tomorrow afternoon at the laboratory, and I'll fix him up so it won't bother him any more."

Smiling under the ecstatic barrage of thanks, Reed waved

the sisters good-by from the gate and went up the walk, his arm through Blossom's.

"How's my patient?" Reed greeted Lily and Shirley the next afternoon when they appeared at the laboratory.

"He's calm, thank you," Lily told him. "He has the greatest confidence in his new doctor."

"Well, I'll try to justify it. Come along in here."

Lily watched the doctor's adroit, gentle hands with admiration. He was one of the busiest medical officers in the Army, and he took the time, personally, to operate on an injured dog. Shirley lay quiet under ether while Reed worked. The protruding bit of bone was off now, a flap of skin tucked over the end and a neat bandage adjusted over the wound.

"There! That oughtn't to trouble him any more, as soon as it heals," Reed remarked.

"I can't thank you enough, Major Reed," Lily faltered, as he showed her, with that attentive courtesy she and her sisters found so charming, to the door. "When you're so busy, to go to this trouble . . ."

Reed dismissed the thanks with his warm smile. "Not at all, my dear. We couldn't have Shirley an invalid for the rest of his life, could we?"

Shirley, it may be added here, was from then on almost as good as new. He quickly learned to run, dodge and throw himself into reverse with one hind leg as well as he had with two, and he lived, with Carter, to a hale and rowdy old age.

The little steamer ran from the mainland to Key West three times a week, carrying passengers, mail, food and sometimes water. Waiting on the pier as the few passengers debarked, Dr. Jefferson Randolph Kean scanned them for the medical officer from Washington. Kean, although he had never seen him, recognized him at once, and smiled to notice how closely

They crossed over to meet him.

his appearance corresponded with descriptions of him he had heard ten years before at Fort Robinson. The mustache was heavier and he was unprepared for the blueness of the eyes, but he could have picked him out of a much larger crowd than this.

Sitting in the evenings on the veranda of Kean's quarters at Key West Barracks, the two officers and Mrs. Kean, her dress a pale graceful blur in the dark, talked, or fell into the silences which congenial people do not fear. Reed was enjoying his stay at Key West so much, he told them, that this detail was as good as a holiday.

He had been sent toward the end of July, 1896, by the Surgeon General to investigate an epidemic of smallpox at Key West, to see if he could find in the blood of those actually suffering with the disease the same microscopic, one-celled body which he had found in the laboratory in the blood of children and monkeys inoculated against it.

The results of the study were negative, but everything else about his two weeks on Key West was successful. A large part of each day he spent at the Army hospital making microscopic examinations of blood. In the late afternoons he enjoyed playing with the Keans' baby—"that dear little girl," he called her—and demonstrating to her admiring parents that, although he had had little practice in the last ten years, he could still soothe a fit of weeping with enviable skill. He even learned to eat mangoes, to the amusement of the Keans, with no more than a little distaste for their slight turpentine flavor. But the pleasantest thing of all about the trip was the friendship it developed with Kean, a cultivated and delightful man who, like Reed, was a product of Mr. Abbot's preparatory school and Mr. Jefferson's University.

Back in Washington again, Reed was busy, as usual. He occasionally saw Welch, who came to the capital to combat, successfully, the anti-vivisection legislation then pending, and other Hopkins friends who came down on various errands. In May, 1897, Kean and his wife, on their way to Fort Warren, Boston, stopped for a few days at Number 5 Cooke Place. Laboratory investigations, classes, examining boards filled his time. In the evenings he taught at Columbian University, or read or wrote or studied Italian, which he was learning so that he could follow the work on malaria then being done in Italy. Occasionally he, with his wife, dined with the Sternbergs or some other friends, or went to the theater. The children were growing up: Lawrence was almost twenty, Blossom fourteen. Reed himself was close to fifty.

The quiet, obscure years were running out. As if to put a period to their passing, Reed's father died shortly before Christmas, 1897, in Farmville, the little Appomattox town where the minister's family had lived forty years earlier. He was an old man, and he left behind him the pleasant memory of a useful and unselfish life—such a memory as his youngest son hoped would survive him at the close of a life of unfaltering service to the sick and to science. It would be enough to know that he in his field, like Pa in his, had been able to accomplish some little good for humanity.

The eclipse of this humble ambition by the brilliant climax of his career was an event which no premonition suggested to the Army doctor. It threw no shadow before it, but now his fame was almost upon him.

CHAPTER EIGHTEEN

HISTORY, OF COURSE, had not been standing still during the years that Walter Reed was unwittingly treading the path to fame. Since the Civil War the United States had undergone great changes, the greatest of which were the passing of the frontier and the country's shift from a primarily farming to a primarily manufacturing economy.

By 1898 the last of the Indian outbreaks was eight years behind us, and the fearful Geronimo was soon to join the Dutch Reformed Church. The Union proudly numbered forty-five states. The population had doubled. Tourists and traveling salesmen could go by rail almost anywhere in the country.

Manufacturers were making more and more goods for home consumption and for export abroad, and our new industrial economy was giving the country new wealth, new power, new horizons. Our interest in foreign affairs, already whetted by our need for overseas markets, was suddenly riveted to them by the outbreak of the Spanish-American War early in 1898.

We had been wrangling with Spain off and on for some years about her island Cuba, which was just then in a state of armed revolt against the aged and feeble monarchy. After the *United States Ship Maine* was blown up in Havana harbor on February 15, 1898, the wrangling stopped and the fighting began. War was declared on April 25th. Thousands of enthusiastic young men hurried to enlist.

Lawrence Reed was one of them. He had been out of school almost two years, working for a local coal company. He still wanted to go into the Army, but had failed to obtain an appointment to West Point. There were, at that time, two ways of getting a commission besides being graduated from the Military Academy. One was to enlist, and after two years' service take the examination for a second lieutenancy. The other was to be designated as a civilian by the War Department to take the examination. Someone, however, had to recommend you to the War Department before it would select you as a candidate. Lawrence's employer, Mr. Parke Agnew, was a friend of President McKinley's. He thought a great deal of his young employee and asked him if he would like to have a letter from McKinley recommending him for the examination. Lawrence, naturally, could have liked nothing better. When the letter came, he hurried downtown to file it at the War Department. Unfortunately, there were so many young men who wanted to take the examination, and so many genial political gentlemen who recommended them, that the War Department was flooded with their letters. It therefore announced that no recommendations would be considered except those having a red line under the aspirant's name. Mr. Agnew again applied to the President and obtained another letter, this one with Walter Lawrence Reed clearly underscored in red. Lawrence filed it at the War Department, too, and waited for the announcement of the list of lucky men who would be permitted to compete. In due course it was published. His name was not there.

This called for explanation. The President himself had recommended him, and he wanted to know why he had been passed over. He decided to find out.

The horse car let him off near the State, War and Navy Building and he ran up the wide flight of steps into the building. It was a beehive these early June days. Elderly clerks who looked as though they had been under wraps since the Civil War scuttled nimbly through the corridors. Voices murmured and rose in the offices. Doors slammed, footsteps were brisk, official brows knit. Lawrence went to the fifth floor to see the clerk with whom he had left his letter.

An elderly man, he had a mouth hedged about with gray whiskers, and mild eyes protected by spectacles. When Lawrence explained his errand, he looked stricken.

"It was just a mistake, Mr. Reed," he said miserably, "a most unfortunate oversight."

"Can't it be corrected now, sir?" Lawrence wanted to know. "I'm pretty anxious to try for a commission."

"I suppose it could be," the old man admitted reluctantly, "if you want to bad enough. If you care to take the matter higher up, you can probably get on the list."

"Well, what's wrong with that?"

"Nothing, I suppose. Except that it would put this office in a very bad light, make trouble for it."

"For you?"

"Well, yes. It seems to have been my fault. But you go ahead if you want to."

Lawrence looked at him and noted his mild, weak eyes, his clerical stoop, his shiny coat. You couldn't get a poor old fellow like this in trouble, he thought wretchedly, it would be inhuman. There went his chance for a commission, but there wasn't any choice that he could see.

"Never mind, then," he said gruffly. "Let's forget it. Good-by."

"Wait a minute, son!" The relief in the old gentleman's voice was almost touching. "What are you going to do?"

"I'm going down to Washington Barracks and enlist! I'll earn my commission!"

An hour later, hot and flushed, Lawrence arrived at the Army Medical Museum and went to his father's office. Reed looked up from his work in surprise—it wasn't like his son to pay unexpected calls at the laboratory.

"Hello, Lawrence. What brings you here?"

"Father," Lawrence came abruptly to the point, "will you give me your permission to enlist? I've just been to the barracks, and Dr. de Schon turned me down because I'm not twenty-one. I need your permission."

"And why do you want to enlist?"

"I want to earn a commission."

Reed got up slowly and eyed the tall young man. In words his son never forgot, he inquired, "Young man, if the President of the United States would accord you the unusual privilege of selecting your own examining board, do you think that you could find three officers who would pass you?"

The reproachful query conjured up the guilty memory of neglected studies and mediocre marks. His father questioned his ability to earn a commission, Lawrence realized with a pang. If he answered no, his father would withhold permission. He would have to say yes.

"I think so, Father," he answered steadily.

"Very well, Lawrence," Reed agreed quietly. "I'll give you a note with my permission. You can take it back to de Schon."

The United States Army in June, 1898, accepted Walter Lawrence Reed as a buck private. When he retired from it forty-two years later, he had risen to the rank of major general. Events had not justified his father's misgivings.

With the war in progress, disease, the United States quickly found, was a far more dangerous enemy than Spain. Only seven hundred American soldiers were killed in action, or died of wounds, in the whole course of the fighting, but the mortality from illness was frightful. Everybody seemed to get sick in the camps. Malaria, typhoid, dysentery ravaged the untrained, ill-equipped troops hastily assembled with almost no sanitary precautions in the big training camps in the United States. As the death rate climbed steadily through the hot summer of 1898, and the Army's under-staffed, under-equipped

The mortality from illness was frightful.

medical department struggled stoutly to keep up with its duties, the costliness of the penny-pinching policies applied to the Corps for so many years became glaringly apparent.

In the financial panic four years earlier Congress, unimpressed with the increasing prestige and scope of the Medical Corps and eying the War Department's budget with an ax in its ready hand, had lopped fifteen doctors from its already inadequate staff, reducing it to a hundred and ten. At the same time it had prohibited the employment of contract doctors. In spite of this treatment, the Corps had progressed under

Sternberg. So that officers could keep up with current medical developments, important new literature was regularly sent to them, and the use of the Surgeon General's Library was extended to them by mail and express. Modern equipment, including laboratory apparatus and operating rooms, had been installed in post hospitals; and a training school for the Hospital Corps, as well as the Army Medical School, had been established. Sternberg's personal eminence had been emphasized by his election to the presidency of the American Medical Association in 1897.

Faced by war, Congress hastily restored the fifteen officers to the Corps, again authorized the employment of contract surgeons, and set aside the absurdly inadequate sum of twenty thousand dollars, out of a war budget of fifty millions, for use in safeguarding the health of an army suddenly expanded to ten times its normal size. Short-handed, without reserve supplies and nearly penniless, the Medical Corps was almost hopelessly handicapped at the start.

The campaigns of the Spanish-American War were fought in Cuba, Puerto Rico and the Philippines during May, June, July and the first week of August, 1898. At the close of the war, however, the men assembled in training camps were not immediately disbanded for fear that they would spread their diseases all over the country. Early in the war Reed had been anxious to get a responsible position in the field where his knowledge of Army routine and methods of sanitation would be useful. Too often, however, the important medical commands were given by authorities, who should have known better, to civilian doctors who, however patriotic and professionally capable, knew nothing of military procedure and lacked training in camp sanitation.

Swallowing his chagrin, Reed had remained at his teaching post. It was not until mid-August—the war was already over—

that he had an opportunity for valuable service. Then he, with Dr. Victor C. Vaughan and Dr. Edward O. Shakespeare, both eminent sanitarians and majors of volunteers, was appointed to a board to investigate the causes of the typhoid epidemics that prevailed in almost every camp.

By that time everybody had to admit, however reluctantly, that there was some typhoid, although the diagnosis of malaria, or even acute indigestion, was greatly preferred wherever it could decently be made. There was little inclination among the medical officers to irritate the public, already angry over the inefficient management of the whole war, with the news that a dangerous disease was epidemic among the soldiers.

All three board members were thoroughly familiar with the current view of typhoid. It was generally believed that it was caused by a specific germ, Eberth's bacillus, and was spread by contaminated drinking water. It was not known to be transmitted by any other agency, although flies were suspected. It could be diagnosed by a laboratory process known as Widal's test, and, at autopsy, recognized by certain pathological findings. It could also, on the basis of its symptoms, easily be confused with malaria, but malaria itself could be identified by the finding of the malarial plasmodium in the blood on microscopic examination. Given the proper equipment and a doctor who could make Widal's test and recognize the plasmodium, there was no excuse on earth for confusing the two diseases. There were still, however, few medical men in the country so trained, and the Army board found, on arriving at Camp Alger in nearby Virginia on the morning of August 20th, that there was not a microscope in the camp.

By the end of their first day's work, all three men realized that the first thing to do was to get a scientific diagnosis of the fever. The Alger doctors insisted that it was malaria. The three inspectors were sure it was typhoid.

"But, Major Reed," one of the doctors handed him a sheaf of temperature charts, "look at the temperature curves. In each case it's a typical malarial curve, up, down, up, down."

Reed glanced through them. The curve was, undoubtedly, unlike the characteristically steady fever of typhoid victims.

"Mmmmmmm," he said non-committally. "By the way, have you done any autopsies?"

"Autopsies? And have the papers all over us? There's enough public clamor without increasing it by doing autopsies."

In the doherty wagon on the way back to Washington Reed remarked, "Those fever charts, up and down like an intermittent fever—I wonder if they suggest the same thing to you that they do to me?"

Shakespeare smiled. "I guess so, doctor."

"It's typhoid, all right," Vaughan agreed, "in disguise. They're administering drugs to reduce the fever, so of course it goes down. Then when the drug wears off, up it mounts again. The action of the drug gives the steady fever, typhoid, the appearance of the intermittent one, malaria."

"That's the way I see it, too," Reed concurred. "However, Widal's and the microscope will settle it for good."

They did. Each one of the hundred cases at Camp Alger which the board believed to be typhoid, and the camp doctors thought was malaria, turned out on laboratory analysis to be typhoid. Would it be the same at the rest of the camps? the board wondered. They immediately requested the Surgeon General to establish a diagnostic laboratory at each large camp; he agreed to do so, and they left Washington for further investigation.

Traveling in the private car lent them by the Southern Railroad, the three doctors, accompanied by a good chef, an attentive porter and a secretary, arrived early in September at Jacksonville, Florida, where the Seventh Army Corps was encamped under the command of Fitzhugh Lee, a nephew of Robert E. Lee's and himself a Confederate veteran.

The medical officers at Jacksonville, like those at Alger, were sure they were dealing with malaria. Typhoid was a water-borne disease—*everybody* knew that—they reminded the board. Their water supply, from deep artesian wells, was unquestionably pure.

There was no good debating, the three doctors saw. It was proof that was needed, not argument. They requested the medical officers to select two hundred "malaria" cases, and sent them in hospital trains to the Army diagnostic laboratory run by Carroll at Fort Myer, near Washington, and to leading hospitals in Baltimore, Boston and other cities. Every single case was pronounced typhoid. The camp doctors were convinced. They had to be.

The thing "everybody knew," that typhoid was due to bad water, did not explain this epidemic. In scientific research, Reed knew, you could take nothing for granted—least of all the things "everybody knows."

Since water was not causing the epidemic, what was? Reed and his colleagues, trained observers, looked around. They had already been struck by the bad sanitary conditions at the camp. Could they be responsible?

A large tent camp had, naturally, no bathrooms with running water. At Jacksonville the latrines were at regular intervals cleaned and the contents carted away by scavengers. This disagreeable labor, the board noted, was often carelessly performed, so that some of the filth spilled in the roads, dried and mingled with the dust, was tracked throughout the camp and blown about by the wind. Flies swarmed on it, then flew to the camp kitchens and mess halls and lighted on the food. The regiments having the poorest disposal methods also had the highest proportion of typhoid. This certainly suggested, the board members agreed, that both wind and flies might be carrying Eberth's vicious little germ from victim to victim.

If it could be spread by wind and flies, why not by contact with soiled clothes and bedding, even by the touch of a dirty hand? Wasn't it possible that the men were spreading the bacillus directly from one to another by what the board called "comrade infection"? It seemed quite likely that they were.

Now, the investigators felt, they were getting somewhere: the fever was certainly typhoid; just as certainly, it was not being carried by water; there was reason to think that wind and flies and comrade infection were spreading it. The thing to do, plainly, was to attack the possible cause, filth, and see if that did any good.

The board began to inspect the regiments, their camping grounds, kitchens, tents and latrines. It had, of course, no enforcement power, but it could make emphatic recommendations. When they came to the Third Nebraska, of which William Jennings Bryan was colonel, the doctors presented their credentials and invited the commander to join them in the inspection of his regiment. All had been bad; the Third Nebraska was no exception.

"Colonel Bryan," Reed addressed him with his disarming smile, "Vaughan and Shakespeare are on this commission because they know about camp sanitation. I am on it because I can damn a colonel." He proceeded to lecture the astonished orator sternly on the duty of a Commanding Officer to care for the health and cleanliness of his troops.

The episode, Reed supposed, was closed. If only these civilians, suddenly blooming in uniforms, could be made to understand the importance of sanitary measures in military life! It would be worth all the unpleasantness, all the hurt feelings. No one of the board mentioned the incident to Lee, at whose mess they ate.

But he heard of it somehow. It was probably too good a

story to keep—the Army medical officer scolding the loquacious
Boy Orator of the Platte to a standstill. A few days later, Lee,
rather insistently, invited the board to stand with him on the
platform while he reviewed the troops. As the regiments
tramped past the three doctors stood respectfully behind the
general. Finally he turned to them.

"Step up, please, gentlemen. Here comes the Third Nebraska. Salute the colonel as he passes," he suggested, with a
little smile.

Chickamauga, in Tennessee, was the next camp on the list.
Sixty thousand men had camped there during June and July,
some still remained, and not a regiment had escaped typhoid.
Here the water from shallow wells and the river was definitely
contaminated. Also the soil of the whole camp had been fouled
by the carelessness of troops who knew they would soon move
on. The rocky ground made digging latrines difficult, moreover, and the earth was unabsorptive. It was hard to fix the
blame for the wretched and filthy situation, unless it could be
fastened on the ignorance of camp sanitation that prevailed
among the Engineer Corps and the line officers. Most of the
medical men, too, were far from being sanitary experts; and
what good recommendations they could make were usually
snubbed.

The troops still stationed at Chickamauga Park were de-
spondent and ill. Their Commanding Officer was no more
cheerful than his men.

"Doctor," he whispered, drawing Vaughan aside, "do you
know what the word Chickamauga means?"

"No, what?" the plump, matter-of-fact man of science
asked.

"River of Death!"

"You don't say. Interesting, these Indian names."

The officer nodded somberly. "There's no use you fellows

going around trying to figure if it's malaria, or typhoid, or how it comes. It's the Chickamauga fever, and it's from the miasma. Every night you can feel it, a foul damp that rises off the River of Death and creeps through the whole camp."

Giving this explanation the credence it deserved, the board tried an experiment. Observing that typhoid occurred more rarely among regiments that ate in screened tents, they scattered lime in the latrines and then watched flies, their feet white with it, later crawling over tables and food in unscreened messes.

Now they were sure of flies, and equally sure, from further observation, about comrade infection. It would be interesting, they thought, to find out next how long it took the bacillus, from the time it entered a man's digestive tract, to lay him low. Conveniently, fifty trained nurses just then arrived from Chicago; the first came down with typhoid ten days later. The conclusion, later confirmed, was that the incubation period of the germ was about ten days.

Now reports of the board's studies were beginning to reach the camps, and when they arrived at Camp Meade, in Pennsylvania, they found that the camp doctors were disinfecting all bedding, clothes, tents and other possibly soiled articles of each victim. This practice, soon adopted in all the camps, caused a sharp decline in the number of new cases.

From mid-October, when they returned to Washington, until the following June, Vaughan and Shakespeare, working at the Army Medical Museum during the day and in their rented room on K Street at night, went over the huge mass of statistics and other data that they had collected at the camps. From detailed analysis of the records of almost a hundred regiments they were able to draw certain conclusions about typhoid which still stand. They confirmed their orignal beliefs that typhoid is due to Eberth's bacillus and does not develop even in fouled soil in the absence of the bacillus; that Widal's test and autopsy can always identify it; and that it need never be confused with malaria, which can always be identified by the plasmodium in the blood. They altered, however, their earlier belief that it was largely water-borne: air and water accounted for only twenty-two percent of the cases they had studied, comrade infection for sixty-two and flies for fifteen. These findings were the last word on typhoid until the discovery, several years later, of the existence of carriers, people who have recovered from the disease and continue, unaccountably, to produce the bacillus in the intestinal tract.

While his friends toiled over the typhoid material, Reed was assigned to other duties. Late in October he went on a trip to Natural Bridge, Virginia, to see if two hotels there could be converted into military hospitals. Having decided that they could not, he made a hasty trip to Lynchburg, where his brother Jim was then living.

As he grew older, he realized, he valued his association with his oldest brother increasingly, especially since it was fifteen years since he had seen either Chris, who was a judge in Kansas City, or Tom, a merchant in Kansas. Jim, now an elderly minister like Pa, met him at the station, and they started walking together up the hill to the car line. With his empty sleeve, memento of Antietam, pinned in his coat pocket, Jim still walked with the quick long stride of his youth, and laughed when his youngest brother, puffing, mentioned that they were in no hurry.

"You take the hill like a breeze," Reed said breathlessly, "and I'm about winded. How do you keep so young, Jimmy?"

"I didn't spend a hard summer riding all around the country inspecting camps," Jim reminded him, "and the life of a rural minister, although not exactly strenuous, does involve some walking."

"It's good to see you so well, Jim. You seem to feel just as young as ever. I wish I could say as much for myself."

Jim, seeing the lines of weariness and strain in his face that had been absent even a year ago, at Pa's funeral, said anxiously, "You need some rest, Walter. You're tired. We'll spend a quiet evening at home, and if you feel like it, maybe you'll tell us a little about your typhoid work. The children are dying to hear about it. They think their military uncle is quite a fellow."

In Washington again, Reed continued his usual work of teaching and research, and met with Vaughan and Shakespeare as often as possible to discuss the typhoid studies. In the middle of April, 1899, he was sent to Cuba to investigate the epidemic of "pernicious malaria" at the camp at Puerto Principe. It was, of course, typhoid. He was miserably seasick going and coming on this first trip to Cuba, and, poor man, he had many more such excursions ahead of him. By the first of June, 1899, he was back in Washington again, in time to tell Vaughan and Shakespeare good-by.

That month the typhoid board was disbanded. Although its preliminary report, which contained recommendations on the sanitary reorganization of the Army, had been published in January, the board's studies were not completed. Splitting the remaining sick reports between them, Vaughan and Shakespeare took them home, and agreed to meet the next June at Atlantic City to write a full report on the board's findings.

The war, happily, had been short. Hostilities were officially opened late in April, 1898, and the peace protocol was signed the following August 12th. Our lack of preparation and inefficiency had been appalling (the War Department's conduct was later the subject of an investigation), but Spain's decrepitude had been fatal. We won easily.

The war had some interesting results. The United States, now that it had some island possessions—Puerto Rico and the Philippines—and was occupying Cuba, was beginning to think of itself as a world power and to take a livelier interest in foreign affairs. At the same time, much of the lingering bitterness of the Civil War was wiped out in the new unity of national feeling.

A new set of heroes, too, had arisen to replace the tottering gaffers of the Civil War. The image of Teddy Roosevelt, organizer of the Rough Riders, his teeth bared in a strenuous smile, was familiar to every newspaper reader. Dr. Leonard Wood's dizzy ascent from captain in the Medical Corps to brigadier general and military governor of Cuba was known to everyone. Admiral Dewey, for his destruction of the Spanish fleet in Manila Bay, was suddenly subjected to the rigors of unrestrained hero-worship. Young Mr. Richard Pearson Hobson, who had tried—and failed—to bottle up the Spanish ships in Santiago Bay by sinking a collier across the mouth of the harbor, became, for his pains, "the most kissed man in America."

The typhoid board won little public attention, however, and there is no record that any attempts to kiss its members were made by an enthusiastic public. This oversight notwithstanding, their work had not been insignificant. They did much to dispel a dangerous misconception about the spread of a serious common disease, and thus contributed greatly to its prevention.

CHAPTER NINETEEN

THE SLAVE TRADE, fertile source of so much other ill, seems also to have been responsible for introducing yellow fever into the Western Hemisphere. The disease was probably carried in slave ships from the west coast of Africa to the Barbados in September, 1648, where it caused thousands of deaths. It raged through the neighboring West Indian islands of St. Christopher and Guadaloupe, jumped across to Yucatan on the mainland, and then struck disastrously, probably in the summer of 1649, in Havana, Cuba. This was the end of its first eruption in the New World; but the disease had established itself. For the next two and a half centuries it was to be a major affliction.

It was called by different names in different places—American plague, malignant infectious fever, Barbados distemper, *coup de barre* (blow of a rod), yellow fever—and it was equally dreaded in all. In some epidemics as many as eighty-five out of every hundred victims died. One attack, happily, produced immunity.

Its onset came with chills and headache. Severe pains in the back and arms and legs (hence *coup de barre*) followed, with high fever, nausea and vomiting. This feverish stage might last a few hours, or several days, and was sometimes accompanied by the jaundice that gave the disease its name. Next came the "stage of calm," during which the severity of the symptoms subsided and the fever dropped. In mild cases the patient was then on the mend; in more severe ones "febrile reaction" set in. The fever again mounted, the aching in back and limbs became acute, jaundice was pronounced. Bleeding from the kidneys and gums sometimes occurred, and blood vessels occasionally broke into the skin. The most dreaded symptom of all was the "black vomit," the ejection of blood released into the stomach by the breaking of its blood vessels. When a yellow fever patient had the black vomit, his chance of recovery was slight indeed.

Yellow fever scourged our coast from the Rio Grande to Boston for more than two centuries, but did its most frequent, fatal work in the southern ports. One authority tells us that there were ninety epidemics in the United States from the time of the first proven outbreak at New York, in 1668, until its control at the beginning of the twentieth century; another, that in the hundred years between 1798 and 1898 there were three hundred thousand cases and eighty thousand deaths.

One of the worst of the early outbreaks took place in Philadelphia in the summer of 1793. The roads were packed with fleeing refugees, many of whom were turned away from neighboring cities and left to wander and starve in the countryside. Over the city a heavy silence rested, broken by the rattle of the dead-wagons collecting corpses. They were buried, without service or ceremony, in shallow graves dug by the Negroes who carted them away. The living shunned each other and often abandoned their dearest and closest connections at the first symptom. Dr. Benjamin Rush, one of the foremost doctors in the city and a signer of the Declaration of Independence, prescribed for a time for more than a hundred and fifty patients a day, had no time to eat or sleep or rest, and later recalled, with grief, that in passing through the streets he sometimes had to whip up his horse to escape the desperate cries of people imploring help. Whole families were erased, and the untended sick lay in the same room with the decomposing dead until they died themselves. The life of the entire community was halted by the plague. At the sight of a man cutting wood, early in October, for the coming winter, Rush was struck with surprise. "I should as soon have thought of making provision for a dinner on the first day of the year 1800," he said. By the time the pestilence was over, in December, it had killed more than four thousand people, one-tenth of the whole population. "Moschetoes (the usual attendants of a sickly season) were uncommonly numerous," Dr. Rush innocently observed.

In the epidemic at Memphis in 1878 more than half the population fled, and those that remained died faster than they could be buried. The police force was reduced by the disease from forty-seven to seven, and the replacements could not keep up with the deaths. Thieves and criminals swarmed in to loot the prostrated city, and many of them died by the disaster from which they had expected to profit. It has been estimated that the total cost, in loss of trade and money paid out, of the 1878 epidemic, which was widespread in the South, was about a hundred million dollars. There is, of course, no measure of the cost in human grief and suffering.

The worst of it was that, at the end of that epidemic, little more was known about the cause of yellow fever than had been known at the time of the great Philadelphia pestilence. Then some thought the disease was contagious—that is, could be passed from a sick person to a well one by contact; others thought it was not contagious, but was spread through the air by poisonous vapors arising from decaying vegetable and animal matter.

In 1804 a determined University of Pennsylvania medical student named Stubbins Ffirth tried to settle the question. He swallowed pills made of fresh black vomit, inserted small quantities of it into cuts in his arms and legs, and injected blood serum from a yellow fever patient into his own blood stream. These courageous and drastic experiments were negative. He did not contract the disease. We know now, however, that he missed it by a hair. Had he taken blood from a patient in the first three days of illness, he would—unless he himself was immune—surely have been rewarded with yellow fever. In any case, his experiments convinced him that it could not be transmitted by contact, that it was not contagious.

As doctors observed more epidemics and noticed how the people in intimate contact with the sick and their soiled clothes and bedding often escaped the plague, the contagion theory fell into disrepute. But they still could not explain how it was spread.

Some accurate observations had, however, been made about it. It had been remarked, not only by Dr. Rush, that mosquitoes were numerous when yellow fever was epidemic. It was known, too, that epidemics always ended with the coming of cool weather. Thomas Jefferson, and others before and after him, had noticed that the malady was "generated near the waterside, under warm climates," and seemed "pretty exactly circumscribed." It was realized, also, that it was not a filth disease, since rich and poor, clean and squalid neighborhoods were equally victimized.

Doctors kept on making guesses about its cause. Dr. J. C. Nott of Mobile, Alabama, in 1848 suggested that insects might carry it, and was hooted by his professional brethren. By the late 1870's theories far more fantastic than Dr. Nott's were earnestly discussed.

But in more serious scientific circles the idea was gaining ground that it was due to a specific germ; and it was but a step to the conclusion that the germ was carried in *fomites*—black vomit and other emanations of the sick, and articles soiled by them. Thus the contagion theory, in new scientific trappings, was well established again by the end of the 1878 epidemic. Stubbins Ffirth's experiments were forgotten. That *fomites* spread yellow fever was something that "everybody knew."

For twenty years this belief was generally accepted—twenty years in which the bedding and furniture of sick rooms were burned, baggage and wearing apparel of people traveling from a yellow fever zone destroyed or disinfected, houses sometimes burnt to the ground, millions of dollars worth of property destroyed—all to kill the germs thought to be lurking in *fomites*.

For twenty years, too, Dr. Carlos Finlay of Havana kept insisting that yellow fever was spread by the bite of a certain mosquito, the female of *Culex fasciatus*, now called *Aedes aegypti*. Everyone laughed at him indulgently: he was a nice old gentleman, but tiresome about his ridiculous theory. He was known as the "mosquito man."

Surgeon General Sternberg was this country's leading authority on yellow fever. It was his most ardent ambition to identify its germ and to discover how the plague spread. He had an old score to settle with it: it had almost killed him in 1875 at Pensacola, Florida. He had spent fourteen years, from 1879 until he became Surgeon General, searching for the germ in the blood—most expert opinion held that it must live in the blood stream—as well as in tissues and the intestinal tract.

Serving on the Havana Yellow Fever Commission in 1879, he had become a close friend of Dr. Finlay's. Even his friendship and respect for the Cuban doctor, however, did not incline him to take seriously the mosquito theory, when Finlay announced it on February 18, 1881, before the International Sanitary Conference of Washington, and again the next August before the Havana Academy of Medicine. Sternberg persistently pursued yellow fever in Brazil, Mexico, Cuba and the United States, and examined and exploded every claim that the specific agent had at last been cornered. He finally concluded that the only remaining competitor for the distinction of causing the pestilence was a germ which he called bacillus x. He was not sure of bacillus x, since repeated inoculations with it had failed to produce the disease in any laboratory animal, but he regarded it as a possibility. What he was sure of, however, was that yellow fever investigation had gone as far as it could until experiments could be done on human beings.

When the Italian scientist, Giuseppe Sanarelli, electrified the medical world in 1897 by announcing that he had identified the bacillus causing yellow fever, Sternberg was skeptical. He did not see how a germ which was easily seen under a microscope and grown in ordinary cultures could have escaped him for years. He obtained some of Sanarelli's germ, bacillus icteroides, and toward the end of 1897 set Reed and Carroll to work on the problem. Off and on for eighteen months, as their other work permitted, they studied the new germ and experimented with it. Early in 1899 they published a paper asserting that Sanarelli's bacillus was not *it;* it belonged to the group causing hog-cholera, the disease which Welch and the veterinarian Clement had been studying while Reed was working in the Hopkins laboratory in the early 1890's. In the same paper they added that Sternberg's bacillus x also had no connection with yellow fever.

During the same period Aristides Agramonte, a young contract doctor, on orders from Sternberg was trying to find bacillus icteroides in the yellow fever cases he autopsied in Cuba during the war. A Cuban himself and the son of an insurgent general who had been killed in an earlier war between the island and Spain, he had been educated in New York City and graduated from the College of Physicians and Surgeons in 1892. After several years as a sanitary inspector and assistant bacteriologist in the New York City Health Department, he joined the Army and was put in charge of the laboratory at Military Hospital Number One in Havana. He not only failed to find bacillus icteroides in seventy percent of the cases he autopsied, but also he did find it in many that were not yellow fever.

These findings might have disposed of Sanarelli's claim but

for two things: the Italian asserted that Reed's and Carroll's results were due to faulty work and prejudice; and two doctors of the United States Marine Hospital Service (now the Public Health Service) said that they had found bacillus icteroides in almost every yellow fever victim they had autopsied in the past two years. Bacillus icteroides remained a strong contender for the unsavory honor of being the yellow fever agent. Interest in it was very keen throughout the medical profession.

The issue, obviously, had to be settled one way or another. And for that matter, Sternberg thought impatiently, it was about time that something was done to solve the whole question of yellow fever. There had to be an answer *somewhere*. How would it be, he wondered, to appoint a commission to go into the whole matter thoroughly?

Reed, standing with his legs apart to brace himself against the slight motion of the anchored ship, looked curiously at the little pill before he swallowed it. If it was as good as it was supposed to be, he would go to bed in Tampa harbor, and wake up next morning with most of the trip to Havana behind him—and never a touch of seasickness. He popped it into his mouth, washed it down with a gulp of water, wiped his mustache on his handkerchief and got into his bunk.

He woke up in the morning feeling fine. He lay in the narrow bunk for a minute, enjoying the unusual sensation of not being seasick and admiring the bar of sunlight that came through the porthole. As he got up a doubt assailed him. He couldn't feel any engine vibration and, unless he had overslept, they could hardly be in Havana harbor already. He opened the cabin door and looked out. A seaman was mopping the floor.

"Where are we?" Reed inquired.

"In Tampa, sir," the sailor told him. "The sea was so heavy last night we didn't leave port."

Reed closed the door unhappily. He was sick for the whole trip.

General Leonard Wood, the handsome, energetic military governor of Cuba, was making everyone work so hard that the Cubans were poking good-natured fun at him with a rueful rhyme.

> "Don't stop to drink or spit,
>   Or smoke or scratch your ear.
> Go work while the stars are lit!
>   Come home when night is near.
>
> There is no time for food.
>   Write till the ink runs dry!
> The man who works for Wood
>   Is the man who wants to die!"

But they liked him, too. Taxes were honestly collected, justice was more properly administered, prisons were reformed, the insane had been collected out of cellars and jails and placed in an asylum in Havana. The administrative chaos due to the war was straightening out and municipal self-government was being started. The island's cities, which had been in a shocking state of filth and ruin, were being systematically cleaned up.

Reed's mission on this trip in March, 1900, was to report on a disinfectant, electrozone, which was manufactured locally and used to flush the city streets. While he conducted his investigation, he lived at Camp Columbia.

Camp Columbia, where the Seventh Cavalry was stationed, was near Quemados, a suburb some half dozen miles west of Havana. The flat ground of the camp, almost unbroken by trees and shrubs, sloped gradually to the sea. It was healthful, well drained and swept by the wind. Except during midday, when the sun beat directly on the unshaded wood buildings, it was pleasantly cool.

The post hospital, a group of frame buildings, stood by itself at the south end of the grounds. Its buildings included wards, offices, barracks for the Hospital Corps, quarters for the non-commissioned officers, nurses' quarters and small houses for the medical officers who had brought their families with them to Cuba. It was in the long, one-story bungalow, with a wide veranda on all sides, which provided quarters for the bachelor medical officers, that Reed stayed.

It took him only a short time to decide that he did not think much of electrozone. But he enjoyed the camp, the excellent mess at the bachelors' quarters, and the friendly, interesting group of young men. Among them was First Lieutenant Albert E. Truby, clean-shaven, round-faced, smiling, whom he had examined for a commission in the Medical Corps two years before and of whom he had since grown very fond. His friend Kean, Chief Surgeon of the Department of Western Cuba, was at General Fitzhugh Lee's headquarters in nearby Marianao, and another doctor, Jesse W. Lazear, was in charge of the laboratory at Camp Columbia.

A handsome young man with a heavy, close-cropped dark beard, Lazear was a thoroughly trained bacteriologist. Born in Baltimore in 1866, he had been educated at Washington and Jefferson College and at Johns Hopkins University. After taking his medical degree at the College of Physicians and Surgeons in the same class as Agramonte, he had spent most of his time in research, and was a bacteriologist at Johns Hopkins Hospital when he joined the Army as a contract doctor. He was an authority on malaria, which had recently been proved to be spread by mosquitoes, and especially interested in mosquitoes as carriers of disease. Reed, won by his personal charm and his intelligence, spent much time with him in the laboratory where, as a matter of diagnostic routine, Lazear did blood tests of all fever cases.

In the warm, bright evenings after dinner, the young doctors, dressed in fresh white uniforms, sat on the veranda of the officers' quarters and talked to Reed. They had at first been inclined to be a little stiff and diffident with the major—the gap is wide between the rank of lieutenant and major—but his sparkling good humor and genial manner had put them completely at ease. Kean, Agramonte and others of Reed's friends would come to see him and all of them would sit long after the tropical darkness had closed down, talking about their work and especially about yellow fever, in which Reed's interest was tireless.

"It's a fascinating problem," he observed one night, "and one that's ripe for solution now. General Sternberg's discredited all the mistaken ideas before Sanarelli's; and we're pretty sure, from the work done in our laboratory in Washington, and by Agramonte here, that Sanarelli's wrong. The field is clear, now, for the definitive piece of work."

"It's clear," Lazear concurred, "and the relation of mosquitoes to malaria may be the clue to follow."

Reed looked dubious. All the best authorities—except nice, stubborn, old Finlay—said yellow fever was spread by *fomites*, and he believed them.

On May 23, 1900, in Washington, Reed and the Surgeon General had a long talk.

"Then we understand each other on every point, Major?" Sternberg, seated behind his big desk, concluded.

"Perfectly, I think, General," Reed told him.

Sternberg scribbled a memorandum in his sprawling handwriting. "I'll ask the Adjutant General to issue the order today," he promised. "You, Carroll, Agramonte and Lazear. How I wish I could be on the board with you!" He sighed. "For twenty years it's been my dearest hope to lick yellow fever."

"If you hadn't done all the necessary preliminary work so thoroughly," Reed reminded him, "we would have to start 'way back from scratch. It might add several years to our job."

"That's some little comfort," Sternberg admitted. "Now, when the AG's order comes through, I'll give you written instructions. General ones. Needless to say, some of the things we've discussed won't be covered. If the anti-vivisectionists got hold of the news that we were prepared even for human experimentation, as a last resort, they'd scream themselves hoarse; and so would plenty of others, especially doctors."

Reed said gravely, "We'll be prepared to experiment on human beings, provided they give their full consent. But it's a terrible responsibility, General, to take a man's life in your hands and run a deliberate risk with it."

"It is indeed, Major. But it's a responsibility which we shall all share. And I know no man more fit by nature and training to assume it than you."

"One more thing, General. This mosquito theory of Finlay's —do you take any stock at all in it?"

Sternberg smiled. "Major Reed, you know I'm devoted to Finlay. He's a fine old man, and an expert on yellow fever treatment. But frankly, I think you'll be wasting your time if you investigate the mosquito possibility."

"I'm inclined to agree with you. Still, maybe we'd better look into it sometime, just to leave no stone unturned." Reed stood up. "I'll expect the order, then, appointing the commission immediately."

"Tomorrow." Sternberg accompanied his colleague to the door and shook hands cordially. "And, Major . . ."

"Yes, General?"

"The very best of luck!"

On May 24, 1900, the Adjutant General issued the order creating a board of medical officers composed of Major Walter Reed and Acting Assistant Surgeons James Carroll, Aristides Agramonte and Jesse W. Lazear "to meet at Camp Columbia, Quemados, Cuba, for the purpose of pursuing scientific investigations with reference to the infectious diseases prevalent on the Island of Cuba." And the Surgeon General wrote, "You will naturally give special attention to questions relating to the etiology [the scientific cause] and prevention of yellow fever. As you are familiar with what has already been done by other bacteriologists in this field of investigation, I do not consider it necessary to give you any suggestions or detailed instructions."

These papers were the death warrant of epidemic yellow fever in the Western Hemisphere.

CHAPTER TWENTY

ON MAY 23rd, the same day that the Surgeon General put in his request for the formation of the yellow fever board, Dr. Lazear was called to 20 General Lee Street, Quemados.

"He's been complaining of headache all day, doctor," Mrs. Sherwood told him.

"We'll take a good look at him and see what the trouble is," Lazear said reassuringly.

Sherwood was a short, strong-looking man who worked in Havana. His head ached, he said, and he felt hot all over—he supposed he'd picked up a cold some place. Lazear examined him, found his temperature was over a hundred degrees, and took a sample of his blood to examine in his laboratory. A mosquito, buzzing viciously in the doctor's ear, made him shake his head vigorously.

"They don't give a man any peace," Sherwood complained. "They get to be an awful pest about this time of year."

"I'll catch a few of these fellows," Lazear remarked, "and take them along with me. They're wonderful things under a microscope."

Sherwood was not greatly interested. "Do you think I can get back to work tomorrow, doctor? I'm too busy to be sick." He smiled feebly at his pleasantry.

"No!" Lazear's tone was positive. "You must stay in bed—no moving around whatever, and nothing at all to eat. Just plenty of cold water. I'll be out and see you again in the morning."

Back in his laboratory, he took off his uniform coat, laying it on the table with special care for the five mosquitoes, captive in test tubes, that he had brought from Sherwood's room. Quickly preparing a blood smear, he put the slide under the microscope and examined it searchingly. His handsome, bearded face became grave: there were no malaria parasites in it.

"But there's a chance it isn't yellow fever," he muttered out loud. "The Widal test may show typhoid."

The Widal, too, was negative. In the morning Sherwood ached all over and his temperature was higher. Lazear had him moved to the isolation ward of the post hospital. Yellow fever was loose again.

The plague picked its victims with its usual eccentricity. From 20 General Lee Street it hopped around the corner to 102 Calzada Real, where no one from Sherwood's house had entered or was even acquainted. Then it struck again in General Lee Street, skipping, in its passage, over a house inhabited by two non-immunes. A few days later it came back to attack them. It progressed in erratic jumps through the clean, pleasant little suburban town. Sherwood died, more people got sick. The officers of his mess complained to General Lee that Kean shouldn't be allowed to visit yellow fever cases—he might bring it back and distribute it among them. Kean, ordered to keep away from the fever, obeyed—and came down with it himself on the 21st of June.

Havana was having an epidemic too, and the officers of General Wood's staff were falling before it like bowling pins. In the officers' mess they drank their red wine, supposed to have a preventive effect, with the grim toast, "Here's to the ones who have gone. Here's to the next one to go." People were getting frightened. Rigorous sanitary measure, carried out with all the thoroughness of which Major William Crawford Gorgas, the Havana sanitary officer, was capable, failed to check the pest. Its rapid spread made mock of the health officers.

Lazear and Agramonte were kept busy examining blood, and material from autopsies. Lazear, in addition, studied his mosquitoes in the minutest detail, and found nothing. He did not discuss this phase of his work with anyone, but he persisted in it. The authorities could ridicule the mosquito theory all they wanted to—he had a hunch there was something in it.

Reed and Carroll landed on the morning of June 25th at Havana. Carroll had never been in Cuba before, and Reed as they rode through pointed out the sights to him—the long, low Governor's Palace where General Wood now had his head-quarters, the near-by cathedral which had once held the bones of Columbus, the forts, the leper hospital and the parks. The massive architecture of the buildings; the flat, tiled roofs; the ornate balconies and façades; the narrow streets; the shrubs and palm trees; the heat and the brilliance of the tropical color-ing—all made Carroll feel as if he were in another world. But the doherty wagon and the lively mules, switching their tails impatiently at the flies, those belonged to the familiar, unchang-ing world of the United States Army.

The wagon turned off the Calzada Real into the road to the hospital grounds and drew up in front of the officers' quarters. The porch was crowded with doctors waiting to welcome them. Captain Alexander Stark, the chief surgeon of the post, Agramonte, Lazear, Truby, Pinto and Ames gathered enthusi-astically around Reed. Carroll, lingering at the edge of the group, watched Reed's reception with almost personal pride, until Reed, taking him by the arm, introduced him to the men he did not already know. Glancing around as though looking for someone, Reed finally asked,

"Where's Kean? Busy?"

"Major Kean's got it, sir," Ames told him. "Yellow jack."

"No! How is he?"

"Not bad. Would you like to see him? He's been looking forward to your coming. It would do him no end of good."

"By all means, doctor. Right away, if you please."

Roger Post Ames, a contract doctor who was unusually successful in the treatment of yellow fever, always attended the cases that occurred in the camp. He and Reed walked through the hospital grounds and across the footbridge over the railroad cut to the group of small buildings composing the isolation ward.

Reed was startled by Kean's yellow and shrunken appearance. He stayed with him only a few minutes, long enough to twit him affectionately about taking the trouble to demonstrate in person the first case of yellow fever he, Reed, had ever seen.

"Has he had a very severe attack, doctor?" Reed asked Ames when they left. "I'm not able to judge, never having seen it before."

"It was bad enough to worry us," Ames admitted. "Some bleeding from the gums, but he's over the worst now. He's going to be all right."

"Thank heaven! You've cheated yellow jack; now it's up to us to eliminate him."

The same afternoon, June 25th, the Yellow Fever Commission, as it came to be known, met for the first time as a body on the veranda of the bachelor officers' quarters. The wind swept in cool from the sea, and they could look across the grounds to the frame shacks, picked out clearly in the brilliant tropical light, in which Kean and other yellow fever victims were lying.

It was a serious meeting, but it is hardly likely that any of the doctors realized that it was a historic one. Their first decision was undramatic. They agreed to start by looking for the germ of yellow fever; then they would try to discover how it got from person to person. First they would work again on bacillus icteroides, to check their previous conclusion about it. Agramonte would continue to work in his laboratory at Military Hospital Number One in Havana, and the rest of them would work at Lazear's laboratory on the post hospital grounds.

"I think we're going to solve it, gentlemen," Reed told them confidently. "Everything is in our favor: we're well equipped, well trained and a congenial working unit. And our accomplishments, whatever they may be, will be the result of cooperative effort; the credit for them will belong to the entire board."

The epidemic was rampant in both Quemados and Havana. Reed and Carroll, who had never before seen yellow fever cases, had a full opportunity to study them at the Camp Columbia hospital and at Las Animas, the Havana hospital under the direction of Dr. Juan Guiteras, an authority on tropical diseases.

So completely had the experience of the first half of the century been forgotten, that Reed learned with surprise, for the first time, that non-immune nurses who came in closest contact with patients in all stages of the disease seemed to be in no more danger of catching it than anybody else. It made him wonder if *fomites* were as dangerous as they were generally thought to be.

Concentrating on its efforts to find bacillus icteroides, the board examined the blood of eighteen people sick with yellow fever in every phase of its progress. No bacillus icteroides. As the epidemic progressed, more people died. The board autopsied eleven cases, and examined the organs with the utmost care. Still no icteroides.

Lazear was not greatly interested in the search for Sanarelli's germ. He was excited about a clue that supported the mosquito theory. It was in a paper by Dr. Henry R. Carter, of the Marine Hospital Service, who was then stationed in Cuba. Dr. Carter, during a recent yellow fever epidemic in Mississippi, had observed that it took two or three weeks for the first case of yellow fever in a community to produce the next case. After that, non-immunes would fall victim within one week of coming into the infected region. The thing that struck Lazear was the two or three weeks that elapsed between the initial case, and the first one to develop from it. Apparently during this period the original case was powerless to spread the infection. His suspicion was strengthened that an insect might be involved in the spread of yellow fever, an insect called, in scientific terms, an intermediate host.

Knowledge that insects were the intermediate hosts of certain disease germs was twenty years old. In 1880 Dr. Patrick Manson had established that a certain kind of mosquito spread elephantiasis. First it fed on the blood of a person with the disease, taking the germs into its own body, where they developed for a time; then it deposited them in the blood stream of a well person by biting him, thus giving him the matured germs—and the disease. Thirteen years later Dr. Theobald Smith of the Department of Agriculture's Bureau of Animal Industry had demonstrated how a particular kind of tick, by a like process, spread Texas cattle fever. In 1898 Dr. Ronald Ross had shown how the *anopheles* mosquito similarly spreads malaria. *In each of these three cases the insect host, even after biting the sick individual, remained harmless for a definite length of time, while the germs it had swallowed ripened, so to speak, inside it. Only when the germs reached a certain stage of development could the insect convey the infection by its bite.*

The insect host theory, Lazear realized, might account for the time that elapsed between the first yellow fever case in a community, and the next: maybe the mosquito bit the first case, remained harmless for a couple of weeks while the germs it had swallowed ripened, and, once they were ripe, gave the pest to everyone it bit. It was just a guess, just a possibility, but what an exciting one!

He discussed with Reed the train of thought that Carter's theory suggested to him. Frowning with interest, the older man listened attentively.

"That does seem to lend color to your favorite theory, Lazear," he admitted. "But if an insect host spreads yellow jack, then *fomites* probably don't—and that *fomites* do spread it is the one thing that practically every expert agrees on."

"Everybody agreed that contaminated water was the only cause of typhoid, sir," Lazear pointed out, "until your board proved otherwise."

"You're right, of course," Reed agreed. "Popular beliefs aren't necessarily Gospel, even when they're held by scientific men. It's an idea worth following up."

Reed was a good scientist, a man who could change his mind when he had reasons. Carter's paper was one reason. Then something happened which provided another.

There had been an extraordinary increase in sickness among the soldiers stationed at Pinar del Rio, the capital of the westernmost province of Cuba. The death rate from "pernicious malaria," as the doctor in charge called it, was remarkably high. Suspiciously high, it seemed to Captain Stark, acting as chief surgeon of the district now that Kean had gone home to recuperate. After consulting Reed, Stark ordered Agramonte to Pinar del Rio to investigate.

Traveling by the narrow gauge railroad across the tropical interior of the island, Agramonte arrived on July 19th and immediately did an autopsy on a "malaria" victim who had just died. Stark's suspicions were woefully confirmed. The "malaria" was yellow fever. The post medical officer was hopelessly incompetent, and the Commanding Officer refused to believe that he had yellow jack at his camp. Agramonte, a contract doctor without authority, wired Stark for official support, and Stark promptly saw to it that he had full authority to enforce precautions. By the time Reed arrived on the 21st, Agramonte had established a tent hospital for yellow fever and put it under quarantine.

The two doctors together questioned everyone who might throw light on the source of the epidemic and examined the sick reports for two months back in an effort to identify the first cases. There had been thirty-five, altogether, with eleven deaths, and the original infection had apparently come from the town of Pinar del Rio.

"Now here's the interesting thing," Reed pointed out to his colleague as they sat in their tent working over the records, "none of the usual precautions of disinfecting bedding and clothes were taken here, since yellow fever wasn't suspected. Yet you'll notice that the nurses, and the other patients in the wards, and the three men who do the hospital laundry all escaped infection. Some of them, at least, must have been exposed to *fomites*."

"That, of course, confirms what we've already observed in Havana and Camp Columbia. It's certainly mystifying." Agramonte, puzzled, twisted the upturned end of his long mustache and ran an agitated hand through his dark pompadour. "And then the guardhouse case, too."

"That one, I think," Reed spoke slowly and carefully, "presents our problem very nicely. Here we have a soldier," he placed a penny on the table, "under close guard for six days with eight other men." He arranged eight coins around the penny and traced an imaginary line around them with his finger. "Neither he, nor any of them, has been in contact with a case of yellow fever, or with *fomites*. Our soldier, and he alone, gets yellow jack; he dies, poor fellow," Reed flipped the penny back in his pocket, "after six more days, and his eight cell mates remain in perfect health. Now, how did the infection get to this one man, and how did it happen to spare the rest?"

Agramonte sighed. "It looks as if yellow jack just flew in the window and tagged him, and flew out again," he said, discouraged.

"Maybe that's what it did do, doctor," Reed said thoughtfully, "and maybe a mosquito brought it. Dr. Finlay's theory looks much less incredible to me today than it did a month ago. We must see him as soon as we return to Havana."

On August 1st, shortly after the return of Reed and Agramonte from Pinar del Rio, the board again met on the veranda of the officers' quarters. Reed described the epidemic they had just investigated, and told them of their observations.

"Now, gentlemen," he concluded, "we've seen that nurses and others who come in close contact with *fomites* are no more likely than anybody else to get yellow jack; and in this guard house case we've seen that a man who had no contact at all with *fomites* somehow picked up a fatal case. These facts suggest that *fomites* probably don't spread the fever, and that something else does. What?" He smiled at Lazear, who was listening eagerly. "Our best bet, I think, is a mosquito. Dr. Carter's paper suggests an insect host; and all the circumstances surrounding an epidemic—low, moist location, warm weather, the way the disease skips around—suggest that the mosquito *may* be the carrier. It seems to me now that we should tackle our problem from a new angle—try to find out how the germ is spread, rather than what it is. We must prove, or disprove, an insect host."

"And to do that," Lazear interposed quietly, "we shall have to experiment on human beings, as you and the Surgeon General foresaw. Unless, Agramonte. . . . ?" he ended on a question.

Agramonte shook his head. "No. I've been trying them all—guinea pigs, dogs, cats, rats. I can't infect any of them. My results are all negative, just like General Sternberg's. I think yellow jack likes only human beings."

"So it appears," Reed agreed. "No one has ever succeeded in giving it to a laboratory animal. I don't have to point out to you the dreadful responsibility we all assume in experimenting with men's lives," he went on. "If we lose any cases we'll be ruined, branded as murderers. But if we find out how yellow fever is spread, the benefit we'll confer on humanity will make the risk, grave as it is, seem trivial. Hundreds, sometimes thousands, of lives are lost every year, and a huge amount of valuable property is destroyed. By risking a dozen lives we may be able to put a stop to that forever. Do you think we can take such a chance to gain such an end?"

"I don't see how there can be any question about it," Carroll said. "I think, though, that the board members must take the first risk. We can't expect other men to do it if we don't. Agramonte, you're immune, I suppose?"

Agramonte shrugged. "Probably. Many Cubans are, from unrecognized light cases in childhood. I wasn't much more than a baby when we went to the United States, so it's just possible that I've never had it."

"In any case," Reed asked them, "we're all agreed to make the first experiments on ourselves?"

The agreement was unanimous. Carroll smiled.

"Somehow, Major," he said to Reed, "I can't feel very alarmed at the prospect. It's going to take a lot of proof to convince me that *fomites* aren't responsible. Even the Surgeon General's sure of it."

"We'll see," Lazear grinned happily. He was delighted at the new turn in the work.

In the end they agreed that Reed should supervise all the work; Lazear, because of his experience with malarial mosquitoes, should do all the mosquito work; Carroll should continue the earlier line of bacteriological investigation; and Agramonte, whose time was already filled by his duties at the Military

Hospital in Havana, should do autopsies and pathological study. The first move would be to call on Finlay and ask him about the mosquito.

Dr. Carlos Finlay, trying to prove that mosquitoes carried yellow fever, had made about a hundred experimental efforts to inoculate human beings. His results had been unconvincing, since he had not guarded the subjects of his experiments against other sources of infection. Only his wife and his assistant, Dr. Claudio Delgado, believed in his theory. Yet, although he had not supported it by convincing demonstration, he had good reasons, based on the observation of many epidemics, for holding it. It explained the frequently remarked presence of mosquitoes during an epidemic; the fact that the epidemic, along with the mosquitoes, disappeared with the first cool weather; that the disease existed only near water and in warm weather; that it moved jumpily, often skipping over houses occupied by non-immunes and attacking people who had had no contact with the sick or with *fomites;* that no sanitary measures had ever been able to arrest it; and that the high and breezy sections of a city were not subject to it, even though it might be flourishing along the waterfront.

Finlay had been a middle-aged man when he first advanced his theory. Now he was sixty-seven, with white side whiskers and a benevolent face. The son of a French mother and a Scottish father, he had been born in Cuba, and educated in France, England, Havana and the United States. As a medical student at Jefferson College in Philadelphia, he had made a friend of S. Weir Mitchell, a distinguished doctor noted also as a writer of historical novels. All through his life he had many friends among the top rank doctors in the United States. Although everyone smiled at his theory, the smile was kindly: his personality was gentle and endearing, and his professional standing high.

The board members found the elderly Cuban doctor in the study of his pleasant home in suburban Vedado. When he heard that they proposed to test his beloved theory, all the more cherished for the ridicule it had always drawn, his kindly face lighted with pleasure.

"I am perfectly sure, gentlemen," Finlay told them, and in his delight and earnestness his slight stammer became a shade more pronounced, "that you will end by convincing yourselves. If only you can also convince the rest of the profession, and the world!"

"It's your opinion, isn't it, Dr. Finlay," Reed asked, "that only one type of mosquito spreads the malady?"

"Yes. The female of *Culex fasciatus*. *Fasciatus* and *pungens* are the common mosquitoes down here, and *pungens* is harmless—in yellow fever, anyway. Our villainess is an interesting little creature, with distinctive habits. She's a daytime mosquito and does not bite after dark. The male doesn't suck blood at all, and the female does it only after mating—she has to have a meal of blood before she can lay her eggs. I have some here." He took a bowl, partly full of water, from the window sill and set it on the table before them. Leaning over it, the doctors saw a number of tiny, jet black cylinders clinging to the side of the bowl where evaporation of the water had left them stranded.

Lazear picked one of the tiny eggs up and rolled it between his fingers thoughtfully.

"Where do they breed, doctor?"

"Oh, rain barrels, the pan of water you put on the porch for the dog, a sagging gutter, a vase of flowers that's been standing in your parlor—any container holding stagnant water."

"Then she's not a roughneck like *anopheles?* She's more a domestic mosquito, and you don't find her in swamps and woods?"

Finlay beamed. "That's right. She's a fragile, domestic little thing. She sticks close to the house. Her wings are delicate, and she can't stand wind. She's rather striking-looking, too, handsomely striped across the back and legs. You've undoubtedly noticed plenty of them."

They all nodded grimly. It was impossible not to notice mosquitoes in Cuba unless you were armor-plated.

Finlay was absorbed in his subject, and thrilled to meet, after almost twenty years, serious attention instead of good-natured skepticism. He explained how the female lays her eggs, at night, on the surface of the water; and how the eggs, very resistant to outside influences, can be hatched even after drying for three months or freezing, when restored to proper conditions of warmth and moisture. It took them, he told his attentive audience, about three days to hatch; the larva stage lasted about a week; and the pupa, usually called the "wiggler," lasted two more days. Then you had the full-grown mosquito, ready to mate, bite, lay, and, if it had bitten a yellow fever case, to spread yellow jack.

When they left, Finlay gave them the bowl of mosquito eggs and promised to help them in any way he could.

Reed had to smile at Lazear's elation. Carrying the little bowl as though it held a million dollars, he looked as if he could hardly keep from skipping. What a dear, enthusiastic fellow, Reed thought warmly, and what a keen man—here was one who would make his mark in the scientific world.

"You look as though you'd swallowed the canary, Lazear," he teased him. "You know, there may be nothing in it at all."

Lazear laughed. "We're on the right track, Major, and I believe you're convinced of it yourself. Cheer up, Carroll, we've as good as got yellow jack in our pockets already. You won't be skeptical much longer."

CHAPTER TWENTY-ONE

REED HAD BEEN WORRYING about the typhoid study. Shortly before he was to have met Vaughan in Atlantic City to write the report, Shakespeare had died. The board had not yet published anything except its recommendations on the Army's sanitary reorganization. Reed therefore requested Sternberg to order him back to the United States so that he and Vaughan could, finally, announce their conclusions in a formal report. Sternberg did so, and the first week in August, just after the visit to Finlay, Reed returned to Washington, traveling on a transport with Truby, who was able to cheer him somewhat during his usual seasickness.

The Quemados epidemic was subsiding, so the three remaining members of the board had to rely on the cases which kept coming into Las Animas and Military Hospital Number One in Havana. Lazear had hatched the eggs given them by Finlay and sent some of the mosquitoes for further information to Dr. L. O. Howard, the insect expert who was head of the Department of Agriculture's Bureau of Entomology. With the mosquitoes he kept, and their offspring, Lazear made almost daily trips to Las Animas where, with Guiteras or Agramonte or Carroll, he would go into the yellow fever ward and feed his "birds."

The technique, which Finlay had worked out, was simple. Each mosquito was carried in a test tube stoppered with a piece of gauze. When he was going to feed one, Lazear would turn the test tube upside down so that the mosquito flew upward, toward its bottom. He would then pull the stopper and press the open end against a patient's arm or abdomen. When the mosquito had settled and drawn blood, Lazear would tap the tube, causing it to fly up again, and replace the gauze. Each tube was labeled, and Lazear kept careful track of each biting.

Being reluctant to introduce mosquitoes of whose dangerous powers he was already half convinced among Camp Columbia's fourteen hundred non-immunes, he kept them at Agramonte's laboratory and carried them in their test tubes to and from Las Animas, where he tried to infect them.

Pinto, one of the Camp Columbia doctors, was bitten by these presumably infected mosquitoes without result. On August 16th Lazear himself fed one that twelve days earlier had bitten a victim on the fifth day of his attack. Altogether, nine men volunteered for the experiment and were bitten. Nothing happened. Finlay was upset—surely it was the technique of the board, not his precious theory, that was at fault. The Cuban doctors, who earlier had watched their own "mosquito man" try similar experiments, observed the efforts of the American board with keen, and skeptical, interest. When the insects failed to produce any infections, it began to look, even to Lazear, as though the skepticism, rather than the interest, was justified.

His scruples about taking the mosquitoes to Camp Columbia dwindled. Apparently they were not dangerous; even if they were, he could trust the hospital steward assigned to his laboratory, John Neate, an intelligent and capable man, to take conscientious care of them.

It was after lunch on the 27th of August, and Carroll and Lazear were at work in the Camp Columbia laboratory. Lazear was preparing the stomach of a mosquito for microscopic study, and Carroll, at the work bench, was examining a blood culture that he had got three days earlier in Agramonte's autopsy room. Jenny, the little rhesus monkey kept in the laboratory for experiment, watched the two scientists with alert and meaningless curiosity and scratched her head.

"It doesn't seem to be a very fruitful line of investigation, so far at least, you'll have to admit," Carroll was remarking.

"It's far from exhausted when we've made only nine tries," Lazear argued, scowling into the eyepiece of his microscope.

"That's one hundred percent failure," Carroll observed.

"It is, and it's discouraging," Lazear admitted. "That reminds me—I was in a hurry before lunch and didn't leave my mosquitoes at Agramonte's lab. One of them didn't bite at Las Animas—seemed listless. I'd hate to lose her." He went over to the bench where the mosquitoes, each transferred to a large jar from the test tube in which she traveled, were kept.

"Yes. She's looking dopey, all right. Too bad." He took his little record book out of his pocket, and consulted it. "Twelve days ago she bit a case in its second day. Then she bit cases again on the 21st and 23rd and 25th. If there's anything in this theory of Finlay's she ought to be well loaded with yellow jack after all that."

Carroll left his microscope and walked over to look at the ailing insect. "Maybe she is," he said. "How about trying her out on me?"

"She may give you yellow fever," Lazear warned him soberly.

Carroll smiled. "I'm seriously afraid, old man, that there's not much danger of it. Whatever the risk, I'm willing to take it, anyway."

The top of the jar was covered with a gauze sleeve closed by a drawstring. Reaching in, Lazear captured the mosquito in a test tube and brought her out. Carroll rolled up his sleeve and sat on a high stool, while Lazear held the mouth of the tube to his arm.

The mosquito clung to the side for a moment, then dropped

onto Carroll's skin. Lazear, his face intent, watched her and held the tube steady so as not to disturb her. The mosquito sat motionless. No one spoke. Neate moved closer to see, and the monkey in a sudden frenzy of activity sprang screeching across her cage. Carroll, perched uncomfortably on the stool, shifted a little and the mosquito hopped and settled again.

Lazear sighed. "It looks as if she wouldn't bite."

"Hush!" Carroll whispered. "Here she goes now."

The mosquito, her legs drawn up, assumed her biting position and introduced her sting. When she finished, Lazear put her back in the jar.

"This is going to make a monkey out of you, Lazear," Carroll assured him good-humoredly.

"I almost hope it does," Lazear answered seriously. "I'd hate to think I'd given you yellow jack."

Two afternoons later, Carroll didn't finish the tour of the Las Animas ward with Lazear and Agramonte. "I'll wait for you on the porch," he said. "I'm feeling rather used up today."

The next evening Lazear telephoned Agramonte. His voice sounded strained.

"Carroll's sick," he announced. "He went swimming at the beach this afternoon, and had a chill when he got back." He paused, and added, "He thinks he's got a touch of malaria."

"Suppose I come out in the morning," Agramonte suggested, "and we'll take a look at his blood."

When Agramonte arrived at the camp he found Carroll in the laboratory examining his blood for the malaria plasmodium. He did not find it. His friends made him go to bed in the officers' quarters. Later he was carried off to the yellow fever ward, feebly insisting that he must have picked up his yellow jack in Agramonte's dead room or the Las Animas ward.

Neither Agramonte nor Lazear doubted that Carroll's attack was due to the mosquito bite. Agramonte was almost bowled over.

"Lazear," he exclaimed solemnly, "do you realize what this means? You, *you*, have produced the first case of yellow fever experimentally, by the bite of a mosquito! It's momentous!"

Lazear was distraught. Maybe he had produced the first case of experimental yellow fever on record, but maybe he had killed his colleague doing it!

"He *offered* to feed it," he exclaimed repeatedly. "It was his own idea. How can I forgive myself if he doesn't get well!"

Agramonte tried to comfort him. "Take it easy, old man. Ames will bring him through." He hoped his words didn't sound hollow. Carroll, rather frail at best, was dangerously sick, and yellow fever went hard with a man past forty. They were both getting a new idea of what it meant to assume the terrible responsibility of taking chances with another man's life.

But when the next opportunity for human experimentation came, Lazear did not shirk it.

On the morning of August 31st Private William H. Dean of the Seventh Cavalry lolled, with nothing much on his mind, in the ward of the post hospital. Time passed slowly there for a lively young man no longer ill, and he was glad that he was about to be discharged.

When the bearded doctor came in, Dean saluted briskly.

"'Morning, Dean," Lazear said pleasantly. "You're about to leave us now, aren't you?"

"Yes, sir. Good as new again, too."

Lazear looked at him thoughtfully. "I've a sporting proposition to make to you. You haven't been off the post or near any yellow jack for a couple of months, have you?"

"Nearly that long, sir."

Lazear reached in his pocket and pulled out four test tubes, each holding a mosquito. "How would you feel about letting my birds bite you?" he asked.

Dean stared at him—the doctor must be joking! Then he

realized he wasn't. But what a crazy request! It was certainly funny, he thought, some of the things grown men did for a living.

"If you wish, sir," he said politely.

"Wait till I explain," Lazear warned a little grimly. He explained carefully.

"This is serious, you understand, Dean," he concluded. "This one here," he showed the young man the mosquito sitting innocently on the side of its test tube, "I truly believe has made Dr. Carroll seriously ill, and can do as much—or more—for you."

"That's all right, sir," Dean was skeptical. "I'm not afraid of any little old gnat. Put him on me."

"Her," Lazear corrected him mechanically. He applied that insect and three others to the doubting cavalryman's arm.

Seven days later Dean joined Carroll in the yellow fever ward.

Reed ran up the steps of the brick building at Seventh and B Streets. Beechner, the museum messenger, looked after him as he strode briskly into his office, and reflected that it was nice to see the major looking cheerful again—he had seemed so worried for a while over Dr. Carroll.

The major had reason to feel cheerful. The preliminary typhoid report was finished. Carroll was out of danger and writing glowing letters about his recovery; convinced by Dean's case, he was proud, too, that his was the first case of experimental yellow fever on record. Dean's illness, which seemed almost certainly due to mosquitoes, was mild and progressing satisfactorily. Now, if only Lazear would get well fast! It had been a shock to learn that he had an attack. But he was only thirty-four, in good health, and under Ames' excellent care he should pull out of it easily, Reed thought confidently.

He reached for the stationery and looked at the calendar. "September 25, 1900," he wrote in his clear, quick hand. "Dear Kean: . . . I am so distressed to hear that Lazear is down with yellow fever. . . . I shall await your next [cable] with much anxiety. . . . I somehow feel that Lazear will pull through, as he is such a good, brave fellow." He frowned and moved impatiently as he wrote on. "I am so ashamed of myself for being here in a safe country while my associates have been coming down with Yellow Jack. The [Surgeon] General has suggested that I do not return, but somehow I feel that as the senior member of a Board investigating yellow fever my place is in Cuba. . . .

"Just how far Carroll's and Lazear's cases go to support that conclusion [that a mosquito carries yellow fever] I don't know, but hope to find out when I get there. Personally, I feel that we are on the eve of an important 'find.' . . ."

They were, but Lazear did not share it with them. Toward evening that same day he died.

Reed arrived at Camp Columbia about noon on October 4th. This time the greetings on the veranda of the officers' quarters were subdued. The shadow of Lazear's death was too heavy for any gaiety. None of the younger men had ever before seen Reed look so sad and stern. In this tired face there was no hint of the quick smile, the kindly humor, that usually made the blue eyes sparkle.

"You've heard about Lazear," Truby stated. There was no need to ask. Truby himself had returned to Cuba just a few days before his death.

"We touched at Matanzas yesterday," Reed explained.

Truby nodded. Kean and Havard, the Chief Surgeon of Cuba, had gone there on an inspection trip. They, of course, had met Reed and told him.

"I'd like to see Carroll, first of all, Ames," Reed requested.

When he rejoined the others on the porch, he looked almost bewildered.

"I was quite unprepared for Carroll," he said wearily. "His letters have been so cheerful, so full of energy—he even said he'd done an autopsy."

"We were lucky to save him," Ames said. "He came within an inch of going out, and he's still quite shattered. He didn't want to worry you, Major, with the news that he wasn't convalescing well, and he's been terribly anxious to spare his wife alarm."

"We'll have to send him home on sick leave as soon as he can travel. Now I'd like to have the details of these cases, particularly poor Lazear's."

They first suspected Lazear wasn't feeling well, Ames and Truby told him, when he missed a couple of meals. But he went about his work and didn't complain until the evening of September 18th, when he had a chill. Ames, Truby and Pinto had immediately diagnosed his illness as yellow fever, and had him carried on a litter to the isolation ward.

"You know what a reticent fellow he was, Major," Ames said. "All he'd say was that he 'might' have got it from a mosquito. Although now that I come to think of it, he made quite a point of telling Carroll and Major Gorgas when they visited him that a mosquito bit him on the hand in the ward at Las Animas on the 13th. He didn't bother to brush it off because he didn't suppose it was a *Culex fasciatus*, he said; anyway, he thought he was immune—he was bitten in August, you know, and nothing happened."

Reed nodded thoughtfully. It occurred to him that it was strange that a man as familiar with *Culex fasciatus* as Lazear should "suppose" the mosquito was not of that species. Surely, he would *know*.

"I want to see all Lazear's records," he said.

Reed, going over Lazear's papers, struggled between depression and elation. Lazear—dear, brilliant Lazear, the first man on the board to scent the mosquito clue—was dead; and Carroll, his almost indispensable assistant, was too ill to work on the probability so strikingly and disastrously revealed.

But the probability was almost a certainty! The secret of yellow jack was in their grasp, Reed was sure. He was confident now that *Culex fasciatus* spread the fever. Of course, Lazear's and Carroll's cases were not conclusive, since both had repeatedly been exposed to possible infection in the wards and the autopsy room; but Dean's case was a different story. He had not been outside of Camp Columbia, which was entirely free of yellow jack, for almost two months. It seemed that he could have contracted the disease only through the mosquitoes that Lazear put on him.

Sitting at the portable field desk in his two-room suite in the officers' quarters, Reed frowned, puzzled.

"But if a mosquito does carry yellow fever, why didn't the first nine experimental bitings produce a single case?" he wondered. "Certainly not because the volunteers all happened to be immune; Lazear was one of them—his case settles that."

Where was the explanation?

Reed searched Lazear's papers for his records of the bitings. In the little notebook that the dead doctor had always carried in his military blouse pocket, he found the answer.

Lazear had carefully recorded, in each experiment, how far along the yellow fever case was when the mosquito fed on it, and how many days then elapsed until the insect bit a volunteer. Studying the rows of figures, Reed's well-trained mind suddenly caught at the critical point. There was the answer, staring at him out of the neat figures written in a dead man's hand! How obvious, how beautifully simple, it was! Eagerly he checked through the figures again, to be sure he had made no mistake. No, that must be it!

"A yellow fever victim has the active agent of the disease circulating in his blood stream *only in the first two or three days of his illness!* After that, even when he's dying, it's gone," he exclaimed aloud, slowly. "And at least twelve days must elapse between the time the mosquito bites a yellow fever case in its early stage, and the time it can pass on yellow jack to the next victim. I thank God, I believe that this is our answer!"

The nine experiments that had failed had been performed with mosquitoes that had bitten yellow fever cases at least five days old, or with insects that had fed on yellow jack less than twelve days earlier. Finlay's hundred failures, and Lazear's nine, were explained. Lazear's success with Carroll and Dean, too, was explained. The mosquito that bit Carroll had fed on a yellow fever patient in the second day of his illness; it had bitten the skeptical doctor twelve days later, and the incredulous cavalryman four days after that. It had met all the conditions.

What agency spreads yellow fever, and how does it work was a question two hundred and fifty years old. Walter Reed, studying Lazear's pocket notebook that October afternoon, hit on the answer.

"If only," he thought sadly, "Lazear could be with us still! But even if he can't share our work any more, at least he shall always share the credit."

There was something curious about the notebook, Reed noticed: its final entries were incomplete, and they seemed to indicate that Lazear had himself secretly undergone experimental bitings. It was not like Lazear, an accurate scientist, to keep incomplete records; nor, for that matter, was it like an accurate scientist, who knew the danger involved, to allow himself to be bitten by an unidentified mosquito. How account for these two strangely unscientific pieces of carelessness? Reed could think of only one explanation: both were deliberate.

When he confided his suspicion to Truby and one or two others, they agreed with him: Lazear, realizing that he had given Carroll and Dean yellow fever, determined to take the same risk to which he had subjected them. He must have inoculated himself secretly; then, ill, he had worried lest his insurance be forfeited and his wife and two small children left destitute, if it became known that he had purposely exposed himself to a dangerous disease. He had decided, they guessed, to withhold the facts, and had told Gorgas and Carroll about the stray mosquito so as to lend the fatal experiment the air of accident.

If Lazear wanted his death to appear an accident, an accident it should appear. They would respect their dead friend's unspoken wish, and help to protect his family. This benevolent conspiracy of silence remained in force for more than forty years. Not until the danger feared by the dying doctor was long past were the facts revealed, even to his family.

Reed cast aside his usual deliberation and worked like a whirlwind writing a report of these first yellow fever experiments. He was to leave for the United States October 13th to attend the meeting of the American Public Health Association at Indianapolis, where he intended to read it. Before going, he had, as a formality, to ask the military governor's permission to leave the island, and Kean offered to drive him into Havana to see Wood.

"Do you know why I borrowed the general's team and am going to the city with you?" Kean asked as the carriage, drawn by Fitzhugh Lee's fine horses, rolled along the road.

"No, Kean, why?"

"I have something serious to talk to you about, Reed."

"What is it?"

"I want to persuade you to ask General Wood for a considerable sum of money to pay the expenses of a series of yellow fever experiments, and give bonuses to volunteers. That way I believe you can get a number of Spanish immigrants to offer themselves, especially since they almost always expect an attack when they come to Cuba."

Reed wouldn't commit himself, and all the way to General Wood's office Kean wondered what he would do.

Wood's greeting was cordial. Reed received permission to leave the following day for the United States. Then he said,

"General, I have something else I want to discuss with you."

The two officers moved into the window embrasure which looked over the plaza and the blue harbor, flanked on the one side by Morro Castle and on the other by La Fuerza, forts harmless with antiquity.

Kean, silently watching, caught the quick sense of a historic moment. This informal meeting in the old Governor's Palace between the Army doctor and the military governor could change the medical history of the world, the course of millions of lives. Reed, slender and animated, confronted the massive Wood and told him, with the irresistible clarity already familiar to his former pupil, about the three yellow fever cases. Wood's cool blue eyes did not shift, nor his expression change, as he listened. Reed, his eyes sparkling with enthusiasm, summed up the evidence. He paused a moment, and said very earnestly,

"General Wood, will you give me ten thousand dollars to continue and complete these experiments? I know we have the answer, but we must have conclusive proof."

Wood's answer was unhesitating. "I have this morning signed a warrant for that amount to aid the police in the capture of criminals. Surely this work is of more importance to Cuba than the catching of a few thieves. I will give you ten thousand dollars. If that isn't enough, I will give you ten thousand more."

Reed and Kean, lunching together later, congratulated each other that the military governor was also a medical man who could appreciate the vast implications of the proposed experiments.

Two days later, on October 15th, Kean issued a circular for the departments of Havana and Pinar del Rio, stating that it was now believed that mosquitoes spread yellow fever and directing that their breeding places be eliminated.

"Major Kean, I'm a little worried," General Lee told him confidentially. He was a short, fat man with a little goatee. He had known Kean's father well, and was devoted to the son. "This notion of Reed's about mosquitoes—I hope you won't identify yourself with it. If you'd seen as many yellow fever theories come and go as I have," he shook his head, "you'd hesitate a long time before you'd commit yourself. If it blows up under you, it can damage your professional standing badly."

"General Lee," Kean assured him, "I'm willing to risk all the professional standing I may ever have on the theory that the mosquito is the villain!"

CHAPTER TWENTY-TWO

REED'S ANNOUNCEMENT at the Public Health meeting of his belief that mosquitoes spread yellow fever set no rivers afire—too many claims had been advanced in the past few years, only to be scrapped later. His case was far from established, he knew. One clear demonstration, Dean's, was not enough to break down error entrenched for half a century. It would take the series of experiments, conducted on human subjects, for which Wood had promised funds, to establish this revolutionary theory beyond question.

After consultations with Sternberg, the insect expert Howard, Welch and other Hopkins friends, Reed hurried back to Cuba, where he landed the end of October. He immediately set to work on plans to establish an isolation camp for his experiments. Camp Lazear, it was to be called, in honor of their dead colleague.

On the opposite side of the Calzada Real from Camp Columbia, about a mile from Quemados, was the farm of Dr. Ignacio Rojas. Agramonte thought one of his uncultivated fields would be a good place for the camp. Reed, seeing it, agreed, and they rented it. It was secluded, well drained, and, being almost bare of shrubs and trees, was open to the sun and wind and free from mosquitoes.

Carroll was on sick leave until the middle of November, but Agramonte came to Camp Columbia often to discuss the isolation camp with Reed. Truby and the other young doctors, keenly interested in the coming experiments, followed the plans closely and gave Reed all the help they could, while Kean consulted with him at every step.

There were, Reed explained to them as they sat on the veranda after dinner, to be three phases to the experiments. They would try to infect non-immunes by the bites of mosquitoes which had fed on yellow fever cases in their first stage, by exposure to *fomites*, and by injection of blood taken from yellow fever cases in the first two or three days of illness. In this way he hoped to prove that yellow jack was spread by mosquitoes, that *fomites* were harmless, and that the specific agent of the disease was in the blood. Each experiment was to be carefully controlled, to exclude exposure to any other source of infection than the one directly in question. Each case would be seen by the Havana Yellow Fever Board, composed of Doctors Finlay, Guiteras, Albertini and Gorgas, so that the diagnosis of yellow fever could not be questioned.

Reed drew up the plans for the camp, and the Hospital Corps erected seven tents, while the Quartermaster's Department started to put up two small wooden buildings that Reed ordered. The work was progressing well when Reed had an unexpected setback.

A violent tropical storm, striking in mid-November with heavy wind and rain, dropped the temperature to the low sixties. *Culex fasciatus*, a delicate insect in spite of its fatal power, cannot survive wind or chill. Most of Reed's laboratory mosquitoes died, and he was greatly alarmed that the sudden cold might put an end to the mosquito season and leave him without insects for the experiments.

The younger doctors reassured him: there would still be plenty of warm weather, plenty of mosquitoes to go with it, and plenty of yellow fever. Truby could see, however, that he was still anxious, and wanted mosquitoes, not promises.

"Come on, boys," he suggested after lunch one day. "Let's lay in a supply of mosquito eggs for the major, so he can stop worrying."

He and several of the other doctors set off toward Quemados

on a mosquito hunt. As they passed the Quartermaster's dump it occurred to them to investigate there for discarded buckets or utensils holding water. To the deep embarrassment of young Dr. Amador, the post sanitary officer, the dump was a regular mosquito mine, in spite of the mosquito control measures he was enforcing. Most of the utensils had the sanitary inspector's ax hole in the bottom, but enough still held water to make the dump an ideal breeding place. Eagerly scooping up wigglers and eggs to keep Reed in stock indefinitely, they hurried with their find to his laboratory. Reed, Neate and John H. Andrus, a Hospital Corps man who had recently been assigned to the laboratory, joyfully set to work to rear the wigglers and dry the eggs for future use.

Agramonte, meanwhile, was rounding up volunteers among the Spaniards at the immigration station on Havana bay. Selecting only men who were of age, in good health, and without dependents, the board asked them if they would take a bite. Many of them, attracted by the promised money, the prospect of being cared for by the "senoritas Americanas," as they called the nurses, and the reflection that they were likely to get yellow fever anyway, signed contracts with the board consenting to be bitten for the reward.

Reed, oppressed by Lazear's death, and by the heavy responsibility that he and his board were assuming, was dubious, too, about relying on the Spanish immigrants. Their co-operation, he feared, captured by the money involved, might not survive the proof that the "harmless little gnats" which they were paid to let bite them would give them yellow jack.

His anxiety was unexpectedly relieved.

Breakfast at Camp Columbia was at seven, and by eight Reed was at his desk, working on plans for the isolation camp. The knock at the door, so early in the morning, surprised him.

"Come in," he called.

John R. Kissinger and John J. Moran stepped into the room, stepping at the same time, although no one knew it then, into history.

"Good morning, gentlemen," Reed greeted them. "What can I do for you?" He was slightly acquainted with both young men. Kissinger was a private in the Hospital Corps. Moran, who shared quarters with him, also had been in the Hospital Corps until his term of enlistment expired. Now he was a clerk at General Lee's headquarters.

"We heard you wanted volunteers, sir," Moran said, "to submit to some yellow fever experiments. We talked it over, and we thought we'd like to go in for it together."

"It's good of you to offer," Reed said cordially. "I don't know if you understand just what you're getting into. This is the situation." He described the dangers of the experiment to them carefully, emphasizing that he himself had no doubt that mosquitoes spread the disease. "And of course," he concluded, "every volunteer gets a hundred dollars; if he comes down with yellow jack he gets two."

"Well, you see, Major Reed," Kissinger explained, "we're not interested in being paid. The money isn't the point—it's the opportunity," he flushed a little, "to do something for humanity and science." Moran nodded emphatically. "That's right, sir," he said.

Reed, silent with astonishment, stared at them. He saw two young men in their early twenties—two pleasant, intelligent, unremarkable-looking boys about the age of his own son, with the best part of their lives before them. And they were offering to risk those lives not for military glory, not for reward— certainly not for two hundred dollars—but for "humanity and science"! He saw, too, that they meant it. On the verge of explaining that the money was already appropriated, that they might as well take it, he checked himself. Money could never reward this unselfish gesture.

"My dear boys," he said, and they could tell by his voice that the quiet, self-possessed doctor was moved, "I am proud to accept your brave offer."

Greatly cheered by the offer of Kissinger and Moran, Reed no longer feared a shortage of volunteers. American boys, motivated by interest in the experiments themselves, rather than by the prospect of reward, would not back out, no matter what the danger.

"And when everything's running smoothly," he remarked to Truby, "and my personal direction isn't necessary any longer, then I'll take the mosquito test myself."

Truby's face clouded at the announcement. He hoped ardently that Reed could be dissuaded. The major was not robust, and he had to eat sparingly. The strain of preparation and responsibility showed now and then through his usual composure. It would be a dangerous thing for the doctor approaching his half century mark to tempt yellow jack.

Camp Lazear opened the morning of November 20th, without fanfare. Agramonte was busy at the Military Hospital, and Carroll, just back from sick leave, was needed for important bacteriological studies, so Reed selected Ames to take charge of the camp. Dr. Robert P. Cooke, a tall young contract doctor with straight lanky hair and a humorous expression, had volunteered for the *fomites* experiments and was the only other doctor at the camp. A hospital steward, a Hospital Corps private and an ambulance driver, all immune; Moran, Kissinger and six other Hospital Corps privates, all non-immune; and several non-immune Spaniards completed the camp personnel.

The experiments began immediately. At 10:30 on the morning of the 20th, Kissinger rolled up his sleeve and watched with mixed feelings while the mosquito, in the test tube pressed against his arm, took a leisurely bite. He wondered if the

Reed, silent with astonishment, stared at them.

fragile little thing would really give him yellow jack. It was funny—he could squash her with a finger tip, and maybe *she* could kill *him* just as easily. As he rolled down his sleeve, he sighed. It was a beautiful day, he realized.

The principal rule of Camp Lazear was simple and rigid: no one could leave or enter without Reed's permission. Only the immunes could go out on such necessary errands as getting supplies from Camp Columbia.

The Spaniards, whose only duty was to gather stones off the ground for a low wall about the camp, could take all the time they wanted to rest, and were mystified and delighted with their life in this strange new world. The soldiers, with nothing to do but keep their quarters neat, passed the time in reading, playing cards and taking naps. Kissinger passed it in waiting for his yellow jack. It did not develop.

Three days later he was bitten again; then, on the 26th and 29th, mosquitoes were held to Moran's willing arm. Still no yellow jack.

"Maybe you're a natural immune, Moran, but I'm going to find out before I'm through with you," Reed warned, only half jokingly. "I'm going to save you now for another test, a very important one. You're still game?"

"For anything you want, Major," Moran told him. Reed was his hero; he would have done anything for him. He slaved over the confidential letters to Sternberg that Reed entrusted to him to type, tossing away sheet after sheet of letter-head to get a perfect copy, and considered himself well rewarded when the doctor praised his neatness.

The failure of his first four experiments did not discourage Reed. The weather was cool now, and he suspected, rightly, that the germ took longer to ripen within the mosquito than it did in hot weather. By the end of the month he still had not produced experimental yellow fever, but life was not without incident. A local newspaper on November 21st loosed a broadside against the heartless Americans who were enticing foreign innocents to submit to the injection of deadly poison. The board had foreseen that some such trouble might arise, and it was for that reason that they had drawn up a contract with each immigrant. Reed, Carroll and Agramonte, armed with the contracts, immediately called on the Spanish consul and explained the conditions on which the Spaniards had consented to take the risk. An intelligent and courteous gentleman, the consul smilingly advised the three doctors that, under the circumstances, he had no objection to their experiments.

Agramonte, because his regular work kept him in Havana, was in charge of infecting the mosquitoes at the Las Animas ward. As he was driving out one day to the experimental camp with his pockets bulging with test tubes full of the lethal insects, his horse, frightened by a road-building outfit, bolted and over-turned the buggy. His laboratory assistant, Loud, was pitched out at the first plunge, and the doctor, desperately clutching his infectious mosquitoes, was dumped in a sand pile. He arrived at the camp dusty and disheveled, but loudly rejoicing that his misadventure had not turned a number of loaded mosquitoes loose in the countryside.

The two little wooden buildings, situated at some distance from the tents, were completed by November 30th. Reed had dire and special plans for them. Building Number One, known as the infected bedding and clothing building, was a one-room shack fourteen by twenty feet. The walls were two boards thick, the inner one made of close-fitting tongue-and-groove lumber. Its two windows, both placed in the south wall to prevent through ventilation, were covered with very fine screening, and fitted with wooden shutters to keep out fresh air and sunlight. The building, entered through a doubly screened vestibule, was constructed in every particular to prevent the accidental entrance of mosquitoes. It was closed tightly in the daytime, and its temperature was kept at about ninety degrees by a coal oil stove, while care was taken to keep the atmosphere humid.

In it was undertaken one of the most revolting experiments to which scientific curiosity and loyalty to his superiors ever persuaded a hero. On November 30th, the day the building was ready, three large boxes containing bedding used by yellow fever patients were carried to it. These articles, foully soiled, had been packed for two weeks in tightly closed boxes.

At six o'clock that Friday evening, Cooke and two privates of the Hospital Corps, Levi E. Folk and Warren G. Jernegan, all non-immunes, entered the hot and stuffy little building and started to unpack the loathsome articles. Reed, with interest and commiseration in his face, watched from outside. The three young men opened the boxes, pulled out and shook several sheets and blankets, as they had been instructed to do, then made an unscheduled bolt for the door. Gulping for air, they stopped.

"Oh, poor fellows!" Reed exclaimed sympathetically.

It was terrible in the little house, but the three volunteers weren't quitting. Shaking their heads and grinning ruefully, Cooke and the two others stubbornly re-entered it, made up their cots with the filthy bedding, and gingerly crawled into them.

The major might be confident that *fomites* were harmless, but they still could not help feeling that their experiment was not only much more disagreeable, but much more dangerous, than the mosquito test; "everybody knew"—still—that *fomites* carried yellow fever. They spent a bad night between their horrid sheets, disturbed by evil smells and somber and uneasy thoughts. But for science—and the major—they willingly spent nineteen more nights like it.

Kissinger was a determined young man. He had already been bitten twice without result, but he had volunteered for a case of yellow jack, and he intended to get it.

On December 5th, at two in the afternoon, he rolled up his sleeve for the third time and watched the mosquito bite. This was getting monotonous, he thought.

"Do you think she'll take this time, sir?" he asked. "I certainly hope so!"

"I'll tell you in a couple of days," Reed replied, smiling.

By evening three days later, the young volunteer had a headache; the next day, December 9th, he was carried on his bed to the yellow fever ward. Kissinger, at last, had his yellow jack. "In my opinion this exhibition of moral courage has never been surpassed in the annals of the Army of the United States," Reed said.

Reed, his belief in the mosquito as intermediate host of yellow fever finally confirmed, was overjoyed.

"Rejoice with me, sweetheart," he happily wrote his wife that night, "as, aside from the anti-toxin of diphtheria and Koch's discovery of the tubercle bacillus, it will be regarded as the most important piece of work, scientifically, during the 19th century. I do not exaggerate, and I could shout for very joy that heaven has permitted me to establish this wonderful way of propagating yellow fever."

There was no self-satisfaction or personal pride in his modest and generous spirit, only thankfulness. Too excited and happy to sleep, he was up early the next morning and dashed off a note announcing the news to Truby, who had been sent across the island to Rowell Barracks at Cienfuegos as post surgeon. Truby told the news to Lawrence Reed, who was now a second lieutenant and shared quarters with him. Kean, almost beside himself with joy at his friend's conclusive demonstration, carried the tidings to General Wood. The good news was on the wing.

When the volunteers for the *fomites* experiment heard it, the gravity of their bearing disappeared in a rush of uproarious high spirits. They felt as if a death sentence had been lifted. Reed was feeling wonderful. The Havana Yellow Fever Board declared that Kissinger had unmistakable yellow fever—one of its members had earlier declared the mosquito theory "wild and improbable" and reluctantly ate his words—and, to make everything perfect, Kissinger was getting well.

Reed was deeply grateful for his recovery. As a good officer he hated to expose one of his men to a danger he did not share; as a good doctor he hated to gamble with a human life; and as a scientist he feared that the experiments could not continue if one of the cases died. Volunteers would probably be frightened away, and public opinion would force him to stop the work. He desperately hoped that his luck—and his volunteers' luck—would hold.

Within the next week three Spaniards, exposed to mosquito bites just as Kissinger had been, came down with yellow fever. Agramonte, still hopeful of inoculating a laboratory animal, held some of the mosquitoes that had infected them to the abdomen of Jenny, the laboratory's rhesus monkey. Her temperature remained normal, her simian spirits undimmed. The effort to give her yellow jack was a failure.

All the Spaniards recovered. One of them, an engaging young man named Antonio Benigno, whom Reed always called Boniato, Spanish for sweet potato, because of his liking for that vegetable, was overjoyed when he received his reward, which represented huge wealth to him, in ten- and twenty-dollar gold pieces. Several of the Spaniards, however, were convinced by their countrymen's illness that the "little flies" were really dangerous. They forgot, as Reed put it, "their own personal aggrandizement and incontinently severed their connection with Camp Lazear. Personally," he added, "while lamenting to some extent their departure, I could not but feel that in placing themselves beyond our control they were exercising the soundest judgment." No shadow of doubt as to the guilt of mosquitoes could linger now.

Nor could anyone but a thorough skeptic doubt the harmlessness of *fomites*. On December 19th, after twenty nights passed in the most contaminated surroundings, Cooke and Folk and Jernegan emerged from the infected bedding building in their usual good health. They had even put on a few pounds. Two more non-immunes, James Hanberry and Edward Weatherwalks, took their place as subjects of the revolting but harmless demonstration, and were themselves later relieved by James Hildebrand and Thomas M. England. This line of experimentation, having failed to produce a single case of yellow fever, was finally abandoned after two months.

The seven brave and patient men who underwent this horrible ordeal were at no time in danger of contracting yellow fever, but that comforting fact was something of which they could not be sure until it was all over. It took just as much courage to disprove the virulence of *fomites*, in which the best authorities believed, as it did to prove that of mosquitoes. The practical value of the experiment was immense, since it clearly showed the uselessness of destroying valuable property in an effort to check the spread of yellow fever.

The Havana medical men, abruptly won over by Reed's conclusive results, hurried to do belated honor to their own neglected prophet, Dr. Finlay. They gave him a banquet at Delmonico's in Havana on the night of December 22nd, which was attended by seventy or eighty Havana doctors, Reed's board, Wood, Kean, Gorgas and other military doctors. Dr. Juan Guiteras tactfully distributed the honors to everyone's satisfaction. Dr. Finlay, he said, was like Sir Patrick Manson, who had advanced the theory that mosquitoes carried malaria; and Reed was like Sir Ronald Ross, who proved Manson's theory and gave it practical value.

Finlay, benign and happy, smiled around at the doctors gathered in his honor, doctors who had laughed at him until a few days ago. After twenty years, thanks to the clear, brilliant demonstration of the middle-aged American medical officer, his cherished theory was accepted. They had been long years, and discouraging sometimes, but this—the cheers and applause roared musically in his ears—this wiped out every painful recollection.

Reed, happy as Finlay, was looking ahead—far ahead to a day when his demonstration would bear fruit, when mosquito control measures would wipe the plague from the earth.

Reed was ready for the next step in his demonstration.

"Now we want to show that the difference between an infected and an uninfected house is due only to the presence of loaded mosquitoes. This is the experiment I've been saving you for, Moran," he told his only civilian volunteer.

"Good," Moran said. He was determined, too, like Kissinger. He had bargained for yellow jack, and he meant to get it.

Across a slight depression and eighty yards distant from the infected bedding building, was the second of the small houses that Reed had had built. Building Number Two, or the infected mosquito building, was like Building Number One, except that its windows were placed so as to afford good ventilation, and it was partitioned inside by a very fine wire screen through which mosquitoes could not pass.

Into one of the two rooms formed by the screen partition Reed liberated, on December 21st, fifteen insects which had previously fed on yellow fever cases. Moran, fresh from a bath and in a clean nightshirt—he felt a little like a sacrificial lamb—promptly at noon went into the mosquito-infested room and lay down on a clean cot. The board members, with two non-immune volunteers who were to remain on the mosquitoless side of the partition, watched through the screen.

In a few moments the insects were buzzing close about Moran. Repressing an almost overwhelming impulse to swat them, he winced as they bit him about the face and hands. He lay still for half an hour, while they deliberately settled on him and fed.

"Good boy," Reed commended him. "That should just about do for now. We'll do it again this afternoon and tomorrow. And I think you'll have that yellow jack you've been asking for."

When Moran's three ordeals were over the two non-immunes who had watched the ceremonies with the doctors remained on the other side of the room, separated from the mosquitoes only by the wire screen, but otherwise exposed to exactly the same influences as Moran had been. Moran went back to his tent, took his temperature and pulse every three hours, and waited as patiently as he could for his yellow jack. He felt pretty sure of it this time.

Christmas was warm and cloudy. Reed, unable to get to Camp Lazear in the morning, drove out in the afternoon. He wondered how Moran was feeling. It was about time for him to come down with the fever, he reflected, as he approached the young man's tent. He had already made a stop at the mosquito building, and found the non-immune controls in excellent health and Christmas spirits.

"Merry Christmas, Moran!" Reed said as he entered the volunteer's tent. Moran, lying on his cot, struggled to his feet.

"And to you, sir," he answered.

"Anything new?"

Blinking with headache, Moran pointed to his temperature and pulse chart. Reed glanced quickly at it—fever a hundred and one, pulse fast, he saw—and looked closely at Moran, noting his flushed face and bloodshot eyes.

Concern and jubilation struggled in his face. He had done

it again, he had proved his point! Moran was sick, the controls were well—this demonstrated that the mosquito was the essential, the single, factor in making a house infected!

"Get back into bed," he ordered. "Moran," he rubbed his hands gleefully, "this is one of the happiest days of my life!"

Moran, ill as he felt, could not help grinning sympathetically. The major acted as pleased as a young interne—it was almost worth a bout of the fever to see him so elated.

Later that afternoon Stark and his wife, and Kean and Mrs. Kean, who had come with him to Cuba when he returned from sick leave, had a Christmas party for a few of the officers. A guava bush, brightly trimmed, acted as Christmas tree, and all the children under six on the post were invited to receive presents. Reed was the gayest person there.

When the children's gifts had been distributed, the two hostesses produced comic ones, accompanied by doggerel verse, for several of the men. A major of convivial habits was given a toy water-wagon, and Stark, a skeleton of a man, got a cake of "obesity soap," capable, so its makers alleged, of washing away the unwanted pounds.

And the great new discovery in yellow fever was suitably recognized. Dr. Amador, the sanitary officer, was presented with a can of kerosene, fatal to mosquito wigglers, with the jingle:

> "Sing a song of kerosene,
>   Of barrels deep and wide.
> Doctors have become so mean
>   Mosquitoes have to hide.
>
> She thinks she finds a haven
>   But the doctor's eagle eye
> Falls on the poor mosquito
>   And she will have to die."

For Reed there was a fragile package that seemed to be all ends.

"What a work of art!" he laughingly exclaimed, as he got the wrapper off, and held it up for everyone to see. It was a handsome mosquito, fashioned of a champagne cork and toothpicks, with a formidable stinger, and legs and body realistically striped to resemble *Culex fasciatus*. He read his rhymes out loud:

> "Over the plains of Cuba
>   Roams the mosquito wild.
> No one can catch or tame him
>   For he is Nature's child.
>
> With Yellow Jack he fills himself
>   And none his pleasure mar
> Till Major Reed does capture him
>   And put him in a jar.
>
> And now, alas for *Culex*.
>   He has our sympathy,
> For since the Major spotted him
>   He longs to be a flea!"

It was a happy Christmas, Reed thought as he went to bed, one of the happiest of his life. The guilt was firmly pinned on *Culex fasciatus*, and they knew how to deal with mosquitoes. "With Howard and kerosene," as he wrote the insect expert, Dr. Howard, they could practically eliminate the yellow fever mosquito. *Culex* and *anopheles*, what a gay old pair of troublemakers they had been! But now their days were numbered.

Moran slowly emerged from his feverish stupor to realize that the quiet, insistent voice of which he had been faintly aware for some time was Major Reed's, and that it was speaking to him. He squinted, focusing his aching eyes, and tried to catch the sense of the words.

"Are you in pain, Moran?" the doctor repeated the question.

Moran weighed the form of his answer, whether to nod his bursting head, or speak through the dreadful taste in his mouth.

"Yes," he whispered.

"Can you localize the pain?" Reed persisted, "back, legs, head?"

The sick man noticed that there were other men in the room besides Reed, and his attention wandered briefly to the white side whiskers framing the benevolent face of an old gentleman watching him from the foot of the cot. It was his first glimpse of Finlay.

"No," he answered, a little more clearly, "it's just everywhere."

"You can groan, Moran, or even yell if you want to. It's all right to make a fuss. It may relieve you some," Reed advised him sympathetically. He bent down to catch the mumbled words, ". . . knew what I was getting into . . . not a cry-baby," and straightened, smiling.

Moran, slipping away into stupor again, was still conscious of the murmur of the doctors' voices, and caught the one clear phrase, "a very pretty case." Pretty! He shut his teeth tight against a groan, and turned his head away.

It might be a pretty case, but that didn't mean Reed liked it. He was terribly anxious. Moran knew the major came to see him early and late, but he never knew how often. It was several days before Reed was sure his volunteer would recover from the experiment through which he had put him. "Thank God!" he thought, "it will be a happy New Year after all."

It was New Year's Eve. Reed was seated at his field desk—the same desk at which, three brief months before, he had found the vital clue in Lazear's pocket notebook. He was writing a letter to his wife. His face was tired, and the lines in it were deep and grave from the long strain, but it was serene.

"The prayer that has been mine for twenty years," he was writing, "that I might be permitted in some way or at some time to do something to alleviate human suffering has been granted! A thousand Happy New Years!"

He stopped, his pen poised over the paper, at the first ringing note. The twenty-four bugles, blown in concert, were sounding taps for the old year. There was a moment's quiet, then they sounded reveille—reveille for a new year, and a new century, to which yellow fever would be not a scourge, but a fading memory.

CHAPTER TWENTY-THREE

KISSINGER and the three Spaniards had proved that mosquitoes carried yellow fever. Cooke and the six other volunteers had proved that *fomites* did not. Moran, now happily well, and the two non-immune controls had shown that a house was infected with the fever only when it contained loaded yellow fever mosquitoes.

With all that accomplished, Reed thought thankfully, the end of the experiments was in sight. Next they would inject the blood of a yellow fever patient into non-immunes to prove that the parasite was in the blood, and to find out if passage through the mosquito was necessary to its development. Then they would see how long a loaded mosquito kept the ability to spread yellow jack by continuing the biting experiments with old mosquitoes. And finally, he would himself undergo one of these experiments in which he had risked other men's lives.

So far, they had not lost a single one of their five experimental cases, a remarkable achievement in a disease with as high a death rate as yellow fever. Reed still looked forward to each experiment with dread, and held his breath over every one until the patient was well on the mend. If only their perfect record would hold to the end of this dangerous gamble!

He looked forward longingly to February when his exhausting work would be over and he could go home. After the Pan-American Medical Congress in Havana the beginning of the month, at which he was going to read a paper on the board's work, he would return to the United States—to Emilie and Blossom, to the beloved cottage in the Pennsylvania mountains, to the laboratory and the examining boards, to his classes at the Army school and Columbian. Taking up his old duties, he would finally be relieved of this crushing responsibility.

Meanwhile, he had to get on with his job.

Twenty nights' contact with *fomites* and a number of mosquito bites late in December had not given Jernegan yellow fever, but he kept on trying. Two cubic centimeters of blood from a yellow fever patient brought him down with it in four days, on January 8th. Three days later, William Olson, injected with Jernegan's infected blood, was carried to the yellow fever ward. Wallace Forbes, with half a centimeter from a case of natural yellow fever, was put to bed on the 24th. Just one more case, Reed decided, and the board would stop the injection experiments.

John H. Andrus had swept out the laboratory, given the guinea pigs and Jenny fresh food and water, and was busy with his mosquitoes when the door was thrown open.

"... impossible!" Carroll's voice was raised, his tone pleading.

"It is not only *not* impossible, but it is necessary," Reed answered with a touch of sharpness. He sat down at his microscope but made no move to uncover it.

"It isn't necessary! We can find another volunteer."

"We can't wait. Forbes' blood should be right for the next test tomorrow. When our volunteer got frightened and backed out, he left us in a hole. We can't waste time trying to line up somebody else. I'll take his place. I'm not asking these men to do something I won't do myself."

"Major, you are almost fifty years old. You haven't been well lately. You're tired and run down. If you persist in submitting to this inoculation, you're inviting grave and maybe fatal results."

"Oh, nonsense, Carroll! With a specialist of Ames' ability

to look after me, it's perfectly safe. He hasn't lost a single one of these experimental cases."

"He couldn't save Lazear."

"Lazear didn't go to him until he'd been sick two days. Anyway, there's a chance that I'm immune."

"That's what Lazear thought, too."

Andrus, going quietly about his work, glanced quickly at Reed. His face was set, and he looked as if he were trying not to get angry.

"There's a chance I'm immune," he repeated with irritation, "if Finlay's new theory is correct that the offspring of loaded mosquitoes are themselves loaded. I've fed a dozen next generation mosquitoes, without any bad result."

"Do you believe that theory of Finlay's?"

"The next generation of ticks are loaded with cattle fever, aren't they?"

"I know that. Do you believe Finlay's theory?" Carroll insisted.

"As a matter of fact, no. But that's all the more reason for my being inoculated. If I get yellow jack, it will prove there's nothing in it."

Carroll groaned. "Really, Major! I thought we'd convinced you—Kean and Truby and Stark and Agramonte and the rest of us—that you are too necessary to this work to take this dangerous, needless risk. You have no right to sacrifice yourself!"

"I'm not going to discuss it any more, Carroll. I'll be inoculated tomorrow, and that's the end of it." Reed got up abruptly and strode out of the laboratory.

Andrus spent the rest of the day, and most of the night, thinking hard.

The next morning, January 25th, Carroll arrived first at the laboratory. He looked worried and tired. Andrus wondered if he had slept badly, too.

"Dr. Carroll," he began.

"What is it, Andrus?"

"I've been thinking—won't I do just as well for this blood injection as Major Reed?"

Carroll's face brightened for a moment, then he shook his head.

"No, I'm afraid not. Major Reed wants to test Dr. Finlay's second generation theory, too, you see."

"But I've fed more mosquitoes hatched from the eggs of infected insects than the major has, sir," Andrus objected. "I do it all the time, just to keep them laying." (The mosquito needed, as Finlay had told the board, blood before she could lay her eggs.)

"That's perfectly true. So you do." Carroll looked at the laboratory attendant with fresh interest. "Have you any dependents?"

"No, sir."

"Then I'll ask the major."

Reed, composed again and cheerful, came in a few minutes later. Carroll sent Andrus out on an errand. The soldier wondered what the two medical men were saying. Would Reed yield? Would he let a younger, stronger man replace him? He hoped so. He knew what the work of the board would mean to the world, and he knew that Reed was the engine that made the apparatus run. In trying to take over the risk that Reed had selected for himself, Andrus felt that he was being practical, in an impersonal sort of way. Somebody had to take the chance. He could better be spared than Reed, so it was only sensible that he should take it. It did not occur to him that this was a high order of unselfishness.

When he came back to the laboratory Reed questioned him.

"You understand, Andrus, what you're getting into?"

Andrus' heart jumped. So the major was going to let him take the injection!

"I've nursed yellow fever, sir, and seen men die of it."

"Dear Mother," he wrote . . .

"Why are you volunteering then?"

"I'm interested in your work, Major Reed. I'd like to take some part in it, even just a little one."

That afternoon at Camp Lazear, Andrus, with a cubic centimeter of Forbes' fever-laden blood circulating poisonously in his blood stream, sat on the edge of his cot, a block of paper on his knees.

"Dear Mother," he wrote, "you won't hear from me for two or three weeks, because I have been detailed to accompany a troop of the Seventh Cavalry on a practice march into the interior. I didn't want you to worry. . . ." He finished writing and sealed the letter. He felt awful—he had lied to his mother, lied to her in what might be the last letter he would ever write her. But at least he was sparing her worry.

There was nothing he could do, though, to spare Reed worry when his temperature hung around a hundred and four degrees for three days. Would the boy live or die? Reed wondered desperately. "Should he die," he wrote the Surgeon General, "I shall regret that I ever undertook the work. The responsibility for the life of a human being weighs upon me very heavily at present, and I am dreadfully melancholic." The melancholy, happily, passed; Andrus slowly recovered.

Since the offspring of loaded mosquitoes had failed to infect the non-immune Andrus, Finlay's theory of their infectiousness was definitely disproved. The injection experiments also showed, among other things, that the parasite of yellow fever was in the blood during the first few days of illness, and that passage through a mosquito, although Nature's ingenious way of spreading it, was not necessary to its development.

His scare over Andrus did not prevent Reed from pushing the other phase of the experiments to a conclusion. Levi Folk, who had undergone the *fomites* test, came down with yellow jack from the bite of a mosquito that had fed on yellow fever thirty-nine days before. Another insect which had bitten a patient fifty-one days earlier proved its virulence on Clyde West. James Hanberry, a graduate like Folk and Jernegan of the *fomites* experiment, received an attack from a mosquito fifty-seven days after its contamination. Charles Sonntag was the last subject of this series. The last loaded mosquito finally died seventy-one days after its meal of yellow jack. This demonstration showed why a house or region could remain infectious even after its sick occupants had been gone for more than two months.

The Yellow Fever Commission had, in all, produced at will and under perfect control fourteen cases of unmistakable yellow fever between the opening of Camp Lazear on November 20th and February 10th, without the loss of a single life. Their skill and good fortune in saving every case was pointed up a few months later when another board, under Dr. Guiteras, conducted further experiments. The death of three out of their first seven cases put an immediate stop to the work.

Reed, facing the delegates to the Pan-American Medical Congress on February 6th, turned the page and glanced at his audience. It was a large one—even the doors were packed with listeners—and it was motionless with attention. After reading the report of the experiments, he was ready to announce the conclusions, the conclusions at which he and his board had arrived with such risk and labor.

Raising his voice so that those in the back of the room should miss nothing, he read clearly, "The mosquito *Culex fasciatus* serves as the intermediate host for the parasite of yellow fever.

"Yellow fever is transmitted to the non-immune individual by means of the bite of the mosquito that has previously fed on the blood of those sick of the disease.

"An interval of about twelve days or more after contamination appears to be necessary before the mosquito is capable of conveying the disease.

"Yellow fever can also be experimentally produced by the subcutaneous injection of blood taken from the general circulation during the first and second days of this disease.

"Yellow fever is not conveyed by *fomites*, and hence disinfection of articles of clothing, bedding or merchandise, supposedly contaminated by contact with those sick of this disease, is unnecessary.

"A house may be said to be infected with yellow fever only when there are present within its walls contaminated mosquitoes capable of conveying the parasite of this disease.

"The spread of yellow fever can be most effectually controlled by measures directed to the destruction of mosquitoes and the protection of the sick against the bites of these insects.

"While the mode of propagation of yellow fever has now been definitely determined, the specific cause of this disease remains to be discovered."

It was not the applause that resounded in the crowded hall, or the congratulations of enthusiastic doctors from two continents that gratified Reed most. It was the certainty that the burdensome and momentous work which he and his colleagues had faithfully performed would mean a safer and a happier life for humanity in future years.

CHAPTER TWENTY-FOUR

INVITATIONS to read papers on yellow fever before medical societies, a dinner in his honor given by the Medical and Chirurgical Faculty of the State of Maryland, congratulations from friends and colleagues and strangers, general acclaim—these were the things that met Reed on his return to the United States. Popsy Welch, bursting with pride in his student's achievement, was of the opinion that Reed's researches in yellow fever were the most important contribution to medicine ever made in this country, with the exception of the discovery of anaesthesia. The praise was not extravagant. Modest though he was, Reed could not have been surprised: he appreciated very well the meaning of the work he had directed.

"You lucky man!" Sternberg greeted him feelingly.

"If you hadn't been the Surgeon General, if the military governor hadn't backed us to the limit morally and financially, if Kean and the other medical officers hadn't co-operated so generously, if we hadn't had a number of brave volunteers, if—well," Reed returned the warm hand clasp, "we have so much, so much, to be thankful for. We were very fortunate."

Self-effacing, he smilingly declined to let the newspapers take his picture. "Fools' names and fools' faces, you know, little daughter," he told Blossom.

But when one of his students, thrilled with a new camera, coaxed him to pose, he yielded.

"Oh, all right," he agreed laughing. "Just for practice."

They went up on the museum roof. Reed smoothed his uniform coat, straightened his collar and patted his hair flat with his hands.

"Is this all right?" he inquired, looking into the camera.

The young man adjusted him to the light. "Look across my right shoulder, sir," he directed him. "A little more this way—that's fine. Hold it!" He squeezed the bulb. Reed's image was committed to the sensitive plate. That was his last photograph.

He was pleased by the recognition he received for his work—an M.A. from Harvard in the summer of 1902, an LL.D. from the University of Michigan a little later—more pleased by the results already apparent in Cuba. Gorgas, at first unconvinced that *Culex fasciatus* was solely to blame for yellow fever, had been converted when his own mosquito control measures made Havana totally free of the disease for the first time in more than two centuries. Already the research was paying dividends in lives and money.

Not content to rest on his achievement, Reed worked as hard as ever at his teaching and research and examining boards. He eagerly followed, too, the further research Carroll was conducting in Cuba. Straining infected blood through a porcelain filter fine enough to catch the smallest known bacteria, Carroll injected the serum thus obtained into three non-immune Americans, John R. Bullard, Albert W. Covington and Paul Hamann, and produced yellow fever. This experiment explained at last why the microscopic examination of the blood, pursued so painstakingly by Sternberg, Reed's board and other workers, had had negative results: the agent is sub-microscopic, a filterable virus.

Reed's children were grown. Blossom, happy to have her favorite companion back again, still came to meet him in the evenings at the corner where he got off the horse car. Lawrence, at the promising beginning of his military career, had married one of the Blackford girls, Landon, and in the usual Army routine was being moved from post to post.

Reed was delighted when Kean was transferred to Washington in September, 1902, and persuaded him to move into the apartment house on Nineteenth Street near Q, where the Reed family then lived.

"But it's so expensive here!" Kean complained. "Isn't there some cheaper section of town where I can live?"

"Kean," Reed explained smiling, "there are three things every Army officer has to do: he has to live north of Pennsylvania Avenue and west of Fourteenth Street; he has to have a charge account at Woodward and Lothrop; and he has to keep his money in the Riggs bank. You might just as well reconcile yourself to it now."

Kean, seeing Reed frequently at home and at work, noticed that he seemed tired, and once or twice heard him refer, lightly, to his indigestion. It occurred to no one, however, that he was seriously ill. He continued his usual duties and received, in addition, the appointment as Librarian of the Surgeon General's Library on November 1, 1902. Mental exertion, however, was becoming strangely painful to the alert mind that had always before approached it so buoyantly; and the heavy schedule of teaching and research seemed unbearably taxing to him when he came back in the fall to resume it after a rest at his little mountain home near Monterey, Pennsylvania.

Characteristically, however, he exerted himself to maintain his usual urbanity and cheerfulness—no one should be distressed on his account if he could help it—but he was unable to conceal his suddenly failing strength from his wife. Finally he consulted his doctor, Major W. C. Borden.

When, on November 17th, Borden removed his ruptured appendix, it was already too late. Reed could not rally. The doctor whose brilliant work had saved humanity from a cruel plague could not himself be saved. At the Washington Barracks hospital, where he had so many times brought healing and comfort to others, early in the dark morning of November 23rd, Walter Reed quietly died.

The stone that marks his grave on a high knoll in Arlington

National Cemetery is, fittingly, simple. On it is inscribed the citation pronounced by President Eliot of Harvard University in conferring on him the degree of Master of Arts:

"He gave to man control over that dreadful scourge, yellow fever."

Walter Reed has been commemorated in many tangible ways, some trivial, at least one of them great: in the bronze bust that stands at the entrance of the Army Medical Museum in which he once worked; in a United States postage stamp; in the Army Register's Roll of Honor, headed by his name, which lists the members of his board and the American volunteers who underwent the experiments; in a memorial gold medal ordered struck by Congress; in the fine Army medical center in Washington, the Walter Reed Memorial Hospital.

It is his own work, however, that is his best and most lasting memorial. It freed the sea and river ports of the United States, the West Indies and Latin America from the prostrating blight of yellow fever. It opened the way to the investigations of later scientists, who have developed a vaccine for the endemic yellow fever that still lurks in the South American jungles and who, with zeal like Reed's, look forward to the day when the disease shall have been wiped from the face of the earth. It also made possible the construction of the Panama Canal, so vital to hemispheric commerce and defense. Building on the groundwork laid by Reed, William Crawford Gorgas eliminated yellow fever and malaria from the Canal Zone, after the fevers had forced the French to abandon the project as a costly failure, and enabled Americans under the brilliant engineer, George Washington Goethals, to complete the great work. When he was lauded as a great man for this sanitary achievement, Gorgas, modest like Reed and generous, disclaimed the praise. "Not a great man," he said, "merely one who is trying to follow in the footsteps of a great man, Walter Reed."

Walter Reed died too young, at the peak of his ability and before the full measure of his usefulness to science and humanity had been tapped. Even so, he was one of the fortunate ones: the good that he did in his relatively short life will benefit and inspire generations long after the more spectacular heroes of his day are only half-remembered names. His place is safe in history.

APPENDIX

APPENDIX ONE

A great many people interrupted their own work and pleasure to examine their recollections, now half a century old, of Walter Reed, and to set them out in conversations and in letters to the writer. Without this generous help it would have been impossible to write the story of his life, and I am warmly grateful to each one of them. It suggests the affection in which his friends and even his acquaintances held Dr. Reed that they so willingly went to the considerable trouble of making these contributions.

I cannot adequately thank Brigadier General Jefferson Randolph Kean, United States Army, Retired, for his tireless interest and co-operation. A close friend and colleague of Dr. Reed's, General Kean has been unfalteringly helpful in furnishing me with new material, in giving explanations and suggestions and in reading the manuscript.

I am particularly indebted, too, to Dr. Philip S. Hench of the Mayo Clinic, an authority on the history of the yellow fever experiments, which was by no means free from confusion before he started to unravel it. Dr. Hench very kindly made available to me much material that he has collected, told me of new conclusions to which his own researches have brought him and checked the yellow fever part of the manuscript.

Brigadier General Albert E. Truby, United States Army, Retired, has written a memoir, not yet published, of Dr. Reed which is a fascinating eye-witness account of him in action, and of the experiments. Generously indifferent to the fact that I would scoop him on some of his own material, General Truby permitted me to make use of several of the incidents in this document.

The kindness of the late John H. Andrus must be bracketed with General Truby's. Mr. Andrus, too, permitted me to use his unpublished account of his own inoculation, thus enabling me to be the first to publish the full story of an especially interesting incident of the yellow fever experiments.

Major General Walter Lawrence Reed, United States Army, Retired, Dr. Reed's son; Mrs. Walter Lawrence Reed; Miss Blossom Reed, the doctor's daughter; and Miss Alice Reed, a daughter of the doctor's oldest brother, the late James Reed, all kindly and painstakingly supplied me with much information.

I wish to express my gratitude to D. S. Otis, of New York University, for his careful research and assistance in checking the facts and material in this biography.

Others to whom I wish I could acknowledge my indebtedness in greater detail include Mr. Charles M. Abbot, Mr. Pedro S. Abreu, the Right Reverend George A. Beecher, Bishop of Nebraska, Mr. F. M. Broome, Dr. Harold J. Cook, Dr. Robert P. Cooke, Mrs. D. T. (Annie Reed) Elam, Dr. Simon Flexner, Dr. Paul N. Garber, Mr. George E. Gorton, Dr. L. O. Howard, Dr. William T. Howard, Dr. William H. Howell, Major General M. W. Ireland, United States Army, Retired, Colonel Harold Wellington Jones, United States Army, Dr. Howard A. Kelly, Mrs. John R. Kissinger, Mrs. Jesse W. Lazear, Dr. Archibald Malloch, Mr. John J. Moran, Mr. James E. Peabody, Dr. B. F. Richards, Mr. and Mrs. W. Crosby Roper, Jr., Miss Mari Sandoz, Miss Frances T. Schwab, Colonel J. F. Siler, United States Army, Retired, Dr. James P. C. Southall, Mr. Elmer Sturgeon, Mr. Roscoe M. White, Dr. E. P. Wilson, Dr. Louis B. Wilson and Dr. Robert Yerkes.

APPENDIX TWO

Notes on the Text

Page 125. This episode is based on a tradition rooted in the Reed family. The relation between the record and the tradition is the usual one: they conflict. The records of the Surgeon General's Office, written in an immense book in a fine, clerkly hand and covering in detail the movements of all medical officers, state that Reed was precisely two weeks on his way from Camp Apache to Virginia.

It seems incredible, too, that he should have been ordered to travel by such a difficult route, when he could much more easily have reached a railroad by the comparatively well-traveled Santa Fe Trail.

On the other hand, Mrs. Reed herself is the source of this version—and who should know better than she? It is out of deference to her, to legend and to a good story that it is followed.

Page 208. There is also good authority to conclude that the board decided to investigate the mosquito possibility and called on Dr. Finlay for advice before, not after, the Pinar del Rio incident.

Page 225. The well-established legend to the contrary, Kissinger and Moran did not volunteer together. The traditional version is given here, however, since diligent investigation has not satisfactorily established which was first. The men's own recollections of this incident differ. Whichever was first, the courage of these two first volunteers was equal. A few hours' or a few days' precedence either way cannot change that essential fact.

APPENDIX THREE

Yellow Fever: the High Spots of Its History in the Western Hemisphere

1647   Epidemic yellow fever broke out in the Barbados in September, presumably introduced from the west coast of Africa by a slave ship.

1648   Yellow fever spread from the Barbados to St. Christopher and Guadaloupe by summer. The epidemic lasted for twenty months in Guadaloupe.
The Massachusetts court quarantined West Indian ships. This is the first instance of quarantine in the New World.
Yellow fever invaded Yucatan, with dreadful mortality, in the summer. At Mérida the epidemic lasted two years.

1649 (or possibly 1648)   A severe outbreak of yellow fever occurred in Havana. From that time on Havana was a focus from which yellow fever was repeatedly spread to the mainland.

1668   The first proved outbreak of yellow fever occurred in the United States, at New York.

1793–1900   Reed and Carroll estimated that during these years there were at least half a million cases of yellow fever in the United States, with a hundred thousand deaths. Among the cities that suffered the worst epidemics were Philadelphia (1793), New Orleans (1853), Norfolk, Virginia (1855), and Memphis (1878).

1848   Dr. J. C. Nott of Mobile, Alabama, suggested that insects might carry yellow fever. He is believed to be the first to have advanced the theory.

1881   February 18th and August 11th   Dr. Carlos Finlay of Havana announced his belief that yellow fever was spread by the bite of a mosquito, the female of *Culex fasciatus* (now known as *Aedes aegypti*).

1900 May 24th An Army commission, consisting of Major Walter Reed and Acting Assistant Surgeons James Carroll, Jesse W. Lazear and Aristides Agramonte, was appointed, at the request of Surgeon General George Miller Sternberg, to investigate the causes of contagious diseases, especially yellow fever, in Cuba.

June 25th The Army board held its first official meeting at Camp Columbia, Quemados, Cuba.

July-August The board began work on the mosquito theory.

August 31st Lazear produced the board's first experimental case of yellow fever, Carroll's.

November 20th Camp Lazear, the yellow fever experiment station, was opened.

December 9th John R. Kissinger developed the first case of yellow fever, produced experimentally under careful control, on record, thus establishing that the female of *Aedes aegypti* spreads yellow fever by her bite.

December 25th John J. Moran developed yellow fever, establishing the fact that a house or region is infectious *only* in the presence of loaded yellow fever mosquitoes.

November 30, 1900-January 10, 1901 The experiment was conducted which established the harmlessness of *fomites*.

1901 January 8th Warren G. Jernegan, inoculated with the blood of a yellow fever patient, developed yellow fever. This experiment proved that the specific agent of yellow fever is in the blood and that passage through the body of the mosquito is not necessary to its development.

Summer Carroll proved that the specific agent of yellow fever is too small to be caught in a porcelain filter, and is sub-microscopic.

1901- No important discoveries about the nature of yellow fever
1926 were made in this period. Startlingly successful control measures, however, based on the knowledge of the mosquito as carrier, were widely put into effect.

1927 It was discovered in West Africa by a commission sent out by the Rockefeller Foundation that certain monkeys, among them the common rhesus, are susceptible to yellow fever. (The rhesus the Reed board tried to infect must have been, by the most unfortunate chance, immune.) Later animal experimentation in the United States and England showed the susceptibility of mice and hedgehogs.

1932   Yellow fever was found to be epidemic in the State of Espirito Santo, Brazil, in the absence of *Aedes aegypti*. Other epidemics and isolated cases in *aegypti*-free regions, especially in the Amazon valley, have been observed. The yellow fever transmitted by insects other than *Aedes aegypti* was named jungle yellow fever. It is now believed that this jungle yellow fever is the permanent endemic source of the epidemics by which cities used to be invaded. Animals other than man appear to maintain the endemic infection in the jungles, and seventeen types of mosquito, of several continents, aside from *Aedes aegypti*, have been shown by laboratory experiments to be able to convey yellow fever by biting.

1937   A satisfactory vaccine against yellow fever, called 17D, was produced after long experimentation by scientists of the International Health Division of the Rockefeller Foundation.

1942   Members of the armed forces of the United States are receiving yellow fever vaccinations as a matter of course.

BIBLIOGRAPHY

BIBLIOGRAPHY

Published Sources

AGRAMONTE, ARISTIDES.

 The Inside Story of a Great Medical Discovery. *Scientific Monthly*, v. 1. New York, December, 1915.

 Yellow Fever a Strictly Human Disease. *New York Journal of Medicine*, v. 96. New York, 1912.

AGRAMONTE, ARISTIDES; CARROLL, JAMES; LAZEAR, JESSE W.; REED, WALTER.

 The Etiology of Yellow Fever. A Preliminary Note. *Philadelphia Medical Journal*, v. 6. Philadelphia, 1900.

AGRAMONTE, ARISTIDES; CARROLL, JAMES; REED, WALTER.

 The Etiology of Yellow Fever. An Additional Note. *Journal of the American Medical Association*, v. 36. Chicago, 1901.

 Experimental Yellow Fever. *American Medicine*, v. 2. Philadelphia, 1901.

ANONYMOUS.

 Guiteau's Confession. Being a Full History of This Cruel Crime. How It Was Done and Why It Was Done!! Philadelphia, The Old Franklin Publishing House, 1881.

 Life of Surgeon Walter Reed, United States Army. *Virginia Medical Semi-Monthly*, v. 7. Richmond, 1903.

ASHBURN, PERCY MOREAU.

 A History of the Medical Department of the United States Army. Boston, Houghton Mifflin Company, 1929.

BARRETT, STEPHEN MELVIL, editor.

 Geronimo, Apache Chief. New York, Duffield and Company, 1906.

BEALS, CARLETON.

 The Crime of Cuba. Philadelphia and London, J. B. Lippincott Company, 1933.

BEARD, CHARLES A.; BEARD, MARY R.

The Rise of American Civilization. New York, The Macmillan Company, 1941.

BLANTON, WYNDHAM B.

Medicine in Virginia in the Seventeenth Century. Richmond, The William Byrd Press, 1930.

Medicine in Virginia in the Eighteenth Century. Richmond, Garrett and Massie, Inc., 1931.

Medicine in Virginia in the Nineteenth Century. Richmond, Garrett and Massie, Inc., 1933.

BORDEN, W. C.

History of Walter Reed's Illness from Appendicitis. *Washington Medical Annals*, v. 1. Washington, 1902.

BROWNE, S. M.

Life of Walter Reed. *Southwestern Medicine*, v. 8. Phoenix, 1924.

CARLISLE, ROBERT J., *editor*.

An Account of Bellevue Hospital, with an Account of the Medical and Surgical Staff from 1736-1894. New York, Society of the Alumni, 1893.

CARROLL, JAMES; AGRAMONTE, ARISTIDES; LAZEAR, JESSE W.; REED, WALTER.

The Etiology of Yellow Fever. A Preliminary Note. *Philadelphia Medical Journal*, v. 6. Philadelphia, 1900.

CARROLL, JAMES; AGRAMONTE, ARISTIDES; REED, WALTER.

The Etiology of Yellow Fever. An Additional Note. *Journal of the American Medical Association*, v. 36. Chicago, 1901.

Experimental Yellow Fever. *American Medicine*, v. 2. Philadelphia, 1901.

CARROLL, JAMES; REED, WALTER.

Bacillus Icteroides and Bacillus Cholerae Suis. A Preliminary Note. *Medical News*, v. 74. New York, 1899.

A Comparative Study of the Biological Characters and Pathogenesis of Bacillus x (Sternberg), Bacillus Icteroides (Sanarelli) and the Hog-cholera Bacillus (Salmon and Smith). *Journal of Experimental Medicine*, v. 5. Baltimore, 1900.

The Etiology of Yellow Fever. A Supplemental Note. *American Medicine*, v. 3. Philadelphia, 1902.

The Prevention of Yellow Fever. *Medical Record,* v. 60. New York, 1901.

The Specific Cause of Yellow Fever. A Reply to Dr. Sanarelli. *Medical News,* v. 75. New York, 1899.

CLAIBORNE, JOHN HERBERT.
Seventy-five Years in Old Virginia. New York and Washington, The Neale Publishing Company, 1904.

CLUM, WOODWORTH.
Apache Agent. Boston, Houghton Mifflin Company, 1936.

CULBRETH, DAVID M. R.
The University of Virginia. New York, The Neale Publishing Company, 1908.

CUSHING, HARVEY.
Life of Sir William Osler. Oxford, The Clarendon Press, 1925.

DE KRUIF, PAUL HENRY.
Microbe Hunters. New York, Harcourt, Brace and Company, 1926.

DE KRUIF, PAUL HENRY; HOWARD, SIDNEY.
Yellow Jack, A History. New York, Harcourt, Brace and Company, 1934.

DOMINGUEZ, FRANCISCO.
Carlos J. Finlay, Son centenaire (1933), Sa decouverte (1881). Paris, Louis Arnette, 1933.

DOUGLAS, HENRY KYD.
I Rode with Stonewall. Chapel Hill, University of North Carolina Press, 1940.

FAIRCHILD, D. S.
Major Walter Reed and Yellow Fever. *Journal of the Iowa State Medical Society,* v. 16. Des Moines, 1926.

FARMER, H. H.
Virginia Before and During the War. Henderson (Ky.), The Author, 1892.

FINDLAY, G. M.
The First Recognized Epidemic of Yellow Fever. Transactions of the Royal Society of Tropical Medicine and Hygiene, v. 35. London, 1941.

FINLAY, CARLOS J.
Carlos Finlay and Yellow Fever. New York, Oxford University Press, 1940.

FLEXNER, JAMES THOMAS; FLEXNER, SIMON.
William Henry Welch and the Heroic Age of American Medicine. New York, The Viking Press, 1941.

FLOHERTY, J. J.
Men Without Fear. Philadelphia, New York, J. B. Lippincott Company, 1940.

GARRISON, FIELDING H.
Scientific Work of John Shaw Billings. Washington, 1917.

GILMAN, DANIEL C.
Johns Hopkins University 1876-1891. *Johns Hopkins University Studies in History and Political Science*, v. 9. Baltimore, The Johns Hopkins Press, 1891.
The Launching of a University, and Other Papers. New York, Dodd, Mead and Company, Inc., 1906.

GORGAS, MARIE D.; HENDRICK, BURTON J.
William Crawford Gorgas, His Life and Work. Garden City, Doubleday, Page and Company, 1924.

GREATOREX, ELIZA.
Old New York from the Battery to Bloomingdale. New York, G. P. Putnam's Sons, 1875.

HALLOCK, GRACE T.; TURNER, C. E.
Health Heroes: Walter Reed. New York, Metropolitan Life Insurance Company, 1926.

HENDRICK, BURTON J.; GORGAS, MARIE D.
William Crawford Gorgas, His Life and Work. Garden City, Doubleday, Page and Company, 1924.

HERGESHEIMER, JOSEPH.
Sheridan, A Military Narrative. Boston and New York, Houghton Mifflin Company, 1931.

HOBBS, WILLIAM HERBERT.
Leonard Wood, Administrator, Soldier and Citizen. New York and London, G. P. Putnam's Sons, 1920.

HOWARD, LELAND OSSIAN.
Fighting the Insects. New York, The Macmillan Company, 1933.
A History of Applied Entomology (Somewhat Anecdotal). Smithsonian Institution Reports. Washington, 1931.
The Insect Menace. New York, London, The Century Company, 1931.

HOWARD, SIDNEY; DE KRUIF, PAUL HENRY.
  Yellow Jack, A History. New York, Harcourt Brace and Company, 1934.
HUTCHINS, ALEXANDER.
  Memoir of Dr. J. C. Hutchison. Transactions of the New York State Medical Association for the Year 1887, v. 4. New York, 1888.
JONES, PHILIP MILLS.
  In Memoriam Dr. Walter Reed. *California State Journal of Medicine*, v. 1. San Francisco, 1903.
KEAN, JEFFERSON RANDOLPH.
  William Crawford Gorgas. *Military Surgeon*, v. 56. Washington, 1925.
  Scientific Work and Discoveries of the Late Major Walter Reed. Washington, Government Printing Office, 1903.
  Walter Reed: Dedication of His Birthplace. *Military Surgeon*, v. 62. Washington, 1928.
KELLY, HOWARD ATWOOD.
  Some Lessons from the Life of Major Walter Reed. *Medical Library and Historical Journal*, v. 4. Brooklyn, 1906.
  Walter Reed and Yellow Fever. New York, McClure, Phillips and Company, 1906.
  Walter Reed and Yellow Fever. Baltimore, Medical Standard Book Company, 1906.
  Walter Reed and Yellow Fever. New York, McClure, Phillips and Company, 1907.
  Walter Reed and Yellow Fever. Baltimore, Norman, Remington Company, 1923.
KOBER, G. M.
  The Walter Reed Memorial Fund. *Science*, v. 23. New York, 1906.
LAMB, MARTHA.
  History of New York City. New York, A. S. Barnes and Company, 1877.
LAZEAR, JESSE W.; AGRAMONTE, ARISTIDES; CARROLL, JAMES; REED, WALTER.
  The Etiology of Yellow Fever. A Preliminary Note. *Philadelphia Medical Journal*, v. 6. Philadelphia, 1900.

LINDSAY, FORBES.
  Cuba and Her People of Today. Boston, L. C. Page and Company, 1911.
LUPTON, F. M., *publisher*.
  The Great Empire City, or High and Low Life in New York. New York, 1883.
McCAW, WALTER D.
  Walter Reed, a Memoir. Washington, 1904.
McGUIRE, JUDITH W.
  Diary of a Southern Refugee During the War. New York, E. J. Hale and Son, 1867.
MITCHELL, S. WEIR.
  Biographical Memoir of John Shaw Billings. Washington, 1917.
NUTHALL, G. H. F.
  In Memoriam: Walter Reed. *Journal of Hygiene*, v. 3. Cambridge, England, 1903.
REED, WALTER.
  The Contagiousness of Erysipelas. *Boston Medical and Surgical Journal*, v. 126. Boston, 1892.
  Remarks on the Cholera Spirillum. *Northwestern Lancet*, v. 13. St. Paul, 1892.
  Association of Proteus Vulgaris with Diplococcus Lanceolatus in a Case of Croupous Pneumonia. *Johns Hopkins Hospital Bulletin*, v. 5. Baltimore, 1894.
  The Germicidal Value of Trikresol. *St. Louis Medical and Surgical Journal*, v. 66. St. Louis, 1894.
  A Brief Contribution to the Identification of Streptococcus Erysipelatos. *Boston Medical and Surgical Journal*, v. 131. Boston, 1894.
  An Investigation into the so-called Lymphoid Nodules of the Liver in Typhoid Fever. *Johns Hopkins Hospital Reports*, v. 5. Baltimore, 1895.
  An Investigation into the so-called Lymphoid Nodules of the Liver in Abdominal Typhus. *American Journal of Medical Science*, v. 110. Philadelphia, 1895.
  What Credence Should Be Given to the Statements of those who Claim to Furnish Vaccine Lymph Free of Bacteria? *Journal of Practical Medicine*, v. 5. New York, 1895.
  The Character, Prevalence and Probable Causation of the Mala-

rial Fevers at Washington Barracks and Fort Myer. Reports of the Surgeon General of the Army. Washington, 1896.

The Parasite of Malaria. *Journal of Practical Medicine*, v. 6. New York, 1896.

Serum Diagnosis in Typhoid Fever. Reports of the Surgeon General of the Army. Washington, 1897.

On the Appearance of Certain Amoeboid Bodies in the Blood of Vaccinated Monkeys (Rhesus) and Children, and in the Blood of Variola. An Experimental Study. *Transactions of the Association of American Physicians*, v. 12. Philadelphia, 1897.

On the Appearance of Certain Amoeboid Bodies in the Blood of Vaccinated Monkeys (Rhesus) and Children, and in the Blood from cases of Variola. An Experimental Study. *Journal of Experimental Medicine*, v. 2. New York, 1897.

Typhoid Fever in the District of Columbia; Diagnosis: The Value of Widal's Test, the Dried Blood Method. *National Medical Review*, v. 7. Washington, 1897.

Experiments with Hollister's Formaldehyde Generator. Reports of the Surgeon General of the Army. Washington, 1897.

Splenic Leukaemia. *National Medical Review*, v. 7. Washington, 1898.

Report on the Practical Use of Electrozone as a Disinfectant in the City of Havana, Cuba. Reports of the Surgeon General of the Army. Washington, 1900.

The Propagation of Yellow Fever; Observations Based on Recent Researches. *Medical Record*, v. 60. New York, 1901.

Recent Researches Concerning the Etiology, Propagation and Prevention of Yellow Fever, by the United States Army Commission. *Journal of Hygiene*, v. 2. Cambridge, England, 1902.

REED, WALTER; AGRAMONTE, ARISTIDES; CARROLL, JAMES; LAZEAR, JESSE W.

The Etiology of Yellow Fever. A Preliminary Note. *Philadelphia Medical Journal*, v. 6. Philadelphia, 1900.

REED, WALTER; AGRAMONTE, ARISTIDES; CARROLL, JAMES

The Etiology of Yellow Fever. An Additional Note. *Journal of the American Medical Association*, v. 36. Chicago, 1901.

Experimental Yellow Fever. *American Medicine*, v. 2. Philadelphia, 1901.

REED, WALTER; CARROLL, JAMES.

Bacillus Icteroides and Bacillus Cholerae Suis. A Preliminary Note. *Medical News*, v. 74. New York, 1899.

A Comparative Study of the Biological Characters and Pathogenesis of Bacillus x (Sternberg), Bacillus Icteroides (Sanarelli) and the Hog-cholera Bacillus (Salmon and Smith). *Journal of Experimental Medicine*, v. 5. Baltimore, 1900.

The Etiology of Yellow Fever. A Supplemental Note. *American Medicine*, v. 3. Philadelphia, 1902.

The Prevention of Yellow Fever. *Medical Record*, v. 60. New York, 1901.

The Specific Cause of Yellow Fever. A Reply to Dr. G. Sanarelli. *Medical News*, v. 75. New York, 1899.

REED, WALTER; STERNBERG, GEORGE MILLER.

Report of Immunity Against Vaccination Conferred upon the Monkey by the Use of the Serum of the Vaccinated Calf and Monkey. *Transactions of the Association of American Physicians*, v. 10. Philadelphia, 1895.

ROCHESTER, T. M.

Tribute to the Memory of Dr. Hutchison. *Transactions of the New York State Medical Association for the Year 1887*, v. 4. New York, 1888.

RUSHMORE, J. D.

Memoir of the Late Joseph C. Hutchison, M.D., LL.D. *Transactions of the New York State Medical Association for the Year 1887*, v. 4. New York, 1888.

SANDOZ, MARI.

Old Jules. Boston, Little, Brown and Company, 1935.

SEARS, JOSEPH HAMBLIN.

The Career of Leonard Wood. New York, London, D. Appleton and Company, 1919.

SIMPSON, T. McN.

A Memoir of the Late Lemuel Sutton Reed. Minutes of the 116th Session of the Virginia Annual Conference of the Methodist Episcopal Church, South. Petersburg (Va.), 1898.

SMITH, STEPHEN.

The City That Was. New York, American Public Health Association, 1911.

STERNBERG, GEORGE MILLER.

Walter Reed. *Proceedings of the Washington Academy of Science*. Washington, 1903-04.

STERNBERG, GEORGE MILLER; REED, WALTER.

Report of Immunity Against Vaccination Conferred upon the Monkey by the Use of the Serum of the Vaccinated Calf and Monkey. *Transactions of the Association of American Physicians*, v. 10. Philadelphia, 1895.

STERNBERG, MARTHA.

George Miller Sternberg, A Biography. Chicago, American Medical Association, 1920.

TAYLOR, WALTER HERRON.

General Lee and His Campaigns in Virginia, 1861-1865. New York, D. Appleton and Company, 1877.

THORNTON, WILLIAM M.

A Virginia Schoolmaster. *University of Virginia Alumni Bulletin*. Charlottesville, 1917.

TURNER, C. E.; HALLOCK, GRACE T.

Health Heroes: Walter Reed. New York, Metropolitan Life Insurance Company, 1926.

WALTER REED COMMISSION OF THE MEDICAL SOCIETY OF VIRGINIA.

An Appreciation of the Life and Work of Walter Reed. *Virginia Medical Monthly*, v. 54. Richmond, 1927.

WALTER REED MEMORIAL ASSOCIATION.

Extracts from Reports and Papers in Reference to Major Walter Reed, Surgeon, U.S.A. Washington, 1904.

WELCH, WILLIAM HENRY.

Papers and Addresses. Baltimore, The John Hopkins Press, 1920.

WILSON, CHARLES MORROW.

Wanted: More Walter Reeds. *Harper's Magazine*, v. 183. New York, 1941.

YELLOW FEVER, A COMPILATION OF VARIOUS PUBLICATIONS (SENATE DOCUMENT 822) Washington, Government Printing Office, 1911.

Unpublished Sources

ANDRUS, JOHN H.
The Tale of a Guinea Pig.

LAZEAR, JESSE W.; REED, WALTER.

Manuscript notebook containing, among other records, case histories of various illnesses among United States soldiers at Camp Columbia, Quemados, Cuba, and case histories of yellow fever among the civilian population of Quemados and among the military. Owned by the New York Academy of Medicine Library.

REGISTRY OF MEDICAL OFFICERS 1875-1902. National Archives, Washington.

REED, WALTER; LAZEAR, JESSE W.—CF. LAZEAR, JESSE W.; REED, WALTER.

TRUBY, ALBERT E.

Memoirs of Service in Cuba and Walter Reed's Work in the Etiology of Yellow Fever.

INDEX

INDEX

273